positions asia critique

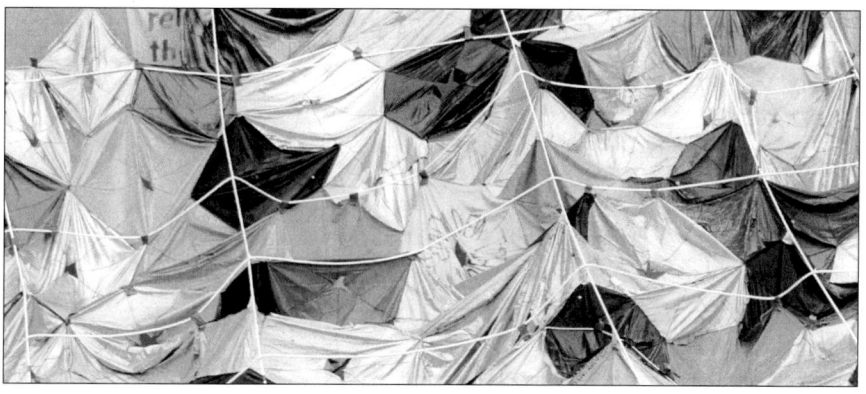

expansive trajectories:
remapping transnationalism in the global china era

volume 32   number 4   november 2024

Contents

Guest Editor's Introduction—Expansive Trajectories: Remapping Transnationalism in the Global China Era

Fran Martin

Introduction

In our current "trans-imperial moment," as the world hangs suspended between US and Chinese hegemonies, expanding transnational engagements by Chinese state and nonstate actors have led to growing interest in how China's rise is reshaping not only macro-level geopolitics but also the micro level of people's everyday experiences in multiple locations around the world (Ching, Shim, and Yang 2023: 737; Katzenstein 2012; Kuehn, Louie, and Pomfret 2014; Shambaugh 2013; C. Lee 2017; Ang 2020; Bailey and Mak 2021; Pieke and Iwabuchi 2021b; Rofel and Rojas 2022; Sun and Yu 2023). Notwithstanding the nation's faltering economy postpandemic, in the era of President Xi's Chinese dream, top-down state initiatives by the People's Republic of China (PRC) continue to expand energetically into

positions 32:4   DOI 10.1215/10679847-11306784
Copyright 2024 by Duke University Press

the global field with the goal of reviving China's historical status as a great world power, while ordinary Chinese migrants and businesses have become increasingly prominent avatars of bottom-up transnationalism in many countries (Pieke 2021). Ching Kwan Lee's (2022a: 313) *global China* concept, referenced in this issue's title, draws attention to these developments, highlighting those "outward flows of investment, loans, infrastructure, migrants, media, cultural programmes and international and civil society engagement" that have so markedly intensified since the beginning of this century. The extension of these transnational flows fundamentally transforms the conditions of culture in many places in the world today.

This issue aims to deepen our understanding of people's lived experiences of the global China era in the Asia-Pacific region and Europe. Contributing to global China studies with ethnographic perspectives on the micro level of everyday human experiences, it focuses on the cultural politics and experiential impacts of PRC state and nonstate actors' intensified extension into transnational fields of activity since the beginning of this century, and especially during the past decade. Collectively, the authors ask: How do growing transnational flows out of and into the PRC affect social identity for first-generation PRC migrants abroad; for ordinary people in China whose lives are impacted by transnational discourses, capital, and state projects; and for overseas communities encountering the increased presence of mobile PRC capital, migrants, and media? How do these differently positioned groups' conceptualizations, practices, and affective experiences of class, gender, "race," nationality, and ethnicity shift and transform as elements of culture become increasingly mobile across the national borders of the PRC?

Focusing on global China marks a significant new direction in the study of Chinese transnationalisms. The first wave of Chinese transnationalism studies, which arose in the 1990s just as China was emerging from a long period of relative cultural and economic isolation, assigned to the PRC at most a peripheral role in transnational cultural economies, focusing instead on analyzing the hybrid energies of Chinese diaspora cultures. Since then, a lot has changed. As Wanning Sun and Haiqing Yu (2023: 1) pithily observe, "A new reality is forcing us to re-introduce China and people from China into the research paradigm," since "China seems to insist on inserting itself into the sphere of Chinese transnationalism, whether the rest of the world wants this or not." This historical shift compels two key conceptual reorientations. First, regardless of how we view recent developments, it is no longer plausible to argue that China's position in the global circuits of Chinese transnationalism is merely peripheral. Second, the PRC state's intentional program of self-globalization complicates assumptions based on the prior regional economic and geopolitical order that transnationalism tends to be a "wild" force working in opposition to the desires of nation-states, and that Chinese transnationalisms tend to support diasporic-hybrid rather than monolithic-China-centric conceptualization of Chinese identity (or identities).

Below, I offer a brief review of the first wave of Chinese transnationalism studies in order to delineate as clearly as possible how this issue's project both is inspired by and departs from that earlier body of work. Our project in this issue rests on the proposal that, although the earlier scholarship on Chinese transnationalisms based in diaspora studies, and more recent studies of global China based in China studies, have tended to operate as two fairly separate subfields, in fact, we must recognize that the phenomena each subfield addresses are historically linked. As the regional centers of transnational capitalism and migration have shifted and transformed, so too have the practices and human cultures of Chinese transnationalisms.

The First Wave of Chinese Transnationalism Studies: Against China-Centrism

Notwithstanding a pervasive China exceptionalism that would cast China's rise as an unprecedented phenomenon driven by some internal logic unique to China (Franceschini and Loubere 2022), in fact, the nation's increased international prominence today clearly hinges on its strategic self-integration into a global capitalist system that predated its "rise"—albeit that the system itself is now being thoroughly reshaped by China's engagement with it. Three decades ago, the regional configuration of transnational capitalism was animated by different and more diffuse energies: those of diasporic Chinese capital, which played a key role in the emergence of the Pacific Rim economy of the late twentieth century. It is this earlier stage in the regional history of global capitalism that gave rise to the first wave of studies on Chinese transnationalism, which has for many years provided the dominant paradigm for addressing the human and cultural aspects of modern Chinese border-crossing practices.

This first wave of Chinese transnationalism studies arose in the early 1990s and focused on the long-established Chinese diasporas of Southeast Asia, emphasizing the hybridity and plurality of their cultural practices and identities. Attention to Chinese transnationalism in multiple disciplines across the humanities and social sciences at that time reflected cross-disciplinary interest in transnational connections, processes, and cultures in the wider context of accelerating globalization. Specifically, this first wave of Chinese transnationalism studies responded to the 1980s consolidation of the Pacific Rim economy with its "four tigers"—the high-growth, export-led economies of Singapore, Hong Kong, Taiwan, and South Korea—and underlined the central role played by transnationally mobile diasporic Chinese elites in this then-booming regional economy and the cultural expressions that accompanied it. The key works in this body of scholarship may be characterized, in retrospect, by two central points of tension. These are, first, their conceptualization of Chinese cultural identity (as a coherent and unitary heritage versus dispersed, hybrid, and multiple), and second, their orientation toward the nation-state and cultures of the PRC (as intrinsically separate from versus connected to the circuits of Chinese transnationalism).

The neo-Confucianist scholar Tu Wei-ming was one of the first to address transformations in contemporary Chinese cultures resulting from the rise of the regional economy. In his now-classic 1991 essay "Cultural China: The Periphery as Centre," which later featured as the first chapter in his edited collection *The Living Tree: The Changing Meaning of Being Chinese Today* (1994), Tu observed the emergence of a diasporic Chinese transnational merchant and financial class along with the rise of the tiger economies. With excitement, he interpreted the capitalist success of non-PRC Chinese societies that retained links to "traditional" culture as challenging common assumptions that modernization equates with Westernization. Tu (1994: 12) held out hope that Chinese economic success in the region promised cultural revitalization, heralding "Chinese culture disintegrating at the centre and . . . being revived from the periphery." "The amazing aspect of all these scenarios," wrote Tu, "is the glaring absence of mainland China," which he proposed had become "largely irrelevant" due to the three decades of being closed off to the wider world and capitalist development during the Mao years (12). Tu therefore prophesied that "the periphery will come to set the economic and cultural agenda for the centre" (12), since "the center no longer has the ability, insight, or legitimate authority to dictate the agenda for cultural China" (27–28).

Tu's argument thus clearly framed the communist PRC as standing in a relation of intrinsic separateness from—indeed, opposition to—the capitalist economic and cultural energies bursting forth from the revitalizing geographic peripheries of Chinese culture. His conceptualization of Chinese *cultural* identity, however, is a little less straightforward. In an article first published in 1998, Ien Ang developed an incisive critique of the paradoxical China-centrism of Tu's schema. She rightly noted that, "placed in the context of Chinese *cultural* history, the assertion of the (diasporic) periphery as the centre is a radical one"; and yet

> the very postulation of a "cultural China" as the name for a transnational intellectual community held together . . . by "a common ancestry and a shared cultural background" . . . is driven by a desire for, and motivated by, another kind of centrism, this time along notionally cultural lines. . . . The aim could seem to be to rescue Chineseness from China . . . [but] the rescue operation implies the projection of a new, alternative centre, a decentred centre whose name is *cultural* China, but China nevertheless. (Ang 2001: 42–43)

Countering Tu's Sinocentrism, metaphorized in the singular trunk and deep roots of his "living tree" of Chinese culture, Ang proposed hybridity, instead, as the key characteristic of plural and fragmented diasporic Chinese identity (or identities). Drawing on examples of diasporic Chinese artists and intellectuals as well as the deeply syncretic, centuries-old *peranakan* cultures of the Malay Archipelago, Ang developed a robustly antifoundationalist conceptualization of transnational Chineseness: "The diasporic paradigm has shattered the convenient certainty with which Chinese studies has been equated, quite simply, with the study of China. 'China' can no longer be limited to the more or less fixed area of its official spatial and cultural boundaries, nor can it be held up as providing the authentic, authoritative, and uncontested standard for all things Chinese" (38). Thus, for Ang, diasporic Chinese identities were characterized both by their separateness from the territory and cultures of the PRC, and by their hybridity and multiplicity. This was a decisively centrifugal model of transnational Chinese cultures, in distinction from Tu's paradoxically centripetal version: Ang's was a model that located the most vital energies in the dynamic and unpredictable *routes* rather than the deep civilizational *roots* of Chinese identities (Hau 2012; Martin 2014).

In developing such a model, Ang contributed to a wider intellectual movement in the 1990s that championed anti-essentialist approaches to modern Chinese cultures and identities, and included the works of prominent scholars such as Leo Ou-fan Lee (1994), Lydia Liu (1995), Xiaomei Chen (1995), Allen Chun (1996), and Rey Chow (1998), among others. Central to this movement were the works of Aihwa Ong and Donald Nonini, whose 1997 edited collection *Ungrounded Empires: The Cultural Politics of Modern Chinese Transnationalism* formally inaugurated Chinese transnationalism studies. Nonini and Ong theorized Chinese transnationalism as a form of alternative modernity in which the border-crossing energies of late capitalism, embodied in the transnational social field of Chinese diasporic elites, were everywhere complexly entangled with the territorializing desires of nation-states (Nonini and Ong 1997; see also Ong 1999). Again, the contexts that produced this form of Chinese transnationalism were those of the post-1970 Asia-Pacific, conditioned by the region's longer Chinese diasporic histories. The hallmarks of Chinese transnationalism as Nonini and Ong theorized it were its intensifying cross-border mobilities (of both low- and high-skilled workers, capital, and media) and its ability to evade disciplining by nation-states. Their analysis was based on an anti-essentialist understanding of "Chineseness" as produced through material practices in the present, albeit conditioned by longer diasporic histories (explicitly contra Tu's centripetal vision of primordial Chinese culture and identity). Chinese transnationalism was, for Nonini and Ong (1997: 11), a "third culture": "an emergent global form that . . . provides alternative visions in late capitalism to Western modernity and generates new and distinctive social arrangements, cultural discourses, practices, and subjectivities." Based on this, their core claim was that "capitalism in the Asia Pacific and its accompanying institutions and practices—flexibility, travel, consumption, multiculturalism, and mass media—are reworking Chinese identities and subjectivities" in ways that tended to subvert national regimes of truth (Nonini and Ong 1997: 16, 26; Ong and Nonini 1997; Ong 1997). Their approach intentionally decentered territorial China: they refused to "accord China a privileged ontological or epistemological position" but rather saw it as "one among many sites within and across which Chinese transnational practices are played out" (Nonini and Ong 1997: 12). In her sole-authored chapter in the same volume, Ong interpreted the then-current capitalist discourse of "Greater China"—a transnational economic zone linking China, Taiwan, and Hong Kong, running on mobile diasporic capital—as inherently antinational, in opposition to the modernist imaginary of the nation-state with its privileging of essentialized identity and territorial fixity (Ong 1997).[1] Thus, the authors were principally interested in the capacity of Chinese transnationalism, as a "wild" form of mobile capitalism, to challenge and subvert the power of nation-states. And the PRC itself—included in their purview largely due to its role as importer of Chinese diaspora capital—remained peripheral to their vision of Chinese transnationalism (Ong 1997: 174).[2]

More recently, Shu-mei Shih (2007, 2011, 2012, 2013) introduced her theorization of the Sinophone, which has become one of the most influential frameworks for scholars working on transnational Sinitic cultures outside China today. In her 2007 book *Visuality and Identity: Sinophone Articulations across the Pacific*, in which she first developed the Sinophone concept based on analyses of screen media, photography, and visual arts, Shih (2007: 4) defined it as "a network of places of cultural production outside China and on the margins of Chineseness, where a historical process of heterogenizing and localizing continental Chinese culture has been taking place for several centuries." Like Ang, Ong, and others discussed above, Shih foregrounded the dispersal, fragmentation, and heterogeneity of "Chineseness," while placing particular emphasis on the deep historical roots of "minor" transnational Sinitic cultures and languages. Also like those scholars, Shih was committed to a critique of China-centrism and specifically Han-centrism—but she did not a priori exclude consideration of cultural phenomena inside China's territorial borders (borders that, she underlined, were established and maintained through colonizing practices on the part of both the Qing dynasty and the PRC [Shih 2013]). Shih's (2012: 5) Sinophone encompassed "minoritised and colonised voices within China, be they Tibetan, Mongolian or Uyghur." Indeed, for Shih, the conceptual relationship between the Sinophone and China as a nation was complex. The Sinophone could "be a site of both a longing for and a rejection of various constructions of Chineseness; . . . a site of both nationalism of the long-distance kind, anti-China politics, or even nonrelation with China, whether real or imaginary" (Shih 2007: 30). And yet while "the Sinophone may articulate a China-centrism . . . the Sinophone is [also] often the site where powerful articulations against China-centrism can be heard" (30). Thus, although the *lived cultures* of some Sinophone sites might be China-centric, for Shih, as an *intellectual framework*, the Sinophone—in this regard similarly to Ong's conceptualization of Chinese transnationalism and Ang's theorization of diaspora—tended to reject China-centrism.

Global China: Transnationalism from Above?

Despite disagreements on the nature and form of cultural identity (or identities), then, by the first decade of the twenty-first century Anglophone scholarly opinion had largely converged on a diaspora-focused understanding of Chinese transnationalisms in which the PRC played a mainly peripheral role, if any.[3] Clearly, this understanding of the transnational social field arose from a particular, late twentieth-century configuration of economic and cultural conditions. By the 1980s, the aftermath of China's three decades of high socialism had left the country economically underdeveloped and culturally isolated from the capitalist world. Meanwhile, with the support of post–World War II American anti-communist developmentalism, its immediate neighbors in the tiger economies embraced industrial capitalism and began to thrive economically and culturally just when the PRC was beginning its post-Mao program of reform-and-opening-up (Glassman 2018). As a result, late-century transnational circuits of capital, culture, and migration were activated several decades earlier across the Chinese societies of East and Southeast Asia and the global diaspora than they were in the PRC itself. Already in 1997, however, Ong (1997: 196) foreshadowed the question of what might happen next: "A synergy of political, economic, and ideological processes is producing a geopolitical center in East Asia. Will the momentary glow of fraternity forged in alternative Chinese modernities, and in renegotiating American global domination, become the Asia-Pacific hegemony of the new century?" Ong hinted presciently at a negative answer: "This 'momentary glow of fraternity' . . . may not outlast China's emergence as a superpower" (196). A decade later, Wanning Sun and John Sinclair (2016: 9) put the question even more bluntly: "Given recent developments that clearly point to China's intention to re-center itself, to what extent can the current transnationalist framework accommodate the rise of China?"

It is precisely this question that we confront in revisiting the Chinese transnationalisms framework today. Whereas in the final decades of last century, the PRC was culturally relatively isolated, today its state and people actively insert themselves into transnational circuits of culture, capital, and human mobility across the world, from Asia and Oceania to Europe, the Americas, and Africa. This is the historical conjuncture addressed by the global China concept, whose prehistory arguably lies in early twenty-first-century migration studies. In their book *Transnational Chinese*, based on a multisite ethnographic study of migration flows between China's Fujian Province and Europe conducted in 1999–2001, Frank N. Pieke et al. (2004: 11) defined what they termed "Chinese globalization" as "multiple, transnational social spaces straddling and embedded in smaller regional or national systems on the one hand and, on the other hand, as a part of a unifying global system." The related concept of global China subsequently emerged from the altered economic and geopolitical contexts of more than a decade later, with the 2017 publication Ching Kwan Lee's book *The Specter of Global China: Politics, Labor, and Foreign Investment in Africa*, and has been further developed in "Inside Global China," a special section of the *China Quarterly* that Lee edited in 2022 (C. Lee 2022b). While the earlier studies of Chinese transnationalisms surveyed above have their disciplinary home in diaspora studies, Lee's approach—like that of Pieke et al. (2004)—originates in China studies and is motivated by the imperative to take seriously the self-extension of the PRC state and its people into a global scope of activities. Lee frames China's "ferocious" outward push over the past two decades as fed by both state and non-state energies (C. Lee 2017: xi). On the one hand, in its global initiatives (discussed below), the PRC state seeks to tackle the twin economic and political problems of excess production capacity and regime legitimation (C. Lee 2022a: 315). On the other hand, the global China phenomenon is also fueled by the private interests of ordinary people and businesses (316). In synergy with a contemporaneous wave of transdisciplinary scholarship on "global Asias" that insists "we cannot restrict the study of Asia to any fixed geographic region" (Chen and Hayot 2015: xi), Lee observes that the notion of global China

> push[es] the empirical boundary of China studies beyond China's territorial borders. China casts an outsize shadow on many different arenas of world development, challenging the field of China studies to abandon its methodological nationalism so as to catch up with China's transformation into a global force. Global China is taking myriad forms, ranging from foreign direct investment, labor export, and multilateral financial institutions for building cross-regional infrastructure to the globalization of Chinese civil society organizations, creation of global media networks, and global joint ventures in higher education, to name just a few examples. . . . Studying global China means reimagining China beyond China. (C. Lee 2017: xiv)

While it is historically and conceptually informed by the earlier studies of Chinese transnationalisms, our project in this issue addresses the particularities of the global China era and, in doing so, also takes inspiration from Lee's framework. From the Chinese transnationalisms scholarship, we draw an abiding mistrust of monolithic and essentialist understandings of Chineseness and an attention to transnational mobility's capacities to (re) make social identities through everyday practices. From the global China scholarship, we draw a heightened attention to the consequences of the PRC's newly central position in the present world order—the ways in which China's global engagements generate complex and unpredictable "new world orderings" (Rofel and Rojas 2022)—and an appreciation of the roles of both state and nonstate actors in shaping the transnational manifestations of Chinese cultures and identities today. For, as Lee underlines, surveying the current configuration of outward flows from China, we find a broad and ambitious suite of state initiatives operating across the spheres of economy, geopolitics, infrastructure, aid, and culture, alongside ever-shifting patterns of transborder movements by ordinary individuals, businesses, and private capital. As Frank N. Pieke (2021: 246) observes,

The Chinese state's strategy of global expansion cannot simply enlist the bottom-up globalization of Chinese enterprises, migrants, institutions, and culture, but neither are the two completely separate. Bottom-up globalization provides both the tools for and sets the limits of state-led strategies and plans; conversely, China's global actors increasingly have to accommodate the plans of the party and the state, both in China itself and abroad.

Thus, top-down state-led transnational engagements and bottom-up private varieties relate to each other in multiple, complex, and sometimes unpredictable ways.

As a result of state initiatives, the direction, volume, and character of transborder flows of Chinese capital and infrastructure have transformed very significantly over the past two decades. In 2000, a year prior to China's admission to the WTO, China's government announced the first iteration of its Going Global Strategy (translated alternatively as Going Out [*zou chuqu zhanlüe* 走出去战略]), supporting the transnational expansion of businesses as a key strategic initiative. This fed a massive increase in outbound direct investment, dominated by state-owned enterprises, such that in 2014 the PRC became, for the first time, a net capital exporter (Wang, Qi, and Zhang 2015; Wang and Lu 2016). The Going Global Strategy was subsequently reoriented under Xi Jinping's presidency toward sci-tech innovation (China Policy 2017). Noteworthy examples of projects launched under this strategy include the *Made in China 2025* industry plan (issued by the State Council in 2015), targeted at developing the nation's high-tech export capacity; and the flagship Belt and Road Initiative (BRI, announced by President Xi in 2013 and incorporated into the Party's constitution in 2017), which aims to build maritime and overland infrastructure, trade, investment, and human linkages to China's south and west, across central Asia to Europe and Africa and through Southeast Asia, with a focus on energy, telecommunications, logistics, law, IT, and transportation sectors (China Policy 2017; Winter 2016). Under the auspices of this initiative, China's government has become a significant player in delivering foreign direct investment and aid to the Global South, including to countries in Africa, the Pacific, Latin America, and beyond (Zhang 2021; Carter 2017). These globalizing initiatives by the PRC state have spawned fast-growing subfields of academic inquiry into their economic, cultural, geographic, and security implications; indeed, the field of global China studies itself arose initially from sociological studies of China's development activities in the Global South (C. Lee 2017, 2022; Sidaway et al. 2020; Rofel and Rojas 2022; Pavlićević and Talmacs 2022).

Meanwhile, in the realm of culture, a soft power–based public diplomacy push by the Chinese government has seen the worldwide expansion of Confucius Institutes and various other arts, cultural, and educational programs (Shambaugh 2015; Breslin 2020; Ptáčková et al. 2021). PRC media have gone transnational, too, including state organs Xinhua, *People's Daily* (which now hosts multiple foreign-language editions online), China Radio International (broadcasting in Mandarin and English, with a multilingual online news platform), and China Global Television Network (a 2016 rebranding of China Central Television's international channels, which broadcasts in multiple languages around the world) (Breslin 2020). This is in addition to innumerable commercial Mandarin-language media channels and platforms run by and for post-1978 PRC diaspora communities. The complex social, political, and industrial implications of this transnational media expansion have been studied in various contexts, including Australia (e.g., Yu and Sun 2019; Sun and Yu 2023), African nations (e.g., Jedlowski and Röschenthaler 2017), East Asia (e.g., Ching, Shim, and Yang 2023), and worldwide (e.g., Thussu, de Burgh, and Shi 2018; Nyíri 2021). Although China's censorship regime, sociocultural specificity, and reputational problems abroad mean it has thus far struggled to exercise international soft power effectively in many countries through direct media exports (Shambaugh 2013; Peng and Keane 2019; Breslin 2020), the production of China-friendly media outside China is supported by practices of self-censorship in coproduction (Ching, Shim, and Yang 2023). And recent major state investment in the development of e-sports means it is conceivable that China's historical status as net pop-cultural importer may be reversed in years to come (Chua 2012; Zhao and Lin 2020; Ismangil and Fung 2021). At the same time, in China's own cities, everyday life has been thoroughly transformed from its character a generation ago as a result of intensified inbound transnational media flows from Korea, Japan, Taiwan, Western Europe, and North America.

Supported by state policies and initiatives, the movements of ordinary people and private capital, too, have intensified and increasingly expanded to a transnational scale, with significant growth in transnational labor mobilities, emigration, and overseas investment by the middle and elite classes, and outbound travel by tourists and students (Oakes and Schein 2006; Xiang 2016; Martin 2022). Annual international departures soared from 3 million in 1990 to 155 million in 2019 (Xinhua She 2020). Pál Nyíri (2010) has made an extended study of how increased human mobility is both a goal and a challenge for the reforms-era Chinese state. Charting the massive increases in domestic and transnational travel in and from the PRC since the 1990s, Nyíri (2010: 6) analyzes the rise of a powerful and state-supported association between human mobility and "the image of the borderless 'globally modern Chinese.'" He frames "new migrants"—those students, workers, undocumented migrants, merchants, entrepreneurs, and others who left the country after 1978—as China's new wave of transnationalists: "Increasingly, the social, economic, and political practices of these migrants are characterized by transnationalism, that is, sustained structural embedding and accumulation and expenditure of various forms of capital both in China and in one or more countries overseas" (59). However, while the state facilitates and rewards citizens' market-mediated mobilities as contributions to China's capitalist modernization, it is simultaneously compelled to find ways of managing the subversive potentials inherent in their increased movement. It thus attempts to channel and discipline human mobilities into a carefully governed system: what we might call a *mobility regime*, rather than a welter of untrammeled flows (Shamir 2005).[4]

In particular, Nyíri (2010: 49) examines how the state seeks to harness migrant energies as a resource for nation-building, based on the presumption of a unitary Chinese identity that "extends the Chinese nation beyond the state's territorial confines." Chinese migrant communities worldwide have been called on to bolster the nation-building project—no longer principally through capital investment as in the 1980s and 1990s, but by promoting China's soft power through telling positive stories abroad. As Yan Tan (2021: 1–2) argues, this illustrates a diaspora engagement policy that "extends to transnational political, social, diplomatic and cultural domains": a kind of "transnationalism from above." In this way, transnational human mobilities, entangled as they are with market mechanisms, are also fundamentally entwined with transnational geopolitics (Nyíri 2010: 60, 164). Thus, in the case of the contemporary PRC, we confront the seeming paradox of a transnational cluster of activities connected at every point with a national project. Here, the unruly energies of transnationalism from below—the multitude of private and nonstate interests, desires, and tactics enacted by ordinary people on the move—meet the reterritorializing desires of the state's transnationalism from above as it attempts to marshal these energies into a support for its vision of global China (Pieke et al. 2004: 12). We might recall, here, Nonini and Ong's (1997) observation of a dialectic of mobility and containment in the diasporic Chinese transnationalisms of the 1990s, where the wildness of cross-border business networks and capital flows challenged the power of nation-states to contain them. In the global China era, a related dynamic may be observed in the case of the PRC itself and the transnational human and capital mobilities that it simultaneously fosters and attempts to discipline.

However, notwithstanding popular perceptions in many countries, ordinary migrants are not simply government puppets, and the reason that the state feels the need to manage their mobilities so closely is precisely because of mobility's potential for disruptive outcomes (Martin 2022; see also Lin Song and Shih-Diing Liu's essay in this issue). It is far from a foregone conclusion that the PRC state's aspirations to exert global influence through its emigrant communities are realized in practice. As Caroline S. Hau forcefully observes, close attention to the complexities of diasporic experience inevitably complicates "the idea of 'Sinicization' as a mainland state-centered and driven process of remaking the world (and the ethnic Chinese outside its borders) in its own image" (Hau 2012: 176): "the evidence for this mainland-driven form of becoming-Chinese—such as the proliferation of simplified Chinese newspapers among overseas Chinese communities, the popularity of mainland Chinese popular culture . . . among non-mainland Chinese migrant communities, de-Anglicization in Hong Kong—exists to some extent; but its capacity to supplant other forms of becoming-Chinese remains debatable" (200).

The situation we now confront, then, is one in which (at least) two types of "Chinese transnationalism" coexist. First, there is the type that was highlighted in the wave of scholarship reviewed above and remains current today: a set of transnational economic flows and social fields activated by Chinese diasporas, which tend to decenter both the nation-state in general and the PRC specifically while foregrounding dispersed and plural iterations of Chinese identities. Second, there is now also a newer type—the one on which this issue principally focuses—that emanates from the PRC itself and is put into motion by the state's self-globalizing policies and initiatives; is played out in the actions of nonstate actors like migrants, investors, students, and others; and is more likely than the earlier form to support Sinocentric understandings of cultural identity (though certainly not predetermined to do so).

The emergence of global China thus underlines two key ways in which the historical specificities of the current era necessitate a reorientation of our understanding of Chinese transnationalisms. First, as I have argued, the PRC can no longer plausibly be viewed as merely peripheral to the transnational (re)production of Chinese cultures and identities. Second, Chinese transnationalisms can no longer be conceptualized as inherently or definitively antinational(ist) or anti-Sinocentric. Rather, they must be seen as a diverse group of processes without any singular or predictable consequence vis-à-vis centering or decentering China—they may do either, neither, or both, in different instances and circumstances.

I hope it is clear by now that our attention to PRC-related mobilities does not entail that contributors to this issue wish to (re)install a China-centric understanding of Chinese identity, fall into methodological nationalism, or ignore the multiplicity and heterogeneity of Chineseness today and the continuing vibrant existence of Sinophone cultural worlds. More simply, our project responds to the radically altered historical conditions of the present, which see novel cross-border movements into and out of the People's Republic materially transforming cultural life at a range of scales across territorial China, the Asia-Pacific region, and the world. As Hau (2012: 198) keenly observes, "'Transnational' approaches that purport to move beyond the strictures of nation- and state-centered analysis . . . [and] invoke 'China' as a self-explanatory straw figure against which transnational or diasporic difference is *then* asserted [thereby] overlook the broader implications of critical disjunctions and historical hybridization." Her point is well taken. In the global China era, there is surely less justification than ever for a priori excluding PRC-related examples from consideration of the multifarious and unpredictable cultural consequences of transnational mobilities.

Transnational Lives in the Global China Era

This issue, many of whose articles were first presented at the "Re-worlding Chinese Transnationalisms" symposium at the University of Melbourne in August 2021, includes studies of transnational phenomena that are unfolding both within and beyond the PRC, addressing the central question of how intensified transnational flows out of and into China this century reconfigure social identities. Geographically, the articles address the Asia-Pacific region—charting trajectories among mainland China, Hong Kong, Taiwan, Malaysia, and Australia—as well as Europe. Many of the articles focus on the PRC's "new migrants" (those who emigrated from China after 1978). In addressing the central question of transforming identities, contributors draw our attention to three core themes: the sometimes unpredictable responses to state policies and initiatives (including but not limited to those of the PRC state) by people living transnationally mobile lives; the transnationalization of class reproduction for both working-class and middle-class subjects as a consequence of new cross-border flows of people, capital, goods, and ideas to and from China; and the revitalization of old forms of racism and the emergence of new ones as a result of evolving transnational mobilities of Chinese media, people, and capital today. The disciplinary backgrounds of the authors range across the humanities from cultural studies and anthropology to media and communications studies and social work. Their methodologies center on ethnographic and interview-based research about the experiences of various groups of people who are subject to and subjects of Chinese transnational mobilities, but also encompass critical analysis of current events and movements as well as policy analysis.

Hau (2012: 199) reminds us that, although hybrid identities emerge especially strongly from diaspora, "Chinese" culture and identity should nevertheless not be presumed to be monolithic or unchanging *within* the PRC itself, since ways of life inevitably hybridize and transform with inflows of media, migration, capital, and discourse. In line with this important observation, the first two articles in this issue consider the reproduction of Chinese working-class subjects and identities through transnational processes shaped by state initiatives. Anita Koo and Ngai Pun analyze the subjectification of Chinese working-class vocational college students training up for China's new high-tech export economy under the Made in China 2025 industry plan, a core initiative of the Going Global Strategy under Xi. Their article thus underlines the human-level effects of capital and commodity mobilities, enacted discursively through training. It explores how the transnationalization of Chinese class (re)production is closely tied to the Chinese government's linking of various sectors of the national economy into the circuits of transnational capitalism. This research sheds light not only on the mechanisms through which working-class identity is reproduced but also how this is entangled with the reproduction of hegemonic gender and, importantly, how women students variously acquiesce to and resist their production as female workers according to the state-sanctioned normative template.

Continuing the exploration of transnational processes' contributions to the reproduction of Chinese working-class women's identities, Shuheng Jin and Haijing Dai examine the new reach of the globally extensive discourse of intensive mothering into the migrant-worker population of southern China. Their fascinating ethnographic study shows that, seemingly against the odds, the imported ideology of intensive motherhood transforms Chinese rural migrant women's understandings and practices of mothering—despite the stark contrast between their own straitened material circumstances and the white, Euro-American, middle-class origin of this ideal. Furthermore, this occurs largely thanks to the active promotion of intensive mothering ideology by local state agencies. The article thus illustrates an intriguing and unexpected alliance between Chinese state power and a transnationally mobile North American discourse in reshaping Chinese working-class women's gendered practices and subjectivities.

Qian Gong and Huan Wu likewise focus on the role of transnational processes in the (re)making of Chinese working-class lives, but their case study concerns workers who themselves become transnationally mobile and whose mobility transfigures their class identity and social and cultural capitals. Their case study is a cohort of skilled tradespeople who moved to the state of Western Australia in response to a skills shortage designated by the Australian government during Western Australia's mining boom. The authors trace the stories of these migrants as they moved, first, from their rural village hometowns to larger Chinese cities, where their social status fell as a result of their lack of urban *hukou* (household registration); and from there to Western Australia, where their income and social status rose significantly, but their cultural capital fell as a result of lack of linguistic and other local knowledge. They compensated for this, in part, by developing both formal and informal associations within their own community, which created localized forms of social capital on which they could draw in daily life in Perth. Gong and Wu thus illustrate how the trade workers engaged in ongoing processes of identity (re)making through their long, segmented domestic and transnational journeys, underlining the need to reconceptualize links between internal and transnational mobilities. Attention to the varied scope of the routes traced by China's increasingly mobile nonmetropolitan subjects prompts us to question the normative division of human mobilities into domestic versus international categories, since the new migrants' multilegged, multiscalar trajectories frequently involve both rural-to-urban and China-to-overseas routes as part of longer, sometimes lifelong mobility projects (Xiang 2022; Çaglar and Glick Schiller 2018).

Lin Song and Shih-Diing Liu, meanwhile, turn their attention to the complex affective and identificatory experiences of mainland students in Hong Kong amid Beijing's assertion of control over the territory's political and social life during the Anti-extradition Law Amendment Bill protests of 2019–20. Proposing that Hong Kong during the student protests could be seen as a minor transnational space of grassroots exchange, in Françoise Lionnet and Shu-mei Shih's (2005) terms, the authors map out the intricate politics of the protests on the ground. They document a "wild" form of affective mobility in the failure of the PRC state to contain the mobile mainland students' political and affective alliances. However, mainland students who supported the movement nonetheless felt excluded from it by virtue of the anti-mainlander attitudes of many of those involved. The authors document the essentializing effects of some forms of Hong Kong localism, which paradoxically meant that the PRC's state nationalism effectively remained dominant in mediating individuals' senses of belonging and alienation in the context of the movement—even when mainland students were originally sympathetic to their Hong Kong classmates' cause. In response, the authors propose the need for a serious and ongoing critical engagement with the concepts of both the national and the local in order to elaborate a minor transnationalist position capable of navigating the complex dynamics of cultural-national (dis)identification in Hong Kong's explosively tense present moment.

The theme of the transnationalization of class reproduction reemerges in the next article. In addition to the working-class identities studied in the three articles discussed above, this also relates to the intensified transnational mobility of a large population of middle-class migrants sometimes called "the new Chinese" (Li 2017), whose experiences and social impacts in Europe and Australia are the subject of two articles. Pál Nyíri and Fanni Beck focus on the new wave of middle-class emigrants from China to Europe—specifically, "golden visa" investment migrants in Hungary. They document these migrants' construction of Hungary as a land of purity and authenticity and a haven from the mental and spiritual exhaustion of high-pressure middle-class life in urban China. Interestingly, in significant part, what these middle-class migrants are fleeing is precisely the unsustainable pressure of upholding the intensive parenting model whose spread is traced among working-class mothers in Jin and Dai's article (discussed above). Significantly, the middle-class migrants' idealized construction of Hungary includes a racial element, as the new Chinese migrants cast nonwhite, non-middle-class migrants—especially Africans, Muslims, and refugees—as endangering the pure land and lifestyle they hope to enjoy in Europe.[5] Nyíri and Beck's article thus charts the reconfiguration of racial, ethnic, and class identities and hierarchies along with evolving patterns of middle-class migration from China.

Christina Ho, Dallas Rogers, and Jacqueline Nelson take up the thread of resurgent racisms in a transformed world. In the context of a growing, transnationally mobile mainland Chinese middle class, they observe that in Australia, Chinese migrants are selected by an immigration regime that actively seeks the wealthy and well educated, courting mobile PRC human and financial capitals. These privileged migrants are in turn highly successful in navigating the marketized fields of housing and education in Australia. Historically entrenched forms of racism have racialized this success, effectively scapegoating "the Chinese" for the effects of the Australian state's neoliberal reforms to secondary education and property investment settings. Forcefully, the authors argue that critical attention must be redirected away from criticizing the Chinese migrants as a racialized group back toward the policy structures that have set up the nation's housing and education markets to favor outcomes that reproduce class privilege.

Among the seven articles, Ting-Fai Yu's contribution on Sinophone media consumption in Malaysia is the one most aligned with the first wave of Chinese transnationalism studies, and also the one that illustrates most clearly the potentials for resistance to global China in diasporic communities. In the broad context of PRC Mandarin media expansion in recent years, his article unpacks the complexities of transnational reception communities that are differentiated both temporally and geographically, and thus trouble interpretive frameworks based on the presumed primacy and homogeneity of nation-states. Yu maps distinct historical waves of Sinophone media popularity in Malaysia, where Cantonese media from Hong Kong dominated during the 1990s, Taiwanese Mandarin media took over after 2000, and PRC Mandarin media have risen to prominence from 2010. Alongside this temporal analysis, Yu explores a geographic dimension through a case study of Sinophone media reception in Johor, which is adjacent to Singapore and where Singaporean Mandarin media has historically dominated and continues to dominate the popular mediascape, thanks to its ready accessibility via tall aerials. Yu highlights how Malaysians' continuing desires for these various non-PRC Chinese-language media resist PRC soft power and challenge the presumptively homogenizing, Sinicizing effects of PRC media expansion (Hau 2012). The affective attachment to Hong Kong media also has direct political implications, as seen when a generation of Malaysian-Chinese audiences habituated to Hong Kong popular music and screen media supported Hong Kong's Anti-extradition Law Amendment Bill movement in 2019–20.

The articles presented in this issue represent one step in what promises to be a far larger and more long-term project of rethinking the significance of plural and dynamic Chinese transnationalisms in the global China era. This is a world in which the status of both the terms *Chinese* and *national* has never been less obvious or more contested. It is therefore also a world in which our critical responses have never been more urgent.

Notes

I am grateful to the Australian Research Council for providing funding that supported the production of this article and special issue (ARC FT140100222; ARC DP230100442).

1 For an overview of further discussions of the conceptual relation between the nation-state and transnationalism, see Willis, Yeoh, and Fakhri 2004.

2 Other contributors to this first wave of scholarship focused on specific cultural sites, texts, and practices in and between territorial China and its diasporas, and they took a variety of positions on both the question of cultural identity and the status of the PRC in transnational circuits. For example, Sheldon Hsiao-peng Lu (1997) focused on cinema histories across mainland China, Taiwan, Hong Kong, and overseas Chinese communities, illustrating tensions between Chinese national(ist) and Chinese transnational (i.e., antinational) forces, insofar as he viewed the endeavor to construct a Chinese national cinema as constitutively haunted by Chinese cinema's unavoidably hybrid origins and its promiscuously transnational routes in the present. Mayfair Mei-hui Yang (2003) was principally interested in the possibility of a transnational public sphere materializing through Chinese women's collective cultural practices and approached "transnational China" somewhat descriptively as a geocultural zone encompassing China, Taiwan, Hong Kong, and diasporic communities. Her characterization of this "transnational China" drew on both roots and routes models: she described it as a "loosely organized" product of "inherited cultural *heritage*" as well as "the ongoing maintenance, renewal, and *reinvention* of cultural connections and a Chinese identity through cultural and material flows across political borders" (M. Yang 2003: 7; emphases added). Also interested in the possibility of a transnational public sphere, Guo-bin Yang (2003) addressed then-emerging practices of Chinese-language discussion and debate online, including the Global Huaren website that was established in response to the anti-Chinese violence in Indonesia in May 1998. Yang drew on Tu's concept of a globally dispersed "cultural China" that shared a "common cultural repertoire" and speculated that "the very confusion about the meaning of being Chinese in this age of globalization" may have precipitated an online Chinese cultural sphere "as a realm for self-clarification" (G. Yang 2003: 486). He drew back, however, from deeper exploration of identity formation to focus instead on the sociopolitical potentials of online communication.

3 In fact, both Ong and Shih expressed misgivings about the concept of diaspora, arguing for the preferability of the concepts of transnationality and Sinophone, respectively (Ong 2003: 87–88; Shih 2007: 26–30). Nonetheless, the broad point stands that their principal focus was on mobile ethnically Chinese people and organizations outside the territorial borders of the Chinese mainland. A partial exception to the "peripheral China" argument in scholarship of that time is found in Pieke et al. 2004.

4 At a domestic level, this was illustrated particularly starkly during the harsh metropolitan lockdowns in response to the spread of COVID-19 in 2021–22, when millions were forcibly immobilized to the point where civil unrest finally erupted at a scale not seen since 1989.

5 For analysis of a related phenomenon among Chinese students in Australia, see Martin 2022: 97–127.

References

Ang, Ien. 2001. *On Not Speaking Chinese: Living between Asia and the West*. London: Routledge.

Ang, Ien. 2020. "Chinatowns and the Rise of China." *Modern Asian Studies* 54, no. 4: 1367–93.

Bailey, Adrian J., and Ricardo K. S. Mak. 2021. "China and the Global Eye: From Globalisation to Everyday Life." In *Asia and China in the Global Era*, edited by Adrian J. Bailey and Ricardo K. S. Mak, 1–20. Boston: De Gruyter Mouton.

Breslin, Shaun. 2020. "China's Global Cultural Interactions." In *China and the World*, edited by David Shambaugh, 137–55. Oxford: Oxford University Press.

Çaglar, Ayse, and Nina Glick Schiller. 2018. *Migrants and City-Making: Dispossession, Displacement, and Urban Regeneration*. Durham, NC: Duke University Press.

Carter, Becky. 2017. *A Literature Review on China's Aid*. K4D Helpdesk Report. Brighton: Institute of Development Studies. https://assets.publishing.service.gov.uk/media/5a5f38d6e 5274a443e00372b/177_China_aid.pdf.

Chen, Tina, and Eric Hayot. 2015. "Introducing *Verge*: What Does It Mean to Study Global Asias?" *Verge: Studies in Global Asias* 1, no. 1: vi–xv.

Chen, Xiaomei. 1995. *Occidentalism: A Theory of Counter-discourse in Post-Mao China*. New York: Oxford University Press.

China Policy. 2017. *China Going Global: Between Ambition and Capacity*. Beijing: China Policy.

Ching, Leo T. S., Doobo Shim, and Fang-chih Yang. 2023. "Editorial Introduction: East Asian Pop Culture in the Era of China's Rise." *Inter-Asia Cultural Studies* 24, no. 5: 737–43.

Chow, Rey. 1998. "On Chineseness as a Theoretical Problem." *boundary 2* 25, no. 3: 1–24.

Chua, Beng Huat. 2012. *Structure, Audience, and Soft Power in East Asian Pop Culture*. Hong Kong: Hong Kong University Press.

Chun, Allen. 1996. "Fuck Chineseness: On the Ambiguities of Ethnicity as Culture as Identity." *boundary 2* 23, no. 2: 111–38.

Franceschini, Ivan, and Nicholas Loubere. 2022. *Global China as Method*. Cambridge: Cambridge University Press.

Glassman, Jim. 2018. *Drums of War, Drums of Development: The Formation of a Pacific Ruling Class and Industrial Transformation in East and Southeast Asia, 1945–1980*. Leiden, Netherlands: Koninklijke Brill.

Hau, Caroline S. 2012. "Becoming 'Chinese' in Southeast Asia." In *Sinicization and the Rise of China: Civilizational Processes beyond East and West*, edited by Peter Katzenstein, 175–206. London: Routledge.

Ismangil, Milan, and Anthony Fung. 2021. "eSports: A Chinese Sport?" In *Global eSports: Transformation of Cultural Perceptions of Competitive Gaming*, edited by Dal Yong Jin, 60–76. New York: Bloomsbury Academic.

Jedlowski, Alessandro, and Ute Röschenthaler. 2017. "China–Africa Media Interactions: Media and Popular Culture between Business and State Intervention." *Journal of African Cultural Studies* 29, no. 1: 1–10.

Katzenstein, Peter, ed. 2012. *Sinicization and the Rise of China: Civilizational Processes beyond East and West*. London: Routledge.

Kuehn, Julia, Kam Louie, and David M. Pomfret, eds. 2014. *Diasporic Chineseness after the Rise of China: Communities and Cultural Production*. Vancouver: UBC Press.

Lee, Ching Kwan. 2017. *The Specter of Global China: Politics, Labor, and Foreign Investment in Africa*. Chicago: University of Chicago Press.

Lee, Ching Kwan. 2022a. "Global China at Twenty: Why, How, and So What?" In C. Lee 2022b: 313–31.

Lee, Ching Kwan, ed. 2022b. "Inside Global China." Special section. *China Quarterly*, no. 250: 313–485.

Lee, Leo Ou-fan. 1994. "On the Margins of the Chinese Discourse: Some Personal Thoughts on the Cultural Meaning of the Periphery." In *The Living Tree: The Changing Meaning of Being Chinese Today*, edited by Tu Wei-ming, 207–26. Stanford, CA: Stanford University Press.

Li, Barry. 2017. *The New Chinese: How They Are Shaping Australia*. Milton, Australia: Wiley.

Lionnet, Françoise, and Shu-mei Shih, eds. 2005. *Minor Transnationalism*. Durham, NC: Duke University Press.

Liu, Lydia H. 1995. *Translingual Practice: Literature, National Culture, and Translated Modernity—China, 1900–1937*. Stanford, CA: Stanford University Press.

Lu, Sheldon Hsiao-peng, ed. 1997. *Transnational Chinese Cinemas: Identity, Nationhood, Gender*. Honolulu: University of Hawai'i Press.

Martin, Fran. 2014. "Transnational Queer Sinophone Cultures." In *Routledge Handbook of Sexuality Studies in East Asia*, edited by Mark McLelland and Vera Mackie, 35–48. London: Routledge.

Martin, Fran. 2022. *Dreams of Flight: The Lives of Chinese Women Students in the West*. Durham, NC: Duke University Press.

Nonini, Donald N., and Aihwa Ong. 1997. "Chinese Transnationalism as an Alternative Modernity." In Ong and Nonini 1997: 3–33.

Nyíri, Pál. 2010. *Mobility and Cultural Authority in Contemporary China*. Seattle: University of Washington Press.

Nyíri, Pál. 2021. "Chinese Correspondents around the World." In Pieke and Iwabuchi 2021a: 271–79.

Oakes, Tim, and Louisa Schein. 2006. "Translocal China: An Introduction." In *Translocal China: Linkages, Identities, and the Reimagining of Space*, edited by Tim Oakes and Louisa Schein, 1–35. London: Routledge.

Ong, Aihwa. 1997. "Chinese Modernities: Narratives of Nation and Capitalism." In Ong and Nonini 1997: 171–202.

Ong, Aihwa. 1999. *Flexible Citizenship: The Cultural Logics of Transnationality*. Durham, NC: Duke University Press.

Ong, Aihwa. 2003. "Cyberpublics and Diaspora Politics among Transnational Chinese." *Interventions* 5, no. 1: 82–100.

Ong, Aihwa, and Donald M. Nonini, eds. 1997. *Ungrounded Empires: The Cultural Politics of Modern Chinese Transnationalism*. New York: Routledge.

Pavlićević, Dragan, and Nicole Talmacs, eds. 2022. *The China Question: Contestations and Adaptations*. Singapore: Palgrave Macmillan.

Peng, Weiying, and Michael Keane. 2019. "China's Soft Power Conundrum, Film Coproduction, and Visions of Shared Prosperity." *International Journal of Cultural Policy* 25, no. 7: 904–16.

Pieke, Frank N. 2021. "The Rise of China and East Asia as the New Center of the World." In Pieke and Iwabuchi 2021a: 245–51.

Pieke, Frank N., and Koichi Iwabuchi, eds. 2021a. *Global East Asia: Into the Twenty-First Century*. Oakland: University of California Press.

Pieke, Frank N., and Koichi Iwabuchi. 2021b. "Introduction: The Many Faces of Global East Asia." In Pieke and Iwabuchi 2021a: 1–10.

Pieke, Frank N., Pál Nyíri, Mette Thunø, and Antonella Ceccagano. 2004. *Transnational Chinese: Fujianese Migrants in Europe*. Stanford, CA: Stanford University Press.

Ptáčková, Jarmila, Ondřej Klimeš, Gary Rawnsley, and Jens Damm. 2021. "Introduction: The Soft Edges of China's Hard Power." In *Transnational Sites of China's Cultural Diplomacy: Central Asia, Southeast Asia, Middle East, and Europe Compared*, edited by Jarmila Ptáčková, Ondřej Klimeš, and Gary Rawnsley, 1–11. Singapore: Palgrave Macmillan.

Rofel, Lisa, and Carlos Rojas, eds. 2022. *New World Orderings: China and the Global South*. Durham, NC: Duke University Press.

Shambaugh, David. 2013. *China Goes Global: The Partial Power*. Oxford: Oxford University Press.

Shambaugh, David. 2015. "China's Soft Power Push: The Search for Respect." *Foreign Affairs* 94, no. 4: 99–107.

Shamir, Ronen. 2005. "Without Borders? Notes on Globalization as a Mobility Regime." *Sociological Theory* 23, no. 2: 197–217.

Shih, Shu-mei. 2007. *Visuality and Identity: Sinophone Articulations across the Pacific*. Berkeley: University of California Press.

Shih, Shu-mei. 2011. "The Concept of the Sinophone." *PMLA* 126, no. 3: 709–18.

Shih, Shu-mei. 2012. "Foreword: The Sinophone as History and the Sinophone as Theory." *Journal of Chinese Cinemas* 6, no. 1: 5–7.

Shih, Shu-mei. 2013. "Introduction: What Is Sinophone Studies?" In *Sinophone Studies: A Critical Reader*, edited by Shu-mei Shih, Chien-hsin Tsai, and Brian Bernards, 1–16. New York: Columbia University Press.

Sidaway, James D., Simon C. Rowedder, Chih Yuan Woon, and Weiqian Lin. 2020. "Politics and Spaces of China's Belt and Road Initiative." *EPC: Politics and Space* 38, no. 5: 795–802.

Sun, Wanning, and John Sinclair. 2016. "Introduction: Rethinking Chinese Diasporic Media." In *Media and Communication in the Chinese Diaspora: Rethinking Transnationalism*, edited by Wanning Sun and John Sinclair, 1–14. London: Routledge.

Sun, Wanning, and Haiqing Yu. 2023. *Digital Transnationalism: Chinese-Language Media in Australia*. Leiden, Netherlands: Brill.

Tan, Yan. 2021. "China's Diaspora Engagement Policy and Its Powerful Effect outside Its Borders." *Melbourne Asia Review*, no. 8. https://melbourneasiareview.edu.au/chinas-diaspora-engagement-policy-and-its-powerful-effect-outside-its-borders/.

Thussu, Daya Kishan, Hugo de Burgh, and Anbin Shi, eds. 2018. *China's Media Go Global*. New York: Routledge.

Tu, Wei-ming. 1994. "Cultural China: The Periphery as the Center." In *The Living Tree: The Changing Meaning of Being Chinese Today*, edited by Tu Wei-ming, 1–34. Stanford, CA: Stanford University Press.

Wang, Huiyao, and Miao Lu. 2016. *China Goes Global: The Impact of Chinese Overseas Investment on Its Business Enterprises*. New York: Palgrave Macmillan.

Wang, Mei (Lisa), Zhen Qi, and Jijing Zhang. 2015. "China Becomes a Capital Exporter: Trends and Issues." In *China's Domestic Transformation in a Global Context*, edited by Ligang Song, Ross Garnaut, Cai Fang, and Lauren Johnston, 315–38. Canberra: ANU Press.

Willis, Katie, Brenda S. A. Yeoh, and S. M. Abdul Khader Fakhri. 2004. "Introduction: Transnationalism as a Challenge to the Nation." In *State/Nation/Transnation*, edited by Brenda S. A. Yeoh and Katie Willis, 1–15. New York: Routledge.

Winter, Tim. 2016. "One Belt, One Road, One Heritage: Cultural Diplomacy and the Silk Road." *Diplomat*, March 29. http://thediplomat.com/2016/03/one-belt-one-road-one-heritage -cultural-diplomacy-and-the-silk-road/.

Xinhua She. 2020. "2019 nian woguo lüyou zong shouru da 6.63 wan yi yuan tongbi zeng-zhang 11%" 2019 年我国旅游总收入达6.63万亿元 同比增长11% ("China's 2019 tourism revenue reaches 6.63 trillion RMB, a year-on-year increase of 11%"). November 3. http://www .xinhuanet.com/travel/2020-03/11/c_1125693570.htm.

Xiang, Biao. 2016. "Emigration Trends and Policies in China." In *Spotlight on China: Chinese Education in the Globalized World*, edited by Shibao Guo and Yan Guo, 247–67. Rotterdam: Sense. https://doi.org/10.1007/978-94-6300-669-9_15.

Xiang, Biao. 2022. "What, When, and How Transnationalism Matters: A Multi-scalar Framework." In *Handbook on Transnationalism*, edited by Brenda S. A. Yeoh and Francis L. Collins, 45–59. Northampton, MA: Edward Elgar.

Yang, Guobin. 2003. "The Internet and the Rise of a Transnational Chinese Cultural Sphere." *Media, Culture, and Society* 25, no. 4: 469–90.

Yang, Mayfair Mei-hui. 2003. *Spaces of Their Own: Women's Public Sphere in Transnational China*. Minneapolis: University of Minnesota Press.

Yu, Haiqing, and Wanning Sun. 2019. "Introduction: Social Media and Chinese Digital Diasporas in Australia." *Media International Australia* 173, no. 1: 17–21.

Zhang, Denghua. 2021. "Messages from China's Third White Paper on Foreign Aid." *Interpreter*, February 5. https://www.lowyinstitute.org/the-interpreter/messages-china-s-third-white-paper -foreign-aid.

Zhao, Yupei, and Zhongxuan Lin. 2020. "Umbrella Platform of Tencent eSports Industry in China." *Journal of Cultural Economy* 14, no. 1: 9–25.

Clashing Gender in the Age of Transnational Infrastructural Capitalism: The Vocational Education and Subject Making of China's Future Workers

Anita Koo and Ngai Pun

Introduction

As we enter the age of Chinese infrastructural capitalism, the transformation of the political-economic system is signaled by the building of physical and digital infrastructures in the Belt and Road Initiatives, resulting in global trade wars on multiple fronts (Pun 2022). Accompanying this new Chinese transnationalism is a new project of subject making: an increasing number of young people, especially those from working-class backgrounds, have entered the expanded urban vocational education system for training as future skilled workers. To prepare for the new imperialistic age, the Chinese state is turning swiftly from labor-intensive manufacturing toward scientific innovation and technology upgrade in order to maximize profits and compete for capital monopoly. In 2015, the State Council of the PRC

positions 32:4 DOI 10.1215/10679847-11306796
Copyright 2024 by Duke University Press

issued an action plan to implement a development strategy called *Made in China 2025* (State Council 2015). An available pool of skilled professionals become the fundamental precondition for upgrading the "Made in China" industrial chain. Correspondingly, the concept of craftsmanship has been promoted in media and policy papers (CGTN 2017), and vocational schools are now regarded as crucial sites for the cultivation of this new generation of Chinese workers (Huang 2017; Zhang and Yao 2015). In contrast to the previous image of feminized workers in global workplaces producing cheap electronics or garments, a new image of masculinized skilled labor capable of inventing and producing high-value commodities is now highlighted (CGTN 2017). The emerging image of a proper laborer is an "innovative brain" equipped with high-level technical knowledge and strong operating skills for the new economy—the achievement of which is "naturally" associated with hegemonic masculinity.

Despite the recent reemergence of a collective craftsman identity bestowed with techno skills, the value and dignity of manual labor are discounted in the dominant ideology of postreform China (Li 2015), and the nation has become embedded in transnational neoliberalism by extolling "self-enterprising" culture since the 1990s (Anagnost, Arai, and Ren 2013). In this context, young people are encouraged to (re)define their gendered subjectivity and individual pathways toward active engagement in market-based competition. The majority of young women in vocational school tend to gravitate toward accounting, secretarial, and tourism training programs, which offer greater assurance of future employment, rather than opting for technical courses that prepare them for manual labor roles. Even some of the male students display a lack of enthusiasm for pursuing skilled labor positions, instead aspiring to managerial jobs or aiming to establish their own small businesses. The new political project of gendered subject making through vocational education thus inevitability clashes with the logics and values of the neoliberal market that go hand in hand with the emergence of gender essentialism. As the enterprising and authoritarian Chinese state forcefully imagineers the epochal "China Dream" of a renaissance of national strength and wealth, it intervenes in mass media and education to create masculinized discourses of nationalistic subjects. Growing up under Chinese transnational infrastructural capitalism, young vocational school students thus experience confusing and ambivalent desires to meet the demands of both state and market.

In many academic discussions, subject making is subsumed under the macro discussion of neoliberal or populist crises in which social and class inequalities predominate and overshadow equally if not more important gender inequalities. In contrast, this article looks at the contestation of the material practices of gender in vocational schools, which produce and repro-duce the new generation of young workers for China's future. Based on our participatory action project in a vocational school, we explore the gendering process in students' vocational learning and training and consider to what extent the production of workers is affected by the tensions between state, school, and market. Gender cannot be seen as a unified concept in China because the state, capital, and education espouse gender logics that some-times run in a consistent direction but more often in opposite directions, which impacts the gendering of younger workers. In this study, we use the concept of "clashing gender" to make sense of the conflictual process of sub-ject making among the new generation of future workers in China's age of rapid transition toward transnational infrastructural capitalism. We argue that in the process of subject making, gender in fact lies at the center of struggles between rising state power, market hegemony, and the education system.

Vocational Education and Nation Building

In China, education is linked to the state's discourse of raising the quality of the population to build a strong nation to compete in the transnational market (Kipnis 2011). The same is true for vocational education, which has been a nationalistic project ever since its introduction (Pun and Qiu 2020). As early as the beginning of the twentieth century, vocational education was regarded as a way to "save the country" (Schulte 2013) by training students to serve society as a labor force for industrial development. This remains relevant today: the system is modeled on and designed for industrial produc-tion (Koo 2016). Since the 1990s, in order to maintain the efficient supply of skilled labor to advance China's market economy, vocational training has taken up a significant role in the postreform education system. With the

"China Dream" and the rise of China as a global player in the circuits of transnational capitalism, vocational education is now being further developed in line with the state's development strategy, *Made in China 2025* (State Council 2015), and serves as an essential human resources lever for the country's economic and social development.

The objectives of *Made in China 2025* are outlined by Premier Li Keqiang as "to seek innovation-driven development, apply smart technologies, strengthen foundations, pursue green development and redouble our efforts to upgrade China from a manufacturer of quantity to one of quality" (Hui 2015). According to Li, the shortage of skilled talents needed for the acceleration of China's industrial upgrading and economic restructuring is becoming more acute, particularly in advanced manufacturing: there will be a severe national talent shortage of nineteen million in 2020 and thirty million in 2025. The *Decision of the State Council on Accelerating the Development of Modern Vocational Education* (State Council 2014) was widely discussed in mass media, elevating the key role of vocational schools in supporting industrial upgrading under the state's innovation-driven development strategy.

China has committed to building a modern, world-class vocational education system in which vocational schools are expected to produce "hundreds of millions of high-quality laborers and skilled technical talent" to upgrade the "Made in China" industrial chain (State Council 2014). State investment in vocational schools continues to grow. By 2017, government funding for vocational education across the country reached 335 billion RMB (Ministry of Education 2019). In April 2019, the State Council announced that another 100 billion RMB would be earmarked to expand the vocational education system (Zhang 2019). Many secondary vocational schools would be upgraded to vocational colleges to equip future workers with higher skill levels for the industrial transformation. In 2021, the state set clearer goals: the enrollment of vocational colleges should reach 10 percent of the total higher education enrollment by 2025, and China's vocational education should be among the best in the world by 2035 (State Council 2021). The further development of vocational education is regarded as a way to facilitate the transformation of China's industrial development and its entry into the highly competitive age of transnational infrastructural capitalism.

Despite all of this, vocational education has long held a lower status than academic education (Hansen and Woronov 2013). In order to attract more students to technical and skills training, the state discourse actively claims that vocational education will open doors to better occupations and higher incomes. The state has also implemented policies to reduce students' tuition fees and provide subsidies for those from disadvantaged backgrounds. An increasing number of students of both genders, especially those from rural and working-class families, enroll in vocational schools after completing their compulsory schooling in order to pursue dreams of upward mobility (Pun and Koo 2019). Over the years of its development, China's vocational system has become the largest in the world, and includes around 11,300 schools that enroll a total of 30.88 million students and produce 10 million graduates per year (*Global Times* 2022). Over 70 percent of workers who enter modern manufacturing and emerging industries are graduates of vocational education institutions (Ministry of Education 2019). Vocational schools are thus the most impactful sites for producing and reproducing young workers for the upgrading of China's transnational economy.

Today, "love the country, upgrade industry, and be a high-tech laborer" has become a prevailing state ideology spread throughout the vocational education system, the talent cultivation platform for China's high-tech manufacturing industry. Vocational school students and graduates are expected to become the "innovative brain" equipped with advanced technical knowledge and strong operating skills, who will be capable of inventing and producing high-value products to boost the Chinese economy. Students are educated to be patriotic subjects to serve the goal of *Made in China 2025*: to work hard to acquire high-value, high-tech professional skills, and sacrifice themselves for national wealth and strength. At the same time, unlike the graduates of the 1980s and early 1990s, whose jobs were assigned by the state, the current generation of vocational students must find their own jobs after graduation. They are expected to embrace the culture of reflexive "self-enterprise" to fit the needs of the neoliberalized labor market.

Gender, Education, and Work in China

In postreform China, young people are highly committed to obtaining educational credentials because they believe that these will assure them a place in the increasingly competitive labor market (Anagnost, Arai, and Ren 2013). The belief in a strong relationship between higher qualifications and securing a better job in future has become a central part of young people's habitus, regardless of gender. The general expansion in education during the economic growth period has also increased the educational attainment level of the new generation and narrowed the educational gender gap (Tsui and Rich 2002). However, the impact of narrowing the gender gap in educational and occupational attainment is mixed. China has a long history under the influence of traditional Confucian values that emphasize distinct gender roles (Gao 2003; Liu 2014). The socialist period witnessed dramatic changes as the government made efforts to promote egalitarian practices. Women were encouraged to work the same jobs as men, and lifetime employment with a wide range of social services and benefits was guaranteed by the state (Hanser 2005). China's female labor force participation rate was among the highest in the world in Mao's era, and the gender wage gap was remarkably small by international standards (Kidd and Meng 2001). Until now, to have a job is standard practice for most urban women. However, following the market transition from the late 1970s, gender relations in the class and employment structure were transformed (Berik, Dong, and Summerfield 2007). On one hand, rapid economic growth and labor market expansion have brought unprecedented employment and mobility opportunities for both women and men. On the other hand, gender disparity in the labor market has increased across both employment status and income level, accompanied by worsening gender segregation (He and Wu 2017). In this sense, the increased female participation in higher education fails to translate to better employment outcomes. Evidence shows that male employees disproportionately occupy more lucrative jobs (Summerfield et al. 2011), and this occupational gender segregation plays an important role in creating gendered earning gaps in postreform China (Xiu and Gunderson 2015).

The declining influence of the socialist ideology of gender equity and the expanding market economy have also led to the resurgence of a more traditional gendered division of labor (Otis 2012; Zuo 2014) and more essentialist gender norms (Koo, Hui, and Pun 2020). Naturalized biological understandings of gender are found in both families and workplaces to justify the gendered segregation in employment (Rofel 1999). Although the one-child policy created a generation of so-called "empowered urban daughters" (Fong 2002; Liu 2014) who did not have brothers to compete with for parental resources, gender identity and gender appropriateness remain central to the childrearing, educational, and occupational aspirations of Chinese youth (Kim, Brown, and Fong 2018). Moreover, studies suggesting the reversal of the gender gap in higher education and numbers of women aspiring to or successfully occupying professional occupations mainly refer to middle-class communities (Liu 2014). The gendered subjectivities of working-class youth in relation to their educational and occupational choices in the context of the rapid development of Chinese capitalism have not yet been examined. To fill this gap, this article focuses on a group of young people with mainly working-class backgrounds and whose education and training focus on vocational skills and practical knowledge.

Both in China and internationally, vocational education has historically been characterized by a high degree of sex segregation (Butler and Ferrier 2006). In contrast to a global trend toward declining gender segregation of higher education majors, vocational programs have been remarkably stable over time in their gender profile, such that women rarely choose programs in crafts and technical subjects, and men rarely choose programs in health and welfare-related subjects. Unlike academic and professional training programs, vocational education does not increase the presence of women in male-dominated jobs, and vice versa. Therefore, while gender stereotyping in subject choice, training, and employment decisions remains hegemonic, the expansion of vocational education and increased enrollments in it may not result in wider vocational choice for Chinese youths.

Our study analyzes the material practices of gender in everyday life and the gendering processes at work among emergent working subjects in a vocational school. In studying these students' educational and occupational choices and opportunities, we highlight the importance of the intersectionality of gender and class. Our focus is on how vocational education promotes girls' and boys' adjustment to the demands of the expanding labor market, and to the limited range of opportunities on offer; and how youths conform to, negotiate with, or resist gender relations as they are called to operationalize the new national strategic plan.

Background and Methodology

The vocational school we chose for this study is an "up-and-coming" vocational institute located in a suburban district of the city of Hangzhou, whose development plan is aligned very closely with local as well as national development strategies. Different from other vocational schools that stereotypically enroll those who fail in public examinations (Woronov 2015), this school is like the academic-track key schools. It receives additional funding from the government to set up model programs that have high thresholds for admission and attract top students. As the provincial capital of Zhejiang Province in southeastern China, Hangzhou is an important manufacturing base and logistics hub for the coastal area. With the development of many new industries including automotive components, electronics, household electrical appliances, and information technology, a number of high-tech industrial zones and incubation parks have been established in the city. Given the increased demand for high-skilled technical workers in manufacturing, the vocational school has created specialty programs such as Robotics Application, Computer Numerical Control (CNC), Tooling Technology, and Digital Control for Advanced Manufacturing. With financial support from various levels of government, classrooms and training workshops in the school have been renovated with an emphasis on the latest techniques, processes, and tools for advanced manufacturing. Many of the school's programs have also been updated to serve the advancement of intelligent manufacturing in Hangzhou. In 2015, the school was upgraded from a skilled workers training school (*jigong xuexiao* 技工學校) to a technical college (*jishi xueyuan* 技師學院), and now provides vocational courses not only at high school but also at tertiary level.

As the Ministry of Human Resources and Social Security has financed and managed the school since its establishment in 1979, the curriculum focuses on teaching the manual skills and practical abilities needed for the state occupational license qualification of skilled workers and technicians. Students who finish a three-year program receive a high school certificate and an official professional license as "middle-level skilled worker." Graduates of five-year and six-year programs are officially qualified as "high-level skilled workers" and "technicians." In the 2016/17 academic year, 2,160 students were enrolled, with 1,660 at high school level and 500 at tertiary level. Programs were organized under three disciplines: Advanced Manufacturing, Intelligent Control, and Modern Services. As over three-quarters of the courses related to machinery and electrical engineering, which lead graduates into male-dominated areas of work, there were only 350 female students. Most of these were enrolled in the three-year programs grouped under Modern Services, such as tourism and accounting.

A local university helped our research team obtain an introduction to the technical college in October 2016. We were welcomed by the principal, who was eager to share with us the school's "successful development story" and its great contribution: cultivating the talents needed by enterprises, local government, and the state. Teachers also provided useful background information about program curricula, class size and gender distribution, students' academic performance, and intern training, which facilitated our data collection. Over the following years, we visited the school five times, with each visit lasting one to three weeks, allowing us to engage in close interactions and in-depth interviews with students and interns of both genders.

In order to understand the gendered processes of subject making in this new generation of Chinese workers, our study set out to explore the learning and training experiences of both female and male students in the male-dominated courses under the disciplines of advanced manufacturing and intelligent control. The courses were described both as syllabus-led and as teaching hands-on skills with highly technical content, training students as skilled manual workers or technicians to help Hangzhou develop an innovative scientific industry and upgrade its industrial structure. We interviewed sixty-two students (twenty-seven girls and thirty-five boys) and seven male graduates aged between fifteen and twenty-four across the two disciplines. We observed lessons held in classrooms as well as training workshops, and participated in various student activities. When analyzing our fieldwork data, we place special focus on students' educational decisions, learning experiences, and career aspirations, and their evolving relation to gender ideologies and identities in the process of crafting selves within social institutions.

Education Plan: Support Chinese Manufacturing, Achieve Successful Lives

The technical college is easily identified by the huge red Chinese characters on the grey wall of its main building, which translate as "Support Chinese Manufacturing, Achieve Successful Lives." This eye-catching motto drew the positive attention of many residents. Throughout the years of upgrading and transformation, the technical college had remained well reputed in the district, attracting many middle-school graduates, both girls and boys, from surrounding areas. Nearly all students were local and rural-migrant children with a working-class background. Many of their parents were factory workers and taxi drivers, and some ran their own small businesses (with fewer than five employees) in the district. When asked about their educational and school choices, nearly all students, regardless of their sex, said they were attracted by the prospect of a career in machine operation or electronic engineering, and hoped to acquire technical skills and become high-skilled workers or industry technicians. Rain, an articulate boy in the second-year CNC machining class, is one example:

> I could have [got into an academic high school] but I preferred to come and receive professional training in high-end practical skills. A future as a technician gives me a clearer direction, to know where I am going. . . . In recent years, the government has shifted its emphasis to vocational schools, so I decided to come here to learn some solid skills. With the forecast of rapid development in the local economy, there will be opportunities around.

During fieldwork, we met a number of students who had achieved marks that would have given them admission academic high schools. They decided to opt for a vocational course instead because they were confident that in responding to the national call to upgrade manufacturing, they would be a privileged group and would benefit from the investment in vocational schools, and be able to get a foothold in a growing industry aligned with the state's development strategy. We also met many male students who were guided toward advanced technical training after completing their compulsory education. They confessed that when they chose the program, they were simply following the advice of their middle school teachers and had no concrete idea of the training involved. Encouraged by their teachers, they "knew" the training in intelligent or advanced manufacturing was their best path for self-development in China: "to prepare for future employment in a booming industry."

For the boys, it was straightforward that the machine operation and electrician courses, which would lead them to male-dominated areas of work, were the best options. For girls, however, enrolling in these courses was regarded as unusual in a highly gender-segregated vocational system. Unsurprisingly, female students were the minority in these two fields of study, and there were consistently only one or two girls in each class of thirty to forty students.

Only Ambitious Girls Enter a Nontraditional Field

In general, the girls in this study were more ambitious and determined and usually performed well in their classes. Many girls declared that the "high quality" of the vocational courses, based on the high marks required for admission and the technical skills involved, attracted them to enter a field traditionally associated with male work. They described their choices as "normal" and "very rational" because the skills and knowledge obtained in the courses were not only needed for national development but also had a high market value, which would bring them high positions in the future.

Nevertheless, we should not forget that these ambitious girls formed minorities in the male-dominated programs. Gender norms related to occupational choice continue to influence the youths' vocational decisions. As the girls recalled, nearly all of their middle-school teachers had recommended they study in female-dominated programs, such as hospitality and tourism, accounting, and electronic business, which would lead to employment in Hangzhou's growing service sector. When we asked the girls to think back, a lot of them admitted that their teachers, friends, and even they themselves had questioned their choice to study in a male-dominated field. "When I realized that I'm the only girl in my class, I was shocked. I was upset that I was left alone. Should I move to another program and join the girls? Is this a course that's really not suitable for girls? I struggled a lot at that time. I worried that I'd made the wrong choice" (Bee). Bee was a second-year student in Tooling Technology, the only girl in the class of thirty-two. After the public examination, most of her female classmates chose to study tourism or secretarial studies and accounting. "Being left alone" by other girls, she felt uncertain about her choice of training and future occupation. But after a year of study, ranking top in her class and being chosen to lead and help other students during training classes, Bee knew that she had made the right choice. However, as she did not share the same aspirations, hobbies, interests, or even outlook as the majority, she had to walk her chosen path alone.

> Girls in other classes always follow the news about fashion and cosmetics on their social media, [which] become their daily discussion topics. But I'm not the type [of girl] that aspires to be an office lady, wearing high heels with short skirts, holding a cup of coffee. Others may aspire to look like that, but I don't. . . . For me, operating a huge machine also looks cool and modern. To them, I look strange.

While the androgynous and austere Maoist women were symbols of advancement during the socialist period, nowadays, such forms of gender expression have become "strange." The subject making of a skillful technician in vocational school—operating huge machines in the manufacturing sector— "clashes" with the cultural image of modern women in current China and other girls' desire to be beautiful, trendy service sector workers with a cosmopolitan outlook. In contrast to the "iron girls" portrayed in the media during Mao's era, who wore the unisex blue trouser suit and displayed strength and bodily comportment no different from their male peers, after the market reforms, beauty is now emphasized (Yang 2011). The new young and fashionable feminine image and modern female office worker identity emerged in the context of intensified global connections. Heavily influenced by the circulation of such images in movies, TV dramas, and fashion magazines, femininity became associated with jobs in the growing service and financial sectors. Complicated by the global consumer culture, this "re-feminization" is often regarded as a new space of "freedom" for women in postreform China, where girls and women are encouraged to indulge in the possibilities and pleasures of feminine expression (Xu and Feiner 2007). And it has been widely noted that when China transitioned from a socialist past to a modern consumer-capitalist society, new employment opportunities arose banking on women's youth and beauty in the service sector, thus creating a so-called "rice bowl of youth" (Hanser 2005: 581).

We observed that most of the female students in the technical college, unlike Bee, wore makeup and happily exchanged their knowledge about makeup techniques and new products in the dorm. On special occasions, such as college ceremonies, they were required to dress up and wear high heels to greet visitors and parents. As a result of the new trend of "re-feminization," a market-based subject-making project (Hanser 2005; Otis 2012), over 90 percent of female students in the technical college enrolled in the three-year high school programs grouped under Modern Services. The much lower entrance criteria for these three-year programs, reflecting the easy entrance into feminized work in the expanding service sector, attracts a large number of female students to the vocational track after their compulsory education. For them, it is a default choice. In both formal and informal curricula in school, these young female subjects actively accommodate themselves to mainstream femininity and beauty, which is believed to secure them gender capital in the fierce competition for social and career success (Wen 2013). In our study, only a minority of girls responded to the state goal of preparing themselves as skilled professionals and technicians to support industrial upgrading. Since gender norms increasingly structure the Chinese job market, gender heavily influences the learning and training experiences and occupational aspirations of those who make nonstandard choices, resulting in more "clashes" during their school-to-work transitions.

Career Aspiration: Who Stays in the Field?

We found that within the advanced manufacturing and intelligent control programs, girls and boys did not differ in their academic achievement or practical abilities. In both formal and informal curricula, both the girls and the boys were fully engaged in learning programming technologies and the operation and control of machinery. Most girls commented that they were treated no differently from male students, and additional support from classmates and teachers was available if requested. For example, when teachers demonstrated the use of advanced computer-controlled lathes in a training workshop, a girl student sitting next to us highlighted that "gender is no longer an issue when the work that requires physical strength is increasingly being replaced by technology."

At the high school level, all of the students in the two disciplines, regardless of gender, were eager to acquire higher qualifications and were entirely positive about the prospect of pursuing careers in their chosen areas. However, many girls left school after receiving the high school certificate and the "middle-level skilled worker" qualification. Boys dominated at the tertiary level of training. There were no girls among the thirty-seven students in their sixth year of study in the "technician classes." In the classes geared toward high-level skilled workers, only 13 out of 462 students were girls. As most girls in the courses were high performers, they should not have had any problems continuing their tertiary education in the technical college. So, where did they go? "They went on better paths, of course. . . . Both girls in my previous class jumped to pursue a university degree. A better path for girls. That's understandable" (Tree, in the fourth-year Tooling Technology class). School teachers explained that most female students and other high performers were channeled into the "examination classes," which would lead them to university, rather than staying at the technical college for tertiary education after high school. When other third-year students were sent to factories for internships, these students stayed in the classroom to catch up with a college entrance examination syllabus especially designed for admission to a "normal university" that trained technical teachers. Most of the female students enrolled in a university after high school graduation. "I love to operate all the machines, and the technical knowledge involved is fascinating. I want to be a female technician, but I don't think I could easily get a job in a factory. I'd worried about that before. So, when the option came up, I was *really* happy and relieved. It allows me to stay in the field" (Lulu, a female student in Machine Operation Examination Class). Lulu had joined the Examination Class along with two female and two male classmates. Initially, she planned to stay on at the technical college for tertiary education, aiming to gain the skilled technician qualification, and look for opportunities to enter the field based on her capabilities. But based on the prior experiences of other senior year students, factories did not welcome female interns in the machinery industry. Without on-the-job training, it was unlikely that they would become technicians or even start a career path in the field. Although girls and boys were trained in the same way in school, and there was no difference between them in their ambitions and performance on the courses, it was very clear that employers either preferred or solely selected male graduates. When the girls' occupational aspirations, based on their interests and individual capabilities, "clashed" with the job market's expectations and demands, many changed their path as a strategy to keep themselves in the field. Some even considered leaving the field, joining the service sector for a "better future."

Moon, the only girl in the fourth-year CNC machinery class, had not arranged for an internship in her third year of study, but stayed on at school to receive the "in-house training." Her classmates and teachers described her as determined and tough. She hoped to work in a local factory over the summer to "practice her learned skills" but was repeatedly told that no girl would be employed. Having no way to gain discipline-related work experience, she "reluctantly" took a part-time job in a coffee shop near her home. To her surprise, the summer job "did not involve any specific skills but the pay was quite high." Her boss even tried to retain her as a full-time employee by doubling her income. Although she went back to school after the summer, she admitted that she had reframed her aspirations after her summer job experience, deciding not to pursue the highest qualification offered at the school, which would have allowed her to become a skilled technician. "In my classmates' description [of their internship experiences], they were working ten-hour days and six-day weeks, with two weeks of morning shifts and two weeks of night shifts. And their pay was lower than mine! . . . After learning this, I told myself: 'There's no need to be stubborn.' In future, if I can get a less tiring job that has higher pay, I will go for it." From time to time, the students were reminded that the state, the local government, and the vocational education system had invested highly in each of them, helping them to acquire the latest high-tech skills to contribute to national development. The school principal also emphasized that the skills students acquired were highly specialized, which would enable them to enter high-level technical positions and thus achieve upward social mobility. However, in reality, the gender ideology of the neoliberal labor market, which naturalizes and even essentializes biological differences between men and women, rejected female graduates in the manufacturing and innovative sectors. As noted above, the abolition of job assignment by the state forces the current generations of vocational school graduates to compete for jobs in the labor market. Female students from working-class backgrounds had to negotiate hard with, if not directly adopt, the dominant gender ideology in their gendered "subject-making" process, which resulted in uncertainty, ambivalence, and even changes of mind.

During fieldwork, many teachers we met actually encouraged their students, especially girls, to "remain flexible" and try to "seize different opportunities offered in the market" after graduation. In a context where the labor market seeks stereotypically young and energetic female workers for the growing domestic service sector, female students were repeatedly reminded to be self-enterprising: be sensitive to the "market's labor needs," and to choose a career path that best fit their personal strengths as valued by the market. Therefore, "when opportunities came," even the best-performing and most ambitious girls who had responded to the state's call to become the engine of industrial growth chose to opt out of further training in engineering and technical innovation.

Diverging Paths?

Within the vocational education system, training and internship were perceived as opportunities for students to develop their skills and commitment to the profession. This training was expected to help students familiarize themselves with the working environment and increase their chances of being employed after graduation. However, on the one hand, we found that almost all of the female students from the two programs were deprived of this on-the-job training. On the other hand, many male students claimed that the internships were discouraging experiences rather than opening new possibilities for them. "They are all simple operations. Not much skill is involved. We just have to put the materials on the machines, and they work on their own. The materials are quite heavy, so it's tiring. And the work hours are long. We only have one day off [per week]. And the pay is low. [*Sigh*] . . . it's harsh" (Cloud, in the fourth-year Tooling Technology class). Most of the boys who returned from internships complained about the restrictive work environments in factories. Many declared that they had to reconsider their "career plan," as they "didn't want to spend their entire life doing tiring and dirty work in factories." During interviews, these students explained the importance of "persistence," as seniority counts for a lot in their fields: "The longer you stay, the higher your income and status." But for the majority, the long working hours and low pay prevented them from persisting or fully committing.

> I'll give myself one year, or two years maximum. By that time, if earnings are still low, if I haven't got promoted to a more senior position, I won't stay [in the factories]. . . . We're twenty [years old] and need to plan for the future. Seriously! If the pay is always so low, [there's] no girl . . . no hope for marriage. [*laugh*] Girls only marry successful men, right? [*laugh*] Anyway, be realistic! As our teacher advises: we have to keep ourselves open, look for better opportunities. (Grass, a graduate of the five-year program in Tool Technology class)

We met Grass with his two classmates on a Saturday afternoon when they returned to technical college for their graduation certificates. All three had finished their nine-month internships and decided not to continue their studies into the sixth-year technician program. They declared that they had lost their commitment and would not invest in the additional year of study. With graduation certificates, their status of "intern" would be changed to "general worker" (*putong gongren*) in the same factory, where they planned to stay for one or two more years. According to these male interns, their credentials qualified them to be employed as "skilled workers" or "high-level skilled workers," but no factory would do so because the wages would be more than double. In their eyes, most factory owners did not properly recognize their skills and qualifications but treated them as general workers with "physical strength" and "some basic knowledge of the industry." In order to be successful—that is, earn higher income to support their future families—they hoped in the long run to run their own businesses, such as trading industrial materials on e-business platforms. Preparing for this plan, they spent every Sunday together learning how to do business online.

Although women's employment is commonly taken for granted due to the legacy of egalitarian gender ideology in socialist China (Koo, Hui, and

Pun 2020), men are still expected to take up the main financial role in families. This creates an intense achievement pressure on young men to "aim high" and "earn more" to become successful (Liu 2019). The low wages of their laboring jobs lead to an unavoidable "clash" between the state's masculine values regarding future workers and the male youths' desire to become rich, flexible, and successful entrepreneurs. And it pushes a number of students and graduates to leave the field at various stages of internship and employment. According to the school's records, only about half its students stay in the field when they finish their on-the-job internships. Less than 20 percent of graduates remain in the field five years after graduation.

In order to retain more of the trained workers in the field, since 2017, the technical college had worked with the local government and official trade unions to regularly send their graduates to Japan for training in transnational companies. Aligning with the state strategy, this overseas training would further equip the trainees with advanced technical skills, allowing them to contribute to the industries after their return. During our fieldwork, many top performers in technician classes showed their eagerness to join the overseas training and sought ways to increase their chances of being selected. All were motivated by a strong belief that going overseas would improve their market prospects, and more importantly would lead them toward managerial positions. Bob, one of the graduates who had just completed the nine-month compulsory internship at a local factory, shared with us: "I finished [the internship] and am eligible [for the training in Japan]. I don't want to stay at the front line and work as a labor forever, you know. After two or three years of training in Japan, even if I returned to the same factory, I would quickly get into mid-level management. Then, move further up. This is my plan." At a time of economic globalization and neoliberal restructuring, willingness or even eagerness to be mobile is portrayed as the dominant valued characteristic of a cosmopolitan and entrepreneurial young agent (Yoon 2014). Similarly to middle-class students who seek chances to study abroad with parental support (Tsang 2013), the working-class youth in our study also aspired to work or train overseas as a basis for upward mobility. It is important to note, here, that the value and dignity of being a manual worker are devalued in the dominant ideology in postreform China (Li 2015). Accordingly, when we discussed career plans with students at the tertiary level of training, they voiced only limited pride in "being a worker" in the manufacturing industry. Building a strong industrial state through the collective efforts of skilled workers and technicians was not their concern. Even those who were committed to remaining in the field were more inclined to aim for a managerial position to support their personal social advancement.

Conclusion

In the new era of Chinese transnational infrastructural capitalism, the strategic blueprint *Made in China 2025* undertakes to transform China from the world's largest manufacturer to its strongest manufacturer. This new direction demands a new working-class subjectivity capable of achieving this, in which gender is central to the process of subject making. Vocational education and training are heavily involved in this national project, since they are envisioned to produce skilled and efficient labor to enhance global competition and national technological upgrade (Pun and Qiu 2020). Vocational school students are presented with an idealized image of "high-skilled, innovative worker" to which they should aspire. With the skills they acquire, they are led to believe, they would contribute not only to their professions and nation building but also to their own future self-development.

However, this study clearly shows that the process of producing a new generation of highly skilled workers for the fulfillment of the China Dream is neither unitary nor straightforward. A top-down approach or policy-led "production" orientation would be inadequate, as the training process involves active learning and becoming by the students themselves, which is not only shaped by the national development strategies and the direction of vocational education but also largely determined by the dominant structures of gender that have emerged in postreform China. In this article, we have framed vocational education and training as a processual political technology of the self, in which gender and other social differences are constituted and reconstituted through multiple, often contradictory discourses and practices. We found that conflicting messages, such as "the spirit of a craftsman" advocated by the state and "the entrepreneurial subject" by the market, were intertwined when they were passed on to the students at school. More importantly, the gender culture and gender ideology involved in the messages generated contradictory learning experiences among the vocational students regarding their active formation of gendered workers' identities. On one hand, students were educated to be patriotic subjects to serve the goal of "industrial upgrading in China," specifically, and the "China Dream" in general. On the other hand, the students were heavily influenced by the belief in being "self-enterprising"—being flexible and self-reflexive (including in their gender identity and performance) in order to seek higher-income and higher-status jobs.

Furthermore, with regard to the production and reproduction of gendered workers in vocational training, we found that the "process of becoming" must understood beyond the traditional perceptions of gender internalized by individuals and the pressure to secure employment following the structural changes in the employment system. The training that working-class youth receive in vocational school reinforces, or even produces, gender-related predispositions in line with the demands of the workplace. In this study, we found gender remains a central axis of youth worker identity in postsocialist China. In the eyes of teachers, as well as employers in the market, girls and boys are suited to different occupations. This widely shared gender ideology runs opposite to the earlier socialist one, which aimed to erase gender differences between men and women while emphasizing female strength and women's contribution to society. It also clashes with the belief in self-investment and meritocracy shared among the female students, who strove consistently for better education and training and sought equal opportunities to enter a male-dominated field based on their personal capabilities. It was the perceived privations of working in the factories, as well as the gendered barriers to entry, that stopped the girls from pursuing a higher level of training and entering the industries they originally aspired to join.

In this context, learning to labor thus entails important contradictory tensions that the students had to negotiate in relation to the masculinized national project, the marketable value of femininity, the call for flexibility and entrepreneurship in global youth culture, and individual aspirations toward independence and self-actualization. The concept of "clashing gender" has been used here to make sense of the subject-making process of

China's new working class as an ongoing conflictual process in which structure, discourse, and subjectivity are all at play at the intersection of gender and class.

Notes

We gratefully acknowledge the financial support from the GRF, Research Grants Council of Hong Kong Special Administrative Region, China: "Gendering the New Generation of Chinese Workers in Vocational Schools" (15601617).

References

Anagnost, Ann, Andrea Arai, and Hai Ren, eds. 2013. *Global Futures in East Asia: Youth, Nation, and the New Economy in Uncertain Times*. Stanford, CA: Stanford University Press.

Berik, Gunseli, Xiao-yuan Dong, and Gale Summerfield. 2007. "China's Transition and Feminist Economics." *Feminist Economics* 13, nos. 3–4: 1–33.

Butler, Elaine, and Fran Ferrier. 2006. "Gender Matters: Perspectives on Women's Work and Training." *Journal of Vocational Education and Training* 58, no. 4: 385–91.

CGTN (China Global Television Network). 2017. "Chinese Premier Stresses Craftsmanship." November 24. https://news.cgtn.com/news/7941444d79637a6333566d54/index.html.

Fong, Vanessa. 2002. "China's One-Child Policy and the Empowerment of Urban Daughters." *American Anthropologist* 104, no. 4: 1098–109.

Gao, Xiongya. 2003. "Women Existing for Men: Confucianism and Social Injustice against Women in China." *Race, Gender, and Class* 10, no. 3: 114–25.

Global Times. 2022. "China Bids to Strengthen Vocational Education amid a New Wave of Industrial Transformation." June 12. https://www.globaltimes.cn/page/202206/1267895.shtml.

Hansen, Mette Halskov, and Terry E. Woronov. 2013. "Demanding and Resisting Vocational Education: A Comparative Study of Schools in Rural and Urban China." *Comparative Education* 49, no. 2: 242–59.

Hanser, Amy. 2005. "The Gendered Rice Bowl: The Sexual Politics of Service Work in Urban China." *Gender and Society* 19, no. 5: 581–600.

He, Gugnaye, and Xiaogang Wu. 2017. "Marketization, Occupational Segregation, and Gender Earnings Inequality in Urban China." *Social Science Research* 65: 96–111.

Huang, Mingrui. 2017. "Premier Li Stresses Vocational Education to Boost 'Made in China' Brand." *Ecns.cn*, September 10. https://www.ecns.cn/2017/09-10/272916.shtml.

Hui, Li. 2015. "Made in China 2025: How Beijing Is Revamping Its Manufacturing Sector." *South China Morning Post*, June 9. https://www.scmp.com/tech/innovation/article/1818381 /made-china-2025-how-beijing-revamping-its-manufacturing-sector.

Kidd, Michael, and Xin Meng. 2001. "The Chinese State Enterprise Sector: Labor Market Reform and the Impact on Male-Female Wage Structure." *Asian Economic Journal* 15, no. 4: 405–23.

Kim, Sung Won, Kari-Elle Brown, and Vanessa Fong. 2018. "How Flexible Gender Identities Give Young Women Advantages in China's New Economy." *Gender and Education* 30, no. 8: 982–1000.

Kipnis, Andrew. 2011. *Governing Educational Desire*. London: University of Chicago Press.

Koo, Anita. 2016. "Expansion of Vocational Education in Neoliberal China: Hope and Despair among Rural Youth." *Journal of Education Policy* 31, no. 1: 46–59.

Koo, Anita, Bryant Hui, and Ngai Pun. 2020. "Gender Ideologies of Youth in Post-socialist China: Their Gender-Role Attitudes, Antecedents, and Socio-psychological Impacts." *Chinese Sociological Review* 52, no. 5: 487–514.

Li, Ju. 2015. "From 'Master' to 'Loser': Changing Working-Class Cultural Identity in Contemporary China." *International Labour and Working-Class History* 88: 190–208.

Liu, Fengshu. 2014. "From Degendering to (Re)Gendering the Self: Chinese Youth Negotiating Modern Womanhood." *Gender and Education* 26, no. 1: 18–34.

Liu, Fengshu. 2019. "Chinese Young Men's Construction of Exemplary Masculinity: The Hegemony of Chenggong." *Men and Masculinities* 22, no. 2: 294–316.

Ministry of Education of PRC. 2019. "Vocational Education in Figures: Funding for Vocational Education." May 30. http://en.moe.gov.cn/features/VocationalEdc/figures/201905/t20190531 _383837.html.

Otis, Eileen. 2012. *Markets and Bodies: Women, Service Work, and the Making of Inequality in China*. Stanford, CA: Stanford University Press.

Pun, Ngai. 2022. "China's Infrastructural Capitalism: The Making of the Chinese Working Classes." *positions politics*, April 28. https://positionspolitics.org/pun-ngai-chinas-infra structural-capitalism-the-making-of-a-chinese-working-class/.

Pun, Ngai, and Anita Koo. 2019. "Double Contradiction of Schooling: Class Reproduction and Working-Class Agency at Vocational Schools in China." *British Journal of Sociology of Education* 40, no. 1: 50–64.

Pun, Ngai, and Jack Qiu. 2020. "'Emotional Authoritarianism': State, Education, and the Mobile Working-Class Subjects." *Mobilities* 15, no. 4: 620–34.

Rofel, Lisa. 1999. *Other Modernities: Gendered Yearnings in China after Socialism.* Berkeley: University of California Press.

Schulte, Barnara. 2013. "Unwelcome Stranger to the System: Vocational Education in Early Twentieth-Century China." *Comparative Education* 49, no. 2: 226–41.

State Council of PRC. 2014. *Decision of the State Council on Accelerating the Development of Modern Vocational Education.* Beijing: State Council.

State Council of PRC. 2015. *Made in China 2025.* Beijing: State Council.

State Council of PRC. 2021. *Guidelines on Promoting the High-Quality Development of Modern Vocational Education.* Beijing: State Council.

Summerfield, Gale, Xiao-yuan Dong, Nahid Aslanbeigui, and Jie Hu. 2011. "Wage Differentials, Occupational Segregation, and Gendered Creativity Perceptions in the Chinese Science and Technology Sector: Beijing and Wuhan." *Eastern Economic Journal* 37, no. 2: 178–96.

Tsang, Eileen Yuk-ha. 2013. "The Quest for Higher Education by the Chinese Middle Class: Retrenching Social Mobility?" *Higher Education* 66: 653–68.

Tsui, Ming, and Lynne Rich. 2002. "The Only Child and Educational Opportunity for Girls in Urban China." *Gender and Society* 16, no. 1: 74–92.

Wen, Hua. 2013. *Buying Beauty: Cosmetic Surgery in China.* Hong Kong: Hong Kong University Press.

Woronov, Terry. 2015. *Class Work: Vocational Schools and China's Urban Youth.* Stanford, CA: Stanford University Press.

Xiu, Lin, and Morley Gunderson. 2015. "Occupational Segregation and the Gender Earnings Gap in China: Devils in the Details." *International Journal of Manpower* 36, no. 5: 711–32.

Xu, Gary, and Susan Feiner. 2007. "Meinu Jingji/China's Beauty Economy: Buying Looks, Shifting Value, and Changing Place." *Feminist Economics* 13, nos. 3–4: 307–23.

Yang, Jie. 2011. "Nennu and Shunu: Gender, Body Politics, and the Beauty Economy in China." *Signs* 36, no. 2: 333–58.

Yoon, Kyong. 2014. "Transnational Youth Mobility in the Neoliberal Economy of Experience." *Journal of Youth Studies* 17, no. 8: 1014–28.

Zhang, Qian, and Chun Yao. 2015. "China Learns to Love Vocational Education." *People's Daily*, July 1. http://en.people.cn/n/2015/0701/c90000-8913746.html.

Zhang, Yue. 2019. "China to Bolster Vocational Education, Expand Enrollment." *State Council of PRC News*, April 30. http://english.www.gov.cn/premier/news/2019/04/30/content _281476637627986.htm.

Zuo, Jiping. 2014. "Understanding Urban Women's Domestic-Role Orientation in Post-Mao China." *Critical Sociology* 40, no. 1: 111–33.

Mismatched: Intensive Mothering in China's Urban Villages

Shuheng Jin and Haijing Dai

Introduction

> What era are we living in? I mean, you need to raise your child scientifically in this society. Why are you insisting on traditional ways? . . . I really admire those experts. What rich experiences they possess! I always tell my daughter: I need to study hard, and you need to study hard too. We both need to study. I didn't like studying before, but now I am willing to learn things about child-rearing.
> —Yingli, from Hunan

We met Yingli, a thirty-year-old stay-at-home migrant mother, when she was playing with her two energetic children in a small park in QH village in Shenzhen, Guangdong Province. Yingli migrated to this new global city in southern China with her husband and two young children in 2017. Although bringing children along on their urban sojourns meant a higher

positions 32:4   DOI 10.1215/10679847-11306808

cost of living, fewer working hours, and lower incomes, Yingli and her husband insisted on migrating with both of their children. "I am afraid that they would hold a grudge if we went out to migrate to work *dagong* 打工 [without them]." As a firm believer in scientific child-rearing, Yingli subscribed to various self-media accounts concerning childcare on WeChat, and she read online constantly. She also occasionally paid for online parenting classes.

Demographic studies have long noted this familization trend in migration among China's rural-to-urban migrants over the past decade (Fan and Li 2019; Yang and Chen 2013). According to the annual report on migrant workers issued by Guojia tongji ju 国家统计局 (National Bureau of Statistics) (2010, 2019), married migrants made up 56 percent of the migrant population in 2009, which rose to 79.7 percent in 2017. In Zhang Liqiong, Zhu Yu, and Lin Liyue's (2017) study based on the *2013 Nian quanguo liudong renkou dongtai jiance shuju* 2013年全国流动人口动态监测数据 (*2013 National Dynamic Monitoring Survey of the Migrant Population*) (with a sample of 198,900 migrants aged from fifteen to fifty-nine), 51.94 percent of the surveyed female migrants and 47.29 percent of the male had migrated with their whole nuclear families. This familization trend suggests that, for a growing number of migrant women, their role as filial migrant daughters delineated in earlier studies has transformed into the role of migrant mothers (Fan 2003; Gaetano 2004; Jacka 2005; Pun 2005). While the previous generation of migrant women tended to give up employment in the cities to undertake caregiving responsibilities in their home villages following marriage, today, more migrant women are trying to manage both employment and childcare while remaining in the cities. Underlying this changing mode of mobility are the new generation of migrants' changing conceptualizations of motherhood and family.

Multiple studies have shown that women's migration experiences are deeply entangled with their mothering values, practices, and emotions (Herrero-Arias et al. 2020; Hoang 2016; Madianou and Miller 2011; Parreñas 2005; Tungohan 2013; Tyldum 2015). Scholars have documented how transnational migrant mothers have made enormous efforts while suffering emotionally in the attempt to fulfill their mothering responsibilities while either separated from their children (Hoang 2016; Madianou and Miller 2011; Parreñas 2005; Tungohan 2013) or living with them in an unfamiliar foreign country (Herrero-Arias et al. 2020). However, with rural women migrants making up roughly one-third of the total rural migrant population in China over the past decade,[1] little has yet been learned about their transforming mothering ideas and practices, with the exception of a small handful of studies (Peng 2018; To, So, and Kwok 2018).

For rural migrant mothers, long distances from hometowns have cut off mutual childcare support practices with female relatives. The child-rearing authority of senior female relatives (particularly mothers and mothers-in-law) based on their own experience has been replaced by professional authorities with academic qualifications. Older-style child-rearing practices that were once considered normal, such as feeding salted food to infants under the age of one and binding a baby's legs to prevent rickets, have been criticized by modern medical professionals as being detrimental to children's health. Similarly, some traditional parenting beliefs that were once highly respected, such as "raising a filial child by means of the rod" (*gunbang dixia chu xiaozi* 棍棒底下出孝子) are now considered by psychology experts to be disrespectful to children and harmful to their mental health. Furthermore, globalization and the booming cultural industries have exposed Yingli and her fellow migrant mothers, most of whom have never been abroad, to a new, imported mothering ideology. The ideology of intensive mothering, a set of theories and standards on childcare that originated in North America (Hays 1996), is profoundly influencing mothers' mothering ideas and practices in contemporary urban China. Best-selling parenting books from abroad, including *Your Pregnancy Week by Week* (*Huaiyun shengdian* 怀孕圣典) by UK gynecologist Lesley Regan (2021), *The Attachment Parenting Book* (*Qinmi yuer* 亲密育儿) by two American pediatricians (Sears and Sears 2011), and *Encyclopedia on Childcare* (*Yuer Baike* 育儿百科) by Japanese pediatrician Michio Matsuda (2010) (松田道雄), have become popular among Chinese parents. For a growing number of migrant mothers, childbearing and child-rearing are no longer merely natural processes under which women's mothering practices are guided by their loving instincts and the experiential knowledge of elder women relatives. Instead, mothering is regarded as a heavy and challenging task about which mothers are expected to "study hard."

Based on the archetype of a white, middle-class full-time mother (John-ston and Swanson 2006), the ideology of intensive mothering holds that mothers should be the primary caregivers for their children and good mothering requires child-centered child-rearing with intensive investment of time, money, energy, and emotional labor under expert guidance (Elliott, Powell, and Brenton 2015; Hays 1996). While it has been suggested that this dominant culture of motherhood is contradictory to capitalist logic (Hays 1996), it actually works well with the neoliberal capitalist system under which families, particularly women, are expected to take the primary responsibility for cultivating proper future laborers for the system. Studies have revealed how mothers with different backgrounds, such as working mothers (Christopher 2012), ethnic minority mothers (Elliott, Powell, and Brenton 2015), and migrant mothers (Herrero-Arias et al. 2020; Hoang 2016; Madianou and Miller 2011; Parreñas 2005; To, So, and Kwok 2018; Tungo-han 2013; Tyldum 2015) have viewed and practiced intensive mothering. As suggested by the new mobilities paradigm (Everuss 2020; Sheller and Urry 2006), mobilities research must move beyond studies on the physical travel of people and materials. With the development of information technolo-gies and the culture industry, the hypermobility of information, ideas, and ideologies within and across borders facilitated by new technologies is now essential for our understanding of contemporary life (Everuss 2020; Sheller and Urry 2006). Keeping this in mind and drawing on the theory of ideal-ization of motherhood and literature on migrant motherhood, this article investigates how the Euro-American ideology of intensive mothering has been preached among rural migrant mothers in China's globalizing cities, and how rural migrant mothers are trapped in the mismatches between this indicatively white, middle-class mothering ideology and their own position in the social class hierarchy.

Migrant Mothers and the Idealization of Motherhood

The idealization of motherhood is a whole set of cultural beliefs on how perfect mothers should behave. In the *Encyclopedia of Motherhood*, Jean-Anne Sutherland (2010: 546) suggests: "The idealization of motherhood is disconnected from the experiences of day-to-day life and pits mothers against mothers. The attempt to live according to a manufactured ideal is fruitless and sets mothers up for guilt and shame." Scholars suggest that globally dominant mothering ideologies, including intensive mothering, illustrate the concept of cultural hegemony described by Foucault and Gramsci (Johnston and Swanson 2006). The idealization of motherhood, in many cases, traps women into a mission impossible (Douglas and Michaels 2004). Depicting the image of an ideal mother as a white, middle-class, stay-at-home mother, the ideology of intensive mothering has ensured the failure of most mothers, including working mothers, single mothers, mothers of color, low-income mothers, and lesbian mothers. Migrant mothers, too, are deeply influenced by the idealization of motherhood. What is worse, with their migrant status, low income, and, in most cases, separation from their children, migrant mothers encounter great difficulties and experience extreme distress in attempting to fulfill the demands of ideal motherhood that they have learned and internalized.

Two themes emerge from the literature on migrant mothers and the idealization of motherhood. The first concerns the harms of the dominant idealization of motherhood for migrant mothers who are physically and economically constrained to maintain their self-image as good enough mothers. Studies on international migrant mothers with left-behind children (Hondagneu-Sotelo and Avila 1997; Madianou and Miller 2011; Moorhouse and Cunningham 2012; Parreñas 2005; Schmalzbauer 2004) have documented how migrant mothers suffer emotionally in failing to fulfill the dominant mothering ideals. Migrant mothers have adopted various strategies to practice intensive mothering across distance via mobile phones (Madianou and Miller 2011; Parreñas 2005) or by delegating part of the childcare responsibilities to female relatives back home (Bloch 2017). Ethe Tungohan (2013) discusses how Filipina migrant mothers in Canada practice "transnational hyper-maternalism" to fulfill their maternal responsibilities by means of financial support and frequent communication with their children. However, such practices do not challenge the existing mothering ideal that presumes women exist solely for their children's well-being—in fact, these migrant mothers are away from home precisely for the sake of their children and families.

Another theme emphasizes migrant mothers' agency by concentrating on their counternarratives contesting the mainstream discourses of ideal motherhood. Although living away from their children makes it impossible for migrant mothers to live up to mainstream standards of good mothering, they find new ways to justify their absence and rearticulate good motherhood with new meanings. Some migrant mothers—for example, those in studies by Guri Tyldum (2015) and Lan Anh Hoang (2016)—frame their migration as an act of self-sacrifice to ensure better lives for their children. Studies in China have also illustrated how migrant mothers reimagine good motherhood as economic support to help their children gain better education and career opportunities (Peng 2018; To, So, and Kwok 2018). Although these counternarratives do not challenge the dominant idealization of motherhood, they at least empower migrant mothers to negotiate the traditional gendered division of labor in their homes and their power relationships with husbands and other family members.

Although it presents us with abundant evidence of how migrant mothers have suffered from and reacted to intensive mothering, the existing literature reveals little about how migrant mothers have learned, accepted, and/or adapted this Euro-American mothering ideology. Coming from different home countries and backgrounds, mothers do not naturally view intensive mothering as the standard of good motherhood. Migration may open a contested site for the fight for dominance between new mothering ideologies and migrant mothers' preexisting mothering ideals. The question for our purposes is how intensive mothering, as a hegemonic mothering ideology originating in North America, has also become dominant among rural migrant mothers in China.

Method

To investigate how migrant mothers in China's urban villages learn and internalize an imported mothering ideology, we must first place their stories and narratives into a larger context. The extended case method aims to push ethnography to "extend out" from the field of the everyday lifeworld to a macro, historical context through a theoretical lens (Burawoy 1998). This study examines migrant mothers' mothering concepts and practices with reference both to the globally dominant culture on motherhood and to China's state policies on family and reproduction that target them as primary subjects. During our eight months of ethnographic research in QH and TD villages in southern cities of China between 2017 and 2018, we used multiple data collection methods to learn about migrant mothers' mothering concepts and practices and the contexts in which these were constructed and constrained.

In-depth interviews were conducted with sixteen migrant mothers and three of their family members (for details on the migrant mothers and their families, see table 1). All migrant mothers in our sample had completed a high-school education, and two had managed to earn junior college degrees. Their migrations started as soon as they concluded their education in their late teens or early twenties. Most of our research participants came from China's central region, including Hubei, Henan, Jiangxi, and Hunan, which are the major out-migration provinces. Most of them were under thirty years of age when we first met them and had had children in their early or mid-twenties. Seven of the sixteen migrant mothers had two children, and the other nine each had one child. The average age of the twenty-three children was 3.5 years.

In this study, observation was a key way to learn how migrant mothers interacted with their children, friends, and family members in ordinary settings. On the one hand, observation helped verify what migrant mothers said about their mothering concepts and practices with reference to what they actually did in their child-rearing and child education. On the other hand, observation of participants in public spaces alongside other migrant mothers who were not part of our sample helped us understand the prevalence of specific child-rearing patterns in migrant communities. This study engaged two kinds of observation sites: public spaces in the parks, sidewalks, and shopping areas of urban villages; and private activities organized by the migrant mothers such as grocery shopping, family dinners, and gatherings with friends.

We used three sources of documents in this study to shed light on the promulgation of intensive mothering ideology and migrant mothers' perceptions of it. These included policy documents and city yearbooks relating to childcare and the migrant population, reading materials concerning child-rearing that the participants introduced to us, as well as migrant mothers' thoughts on mothering and motherhood posted on WeChat Moments.[2] One

Table 1. Informants' basic details

Site	Name	Hometown	Age of child	Husband's hometown	Employment conditions	Husband's job	Monthly income (yuan)	Husband's monthly income (yuan)
TD Village	Panni	Guangxi	1	Jiangxi	Self-employed before childbirth	Manager	5,000 before childbirth	15,000
	Shuangling	Guangdong	4 and 1	Henan	WeChat commerce	Self-employed	Less than 1,000	Unknown
	Suying	Chongqing	6	Shandong	Technician	Passed away	6,000	N/A
	Xutong	Hubei	5	Hubei	Two part-time jobs	Self-employed	4,000–5,000	Unknown
	Fengxi	Jiangxi	5	Jiangxi	Clerk	Technician	5,000–6,000	7,000
	Huangrui	Guangdong	6 and 3	Guangdong	Self-employed	Self-employed	Earn a family income of 6,000–8,000	
	Amy	Jiangxi	4	Jiangxi	Part-time insurance agent	Self-employed	Less than 3,000	In debt from business
	Tanjie	Hunan	5	Hunan	Clerk and part-time saleswoman	Shopkeeper	Less than 5,000	8,000

Site	Name	Hometown	Age of child	Husband's hometown	Employment conditions	Husbands' job	Monthly income (yuan)	Husband's monthly income (yuan)
QH village	Huili	Jiangxi	6 and 2	Hunan	Clerk	Technician	4500	Less than 10,000
	Yanni	Hubei	2	Hubei	Stay-at-home mother	Factory worker	Not working for pay	6,000
	Jiayue	Sichuan	4 and 2	Hunan	Factory worker	Factory worker	4,000	6,000
	Xiaoge	Henan	3	Henan	Stay-at-home mother	Factory worker	Not working for pay	5,000–6,000
	Shumin	Henan	2 and 2	Hubei	Factory worker	Factory worker	4,000	4,000
	Liangyu	Henan	5	Henan	Factory worker	Technician in factory	4,000–5,000	8,000–10,000
	Yingli	Hunan	6 and 2	Hunan	Stay-at-home mother	Chef	Not working for pay	6,000–7,000
	Wanxia	Jiangxi	5 and 2	Jiangxi	WeChat commerce	Self-employed	2,000–3,000	In debt from business

best-selling book and fifty-three articles concerning motherhood and womanhood shared by forty-two migrant mothers, each with tens of thousands of page views, were selected for content analysis. While the migrant mothers admitted that they did not always practice mothering according to these articles' advice, they showed their approval of the ideas in these materials by introducing them to us or posting them on their social media accounts. Moreover, these materials' popularity in itself underlines the idealization of motherhood in popular culture. Through the migrant mothers' expressed ideas about these reading materials and how they put them into practice, we learned how they were influenced by the dominant motherhood ideals and how they negotiated between their perceptions of ideal motherhood and their limited resources.

A third document source was the mothering ideas and stories migrant mothers posted on WeChat Moments. Most migrant mothers we met in the urban villages were active users of WeChat. Not only did they use WeChat to communicate with family and friends, but they also used it as a platform to share their opinions, memorable moments, and other information of interest. Forty-seven excerpts from WeChat Moments passages shared by the migrant mothers between 2017 and 2018 were selected as materials for content analysis. These were mostly shared opinions and feelings about modern motherhood and womanhood. There were also some short stories about daily parent-child interactions. Such materials provide important supplementary information for our interview data.

Insist on Scientific Child-Rearing:
The Promotion of Intensive Mothering

Intensive mothering strongly emphasizes expert guidance, especially from pediatricians and psychologists (Hays 1996). In our study, the state played a critical role in promoting this mothering ideology by making medical and child educational institutions front lines for the proliferation of scientific child-rearing. The Law of China on Maternal and Infant Health Care (Zhonghua renmin gongheguo muying baojianfa), passed in 1994, stipulates that medical institutions must instruct pregnant women on scientific child-rearing. To support this, the Guowuyuan 国务院 (State Council) further promulgated the Measures for Implementation of the Law of China on Maternal and Infant Health Care (Zhonghua renmin gongheguo muying baojianfa shi- shi banfa) in 2001, stipulating that medical institutions must deliver scientific education on reproduction and child-rearing to pregnant women and their families.[3] In 2011, Guojia weisheng jiankang weiyuanhui 国家卫生健康委员会 (National Health Commission) also launched a pilot project with Zhong- guo renkou fuli jijinhui 中国人口福利基金会 (China Population Welfare Foundation), entitled Chuangjian xingfu jiating huodong 创建幸福家庭活动 (Movement for Building Happy Families). The movement has made scientific child-rearing a key focus for building families and urged local health com- missions to provide free prenatal checkups and spread knowledge on scientific child-rearing.[4] To put these policies into practice, in 2008, Weishengbu 卫生 部 (Ministry of Health)—later integrated with Jihua shengyu weiyuanhui 计 划生育委员会 (National Family Planning Commission)—further issued spe- cific instructions for implementing pregnancy education.[5] These instructions set standards for the facilities medical institutions must provide for pregnancy education, and suggest that medical institutions should ensure that 50 percent to 60 percent of the pregnant women attend pregnancy education programs. In Guangzhou and Shenzhen, all obstetrics departments have set pregnancy courses and encourage pregnant women and their families to attend at least two or three classes. Kindergartens, too, have become a site for the promotion of scientific child-rearing. In 2010, Guowuyuan issued Suggestions Regard- ing the Development of Early Childhood Education at Present (Guowuyuan guanyu dangqian fazhan xueqianjiaoyu de ruogan yijian).[6] It stipulated that early childhood education should "insist on scientific child-rearing and respect the natural patterns of young children's development to facilitate their health and happiness."[7] The government's documents concerning childbear- ing and child-rearing thus frame scientific child-rearing as essential for the nation's wider goal of improving *renkou suzhi* 人口素质 (population quality) in both physical and psychological terms. While the government does not explicitly cite intensive mothering in its documents, its measures promot- ing professional instruction in both childbearing and child-rearing and its emphasis on "respecting the natural patterns of children's physical and psy- chological development" are consistent with the fundamental principles of the ideology of intensive mothering. The government's preaching of scientific child-rearing thus facilitates the spread of intensive mothering among people from a wide range of socioeconomic backgrounds.

Local governments are further required to "fully utilize all types of media, including radio, television, newspapers, websites and mobile apps, to popularize knowledge and information on scientific child-rearing and healthy adolescent development" among parents.[8] As a result, public lectures are delivered, service centers for scientific child-rearing are set up,[9] free clinics for pregnant women and young children are organized in various communities, pregnancy schools are established in city hospitals,[10] and free books on childcare are handed out. This campaign on scientific child-rearing can be seen as part of the government's ongoing endeavor to improve population quality since the One Child Policy. Just as in Suzhi jiaoyu 素质教育 (Education for Quality movement) (Kuan 2012), in preaching scientific child-rearing, parents—particularly mothers—are asked to change their parenting methods in accordance with expert advice. In addition, both movements have issued challenges to traditional ways of parenting and teaching (Lin 2011). Instead of respecting the authority of parents and teachers, the new ways of parenting and education emphasize "scientific knowledge" and "the natural patterns of children's physical and psychological development."

Although the rural migrant population is excluded from urban welfare systems (Ouyang et al. 2017; Wang, Guo, and Cheng 2015), it is actively included in the urban government's family planning projects and its promotion of scientific child-rearing. The municipal governments of both Guangzhou and Shenzhen endeavor to equalize the service quality of family planning and health care between the migrant population and urban residents. Thus, migrant women in both cities are entitled to free prenatal checkups and counseling on childbearing from medical professionals. Migrant newborns, whether born in their parents' hometowns or in the cities where they work, are covered by the basic newborn public health care system similarly to their urban counterparts. Parents of newborns are encouraged to take their babies for thorough physical checkups every two to three months up until one year of age, then every six to twelve months until the child is three years old.

Most of the migrant mothers with children under three that we met during fieldwork made use of these free checkups and immunizations provided by the community health centers. Yanni, a twenty-three-year-old full-time mother, had delivered her daughter Lingling in a county hospital in her hometown. She took her then two-year-old daughter to every checkup and immunization, as instructed by doctors. Since bringing Lingling to Shenzhen, she also kept a detailed health record for the little girl in the health log handed out by the community health center. At Lingling's twelve-month checkup, the doctor suggested that Lingling suffered from zinc deficiency. Without further instructions from the doctor, Yanni decided that Lingling needed cod-liver oil and almost immediately asked one of the researchers to buy her some branded cod-liver oil from Hong Kong. We asked Yanni why she thought that cod-liver oil was helpful for Lingling's zinc deficiency. "I just thought it's good for children's development, isn't it? They all use it," she replied. If Yanni had questioned the doctor further about the proper treatment for zinc deficiency, she would have found out that cod-liver oil is used for vitamin (not zinc) deficiency, and that Lingling in fact needed different supplements.

Nevertheless, whether or not Yanni picked the right way to treat her daughter's condition, the way the government put her mothering practices under scrutiny through medical institutions illustrates the ideology of intensive mothering. Migrant mothers, just like their Euro-American, urban, middle-class counterparts, are convinced through their reproductive experiences in urban hospitals, perinatal examinations, pregnancy classes, and follow-up checkups for newborns that good mothering requires them to follow expert guidance in order to ensure their children's health and development.

A significant difference is that migrant mothers, having fewer economic resources and living in crowded urban villages, receive insufficient medical services in contrast with their urban middle-class counterparts. Although the Shenzhen Municipal Government stipulated that there should be one community service center for every ten to twenty thousand residents,[11] public services in urban village communities fall extremely short. With 120,000 migrant workers and 2,000 local villagers in QH village, there were only two small community health centers, each with less than twenty medical professionals responsible for services including but not limited to basic health care, public hygiene education, immunizations, and follow-up physical checks for newborns. Overloaded as the doctors in community health centers were, it could be reasonably imagined that in the absence of further inquiries from Yanni, her doctor would not have the time or energy to give more detailed instructions about treating Lingling's zinc deficiency.

Do It According to the Books:
Imported Ideology and Rural Migrant Mothers

There is a popular saying among young mothers, which we first heard from Shuangling, a migrant mother in TD village: Raise your first child according to books, and raise your second like raising pigs (*diyige zhaoshu yang, dierge zhaozhu yang* 一胎照书养, 二胎照猪养). This suggests that mothers should turn to experts and books to learn how to raise a child when they first become mothers, but once they have acquired the proper knowledge and experience the first time, they can worry less about the next. It is, of course, not actually the case that migrant mothers raise their second children like pigs. However, they do think that expert advice is more appropriate for modern child-rearing than traditional knowledge sources on child-care (that is, mothers and mothers-in-law). Aside from advice from medical experts, books and popular readings on child-rearing have become another important source of knowledge from which migrant mothers learn about scientific child-rearing.

The booming cultural industries and the development of information technology have facilitated the transnational spread of information and ideas (Sheller and Urry 2006). Many parenting books and reading materials from abroad have been translated into Chinese, with a majority of them originating from Europe and America. The latest edition of the parenting book *Caring for Your Baby and Young Child: Birth to Age Five* from the American Academy of Pediatrics is always the fastest to be translated into Chinese and published for sale in China. A considerable proportion of the works on the list of best-selling parenting books are translations from English or Japanese. Every migrant mother in our sample had read some parenting books or articles. They did this using old-fashioned means, like buying books and reading newspaper articles on parenting; as well as more up-to-date ways such as subscribing to dedicated accounts through WeChat and other mobile apps. Some even paid for commercial education services online or offline. Therefore, while most migrant mothers may not have mastered foreign languages, they are still able to quickly access the latest parenting ideas from abroad. Xutong, a self-employed mother from Jiangxi Province with a five-year-old son, even received a stack of books from her sister-in-law as a pregnancy present, among which *Intimate Parenting* (*Qinmi yuer* 亲密育儿) by two American pediatricians was said to be a must-read. Amy, an insurance agent with a four-year-old son, strongly recommended to us the thick book by Michio Matsuda (a Japanese pediatrician). Further, with an associate degree in English, Amy had even visited the website of the American Academy of Pediatrics. "These are all very good. Very pragmatic," she said.

Having graduated from a vocational secondary school, twenty-nine-year-old Shuangling, a full-time mother with two sons, described herself as "not a student who loves reading." However, she became an enthusiastic reader of parenting articles and constantly shared her readings on WeChat Moments. "Everything (regarding childcare) that I do, I do myself, and I do it according to the books," Shuangling said with pride when she told us that her mother and mother-in-law did not come to Guangzhou to help her when she had her first son. For Shuangling and other migrant mothers, it was now the experts from books, instead of rural grandparents, who held the authority to advise on proper mothering.

Not only do the books and articles spread mothering ideas based on research and theories from abroad, but in some cases, they also frame foreign mothers, mostly from developed countries, as models of ideal motherhood in contrast to Chinese mothers. While the "foreign mothers" (*waiguo mama*) are said to prioritize their children's needs and abide by scientific child-rearing, Chinese mothers are depicted as either authoritarian or overprotective. Although many articles do not explicitly specify which "foreign" country they are referring to, we often see images of white middle-class families—often with white people in suburban houses—in the accompanying illustrations. Fengxi, a migrant mother in TD village Guangzhou, shared an article on her WeChat Moments suggesting mothers to "learn from foreign mothers and change their perspectives on children's naughti-

Figure 1 Chinese online articles on intensive mothering showing white children in Anglophone settings (Shishang mabao 2015).

ness or disobedience" (*Xuexue waiguo mama huan yizhong jiaodu lai kandai haizi de wanpi huoshi butinghua* 学学外国妈妈换一种角度来看待孩子的顽皮或是不听话). By illustrating nine parenting scenes, the article suggests that mothers in the West (*xifang mama*) adopt a democratic mothering method which is better at detecting and cultivating children's talents from their so-called misbehaviors (such as drawing on the wall, playing with mud, or getting low scores in exams). By contrast, Chinese mothers are represented as more inclined to violence when training their children (see fig. 1).

Like their North American counterparts, the parenting/mothering experts in China's popular literature use research findings from psychologists, pediatricians, educators, and philosophers to persuade their readers that children are perfect until bad parenting (mothering) turns them bad. Such mothering ideals require mothers to constantly invigilate their mothering practices to ensure their children's smooth development. Agreeing with such ideas, Fengxi became worried about her parenting style when she sometimes lost her temper when interacting with her son: "Sometimes I shout at him. I know it is bad for him. Instead, I should ask about his actual needs. I don't know why; I just can't help it. Especially when he is doing his homework, he just can't concentrate. Something else always attracts his attention, such as people talking outside or his toys" (Fengxi, from Jiangxi).

The proliferation of intensive mothering emphasizing expert guidance and children's innocence does not explicitly target rural migrant mothers: all mothers are surrounded by parenting instructions from various sources. However, urban middle-class mothers act like "cultural arbiters" (Stone 2007: 8) who set up the standards of good motherhood and have the resources to realize idealized motherhood (albeit with tremendous stress and through difficult struggles). On the other hand, popular literature and even government documents in some cases depict migrant mothers as negative examples of mothering (usually on the basis of leaving their children behind in their home villages). By setting up rural or traditional ways of child-rearing as negative examples, migrant mothers' acceptance of the ideology of intensive mothering and their determination to practice it become part of their pursuit of urbanity and resistance to their rural origins.

Huili, a thirty-year-old migrant mother with a six-year-old daughter and a two-year-old son, criticized her fellow villagers for leaving their children behind when migrating for work. She also blamed herself for "not thinking right" in the past, as she had left her daughter with her in-laws for around one year: "In rural areas, these days, in the village of my natal family, many parents are working in cities far away from home. Children without parents (present) are primarily cared for by their grandparents. . . . They [parents] don't think of their children. They take money to be the most important thing. . . . Grandparents . . . cannot fulfill your children's psychological needs the way you do [yourself]" (Huili, from Jiangxi).

Based on her readings on scientific child-rearing, Huili was convinced by the intensive mothering ideal that the mother was the best possible caregiver for her child. Unlike migrant mothers from the older generation, young migrant mothers in our study considered economic support alone as far from sufficient to ensure children's well-being. For Huili and a growing number of migrant mothers who had internalized the intensive mothering ideology, no one could fulfill a child's psychological needs as a mother could. This became the main reason for them bringing their children along on their urban sojourns, despite the economic burden and social exclusion this entailed. Further, by differentiating herself from those who left their children behind in rural hometowns, Huili managed to maintain the self-image of a good mother who could "eat bitterness" (*chiku*) for the sake of her young children.

We Don't Know about That: Disempowerment and Resilience

With all the world apparently on the move, mobility has today become a crucial social issue (Sheller 2018). Not only do people have different opportunities to move, but also the movements of materials, information, and other people have uneven consequences for people of different backgrounds. In our study, the transnational inflow of the intensive mothering ideology into China has differential impacts on mothers of different social economic status. Emphasizing expert guidance and children's innocence, the ideology of intensive mothering pushes mothers to prioritize children's needs over their own interests. Lin Xiaoshan's (2011) study on China's urban middle-class women's experiences in prenatal examinations indicates that medical intervention silences pregnant women's narratives under a professional medical discourse and alienates women from their own bodily experiences. For migrant mothers, such alienation and debasement are even worse. While the urban middle-class informants in Lin's study questioned the necessity of some medical interventions and negotiated with doctors over medical decisions, the migrant mothers in our sample mentioned little about their own opinions on childbirth and health care in hospitals. "We don't know about that," they often said. In Annette Lareau's (2011) landmark work *Unequal Childhoods*, she presents a description of how middle-class children are raised to feel entitled and competent when confronting authority figures, such as doctors and teachers, while working-class children are raised to be obedient and conform to authority. Having been brought up in migrant families in rural China, in most cases as left-behind children themselves, the young migrant mothers in our study had been raised to be just like the working-class children depicted by Lareau. With relatively low education levels, they tended to regard doctors and other experts as authority figures. With their frustrations with the education system and limited experiences with experts and professionals, migrant mothers lacked confidence in front of doctors, teachers, and other professionals. As a result, most of them followed doctors' instructions without question. Yanni, whose story was presented above, even felt so uncomfortable asking for more detailed advice that she ended up giving her daughter incorrect treatment. With the promotion of intensive mothering emphasizing expert advice and scientific knowledge, migrant mothers are further marginalized in their mothering practices.

At the same time, despite the disempowering effects of the idealization of motherhood, migrant mothers do find ways to gain a sense of achievement in mothering and maintain their self-image as good enough mothers using their limited resources: "They say a mother is her child's best doctor. 'Cause the doctor only occasionally checks up on the child, [but] the mother is always there caring for her child. I understand my son's body, so I have my own judgment when he is unwell" (Amy, from Jiangxi).

Amy had learned this quote from a book by the Japanese pediatrician Michio Matsuda. As an enthusiastic reader of parenting books and articles, she had also developed self-confidence based on her everyday mothering practices and interactions with her son, Gaoyi. Instead of taking the doctor's advice no matter what, Amy gave some credit to her own judgment. "Gaoyi has been illness-prone since he was born. He is a typical high-needs baby [*gao xuqiu baobao*, a concept created by the American pediatrician Dr. Sears]. I'm so experienced, you know. When Gaoyi has a fever, now I know exactly when to take him to the doctor and when to just apply physical cooling at home." As a part-time insurance agent and a full-time mother, Amy had no extra money to send her four-year-old son to extracurricular activities. To compensate, she seized every possible opportunity to take Gaoyi to free demo classes at commercial early childhood education centers. For Amy, this was ideal for Gaoyi as he could "develop wider interests" during these classes, such as painting, math, Lego, and so on.

Conclusion

Existing literature on the idealization of motherhood and migrant mothers has paid little attention to the processes through which migrant mothers in the Global South come to internalize the dominant Euro-American ideology of intensive mothering. Inspired by the mobilities paradigm (Sheller

2018; Sheller and Urry 2006), our study pays attention to the impact of the transnational inflow of information and ideas—the ideology of intensive mothering in our case—on the relatively (im)mobile population (rural migrant mothers). We argue that the spread of intensive mothering differs across societies and cultures. In the context of China, we find that the state has played a critical role in the inculcation of intensive mothering through its policy of improving population quality. Through various kinds of free counselings on childbearing and child-rearing, prenatal examinations, pregnancy classes, and public lectures on scientific child-rearing supported by government programs, migrant mothers become more open to learning and accepting this new, imported mothering ideal. In popular parenting readings, urban, white, middle-class mothers in North America and Western Europe are set up as models of good motherhood who attend effectively to their children's needs. The rural or traditional way of mothering, on the other hand, is criticized for its ignorance of modern scientific knowledge. While migrant mothers are not explicitly targeted in the promotion of intensive mothering, they have accepted, even embraced, this new cultural belief system as a means to pursue urbanity and modern motherhood. Like their middle-class counterparts, migrant mothers come to consider it imperative to follow the direction of experts on reproduction and childcare. However, with their limited economic and cultural resources, China's rural migrant mothers experience a far greater degree of alienation and marginalization when learning and practicing intensive mothering.

Notes

This research received support from the Guangdong Planning Office of Philosophy and Social Science (GD22CSH01).

1   According to the "Migrant Workers Monitoring Survey Report 2020" released by China's National Bureau of Statistics, female rural migrants made up 34.8 percent of the total rural migrant population, decreasing slightly from 35.1 percent in 2019. For details, see Guojia tongji ju 2021.

2   WeChat Moments are somewhat like tweets, except that Moments are accessible only to the users' WeChat friends.

3   For details, see Guojia weisheng he jihua shengyu weiyuanhui 2001.

4   For details, see Guojia weisheng he jihua shengyu weiyuanhui renkou ting 2011.

5 For details, see Weishengbu 2009.

6 For details, see Guowuyuan 2010.

7 Translations are by the authors unless otherwise indicated.

8 For details, please see Guojia weisheng he jihua shengyu weiyuanhui 2015.

9 The Shenzhen Government has set up ninety-four service centers for scientific child-rearing in 2016 for services concerning child health care, children's overall development, and parental education (Guangdongsheng weisheng he jihua shengyu weiyuanhui 2017: 236).

10 Guangzhoushi weisheng he jihua shengyu weiyuanhui 广州市卫生和计划生育委员会 (The Health and Family Planning Commission of Guangzhou) has specifically stipulated not only that all levels of medical institutions with obstetrics departments in Guangzhou should set up pregnancy schools but also that are they required to make sure that over 90 percent of the pregnant women (planning to deliver their children in that hospital) attend at least two classes in the pregnancy schools.

11 Shenzhen Municipal Government issued "Shenzhenshi renmin zhengfu guanyu fazhan shequ jiankang fuwu de shishi yijian" 深圳市人民政府关于发展社区健康服务的实施意见 ("Shenzhen Municipal Government's Implementation Suggestions on Developing Community Healthcare Services") in 2006 and has suggested that with every community there should be one community health center. It further suggests that in communities with larger areas and populations, every ten to twenty thousand residents should be covered with one community health center. For details, see Shenzhenshi renmin zhengfu 2006.

References

Bloch, Alexia. 2017. "'Other Mothers,' Migration, and a Transnational Nurturing Nexus." *Signs* 43, no. 1: 53–75.

Burawoy, Michael. 1998. "The Extended Case Method." *Sociological Theory* 16, no. 1: 4–33. https://doi.org/10.1111/0735-2751.00040.

Christopher, Karen. 2012. "Extensive Mothering: Employed Mothers' Constructions of the Good Mother." *Gender and Society* 26, no. 1: 73–96. https://doi.org/10.1177/0891243211427700.

Douglas, Susan, and Meredith Michaels. 2004. *The Mommy Myth: The Idealization of Motherhood and How It Has Undermined All Women*. New York: Free Press.

Elliott, Sinikka, Rachel Powell, and Joslyn Brenton. 2015. "Being a Good Mom: Low-Income, Black Single Mothers Negotiate Intensive Mothering." *Journal of Family Issues* 36, no. 3: 351–70. https://doi.org/10.1177/0192513X13490279.

Everuss, Louis. 2020. "The New Mobilities Paradigm and Social Theory." In *Routledge Handbook of Social and Cultural Theory*, edited by Anthony Elliott, 287–305. New York: Routledge.

Fan, C. Cindy. 2003. "Rural-Urban Migration and Gender Division of Labor in Transitional China." *International Journal of Urban and Regional Research* 27, no. 1: 24–47.

Fan, C. Cindy, and Tianjiao Li. 2019. "Familization of Rural–Urban Migration in China: Evidence from the 2011 and 2015 National Floating Population Surveys." *Area Development and Policy* 4, no. 2: 134–56. https://doi.org/10.1080/23792949.2018.1514981.

Gaetano, Arianne. 2004. "Filial Daughters, Modern Women: Migrant Domestic Workers in Post-Mao Beijing." In *On the Move*, edited by Gaetano Arianne and Jacka Tamara, 41–79. New York: Columbia University Press.

Guangdongsheng weisheng he jihua shengyu weiyuanhui 广东省卫生和计划生育委员会 (Guangdong Health and Family Planning Commission). 2017. "Guangdong weisheng he jihua shengyu tongjinianjian 2016" 广东卫生和计划生育统计年鉴 2016 ("Guangdong Health and Family Planning Yearbook 2016"). Guangzhou: Guangdong renmin chubanshe.

Guojia tongji ju 国家统计局 (National Bureau of Statistics). 2010. "2009 nian nongmingong jiance diaocha baogao" 2009年农民工监测调查报告 ("2009 Report on the Monitoring Survey of Migrant Population"). Zhongguo shehui kexue wang 中国社会科学网 (China Social Sciences Network), April 19. http://iple.cass.cn/ldjjxzt/ldlscdt/201004/t20100419_1949023.shtml.

Guojia tongji ju 国家统计局 (National Bureau of Statistics). 2019. "2018 nian nongmingong jiance diaocha baogao" 2018年农民工监测调查报告 ("2018 Report on the Monitoring Survey of Migrant Population"). April 29. https://www.stats.gov.cn/sj/zxfb/202302/t20230203_1900299.html.

Guojia tongji ju 国家统计局 (National Bureau of Statistics). 2021. "2020 nian nongmingong jiance diaocha baogao" 2020 年农民工监测调查报告 ("Migrant Workers Monitoring Survey Report 2020"). April 30. https://www.stats.gov.cn/xxgk/sjfb/zxfb2020/202104/t20210430_1816937.html.

Guojia weisheng he jihua shengyu weiyuanhui 国家卫生和计划生育委员会 (National Health and Family Planning Commission of the People's Republic of China). 2001. "Zhonghua renmin gongheguo muying baojianfa shishi banfa" 中华人民共和国母婴保健法实施办法 ("Measures for Implementation of the Law of China on Maternal and Infant Health Care"). June 20. http://www.nhc.gov.cn/zwgkzt/wsbysj/200804/29521.shtml.

Guojia weisheng he jihua shengyu weiyuanhui 国家卫生和计划生育委员会 (National Health and Family Planning Commission of the People's Republic of China). 2015. "Guojia weisheng jishengwei bangongting guanyu kaizhan jihua shengyu jiating kexue yuer he qingshaonian jiankang fazhan shidian gongzuo de tongzhi" 国家卫生计生委办公厅关于开展计划生育家庭科学育儿和青少年健康发展试点工作的通知 ("Notice of the General Office of the National Health and Family Planning Commission on Carrying Out Pilot Work on

Scientific Child Rearing and Healthy Development of Adolescents in Family Planning Families"). Zhonghua renmin gongheguo renmin zhengfu 中华人民共和国人民政府 (The Central People's Government of the People's Republic of China) (website), April 24. http://www.gov.cn/xinwen/2015-04/24/content_2852561.htm.

Guojia weisheng he jihua shengyu weiyuanhui renkou ting 国家卫生和计划生育委员会人口厅 (Office of Population Affairs, National Health and Family Planning Commission of the People's Republic of China). 2011. "Guojia renkou jishengwei guanyu kaizhan chuangjian xingfu jiating huodong shidian gongzuo de zhidao yijian" 国家人口计生委关于开展创建幸福家庭活动试点工作的指导意见 ("National Population and Family Planning Commission's Guiding Opinions on Carrying Out Pilot Activities to Create Happy Families"). May 4. http://www.nhc.gov.cn/jtfzs/s7872/201311/7b714b9e4d044da4847134e60ca90ac1.shtml.

Guowuyuan 国务院 (State Council). 2010. "Guowuyuan guanyu dangqian fazhan xueqian jiaoyu de ruogan yijian" 国务院关于当前发展学前教育的若干意见 ("Several Opinions of the State Council on the Current Development of Preschool Education"). Zhonghua renmin gongheguo renmin zhengfu's 中华人民共和国人民政府 (The Central People's Government of the People's Republic of China) (website), November 24. http://www.gov.cn/zhengce/content/2010-11/24/content_5421.htm.

Hays, Sharon. 1996. *The Cultural Contradictions of Motherhood*. New Haven, CT: Yale University Press.

Herrero-Arias, Raquel, Ragnhild Hollekim, Haldis Haukanes, and Åse Vagli. 2020. "The Emotional Journey of Motherhood in Migration: The Case of Southern European Mothers in Norway." *Migration Studies* 9, no. 3: 1230–49. https://doi.org/10.1093/migration/mnaa006.

Hoang, Lan Anh. 2016. "Moral Dilemmas of Transnational Migration: Vietnamese Women in Taiwan." *Gender and Society* 30, no. 6: 890–911.

Hondagneu-Sotelo, Pierrette, and Ernestine Avila. 1997. "'I'm Here, but I'm There': The Meanings of Latina Transnational Motherhood." *Gender and Society* 11, no. 5: 548–71.

Jacka, Tamara. 2005. *Rural Women in Urban China: Gender, Migration, and Social Change*. Armonk, NY: M. E. Sharpe.

Johnston, Deirdre D., and Debra H. Swanson. 2006. "Constructing the 'Good Mother': The Experience of Mothering Ideologies by Work Status." *Sex Roles* 54, no. 7: 509–19. https://doi.org/10.1007/s11199-006-9021-3.

Kuan, Teresa. 2012. "The Horrific and the Exemplary: Public Stories and Education Reform in Late Socialist China." *positions: asia critique* 20, no. 4: 1095–125. https://doi.org/10.1215/10679847-1717681.

Lareau, Annette. 2011. *Unequal Childhoods: Class, Race, and Family Life*. Oakland: University of California Press.

Lin, Xiaoshan 林晓珊. 2011. "Muzhi de xiagnxiang: Chengshi nvxing de chanqian jiancha, shenti jingyan, yu zhutixing" 母职的想象：城市女性的产前检查、身体经验与主体性 ("The Image of Motherhood: Prenatal Examination, Body Experience, and Subjectivity of Urban Women"). *Shehui* 社会 (*Chinese Journal of Sociology*) 4: 113–57.

Madianou, Mirca, and Daniel Miller. 2011. "Mobile Phone Parenting: Reconfiguring Relationships between Filipina Migrant Mothers and Their Left-Behind Children." *New Media and Society* 13, no. 3: 457–70.

Matsuda, Michio 松田道雄. 2010. *Yuer Baike* 育儿百科 (*Encyclopedia on Childcare*). Translated by Wang Shaoli 王少丽. Beijing: Hua Xia.

Moorhouse, Lesley, and Peter Cunningham. 2012. "'We Are Purified by Fire': The Complexification of Motherhood in the Context of Migration." *Journal of Intercultural Studies* 33, no. 5: 493–508.

Ouyang, Wei, Boyi Wang, Li Tian, and Xinyi Niu. 2017. "Spatial Deprivation of Urban Public Services in Migrant Enclaves under the Context of a Rapidly Urbanizing China: An Evaluation Based on Suburban Shanghai." *Cities* 60, part B: 436–45. https://doi.org/10.1016/j.cities.2016.06.004.

Parreñas, Rhacel. 2005. "Long Distance Intimacy: Class, Gender, and Intergenerational Relations between Mothers and Children in Filipino Transnational Families." *Global Networks* 5, no. 4: 317–36. https://doi.org/10.1111/j.1471-0374.2005.00122.x.

Peng, Yinni. 2018. "Migrant Mothering in Transition: A Qualitative Study of the Maternal Narratives and Practices of Two Generations of Rural-Urban Migrant Mothers in Southern China." *Sex Roles* 79, no. 1: 16–35. https://doi.org/10.1007/s11199-017-0855-7.

Pun, Ngai. 2005. *Made in China: Women Factory Workers in a Global Workplace*. Durham, NC: Duke University Press. https://doi.org/10.2307/j.ctv125jkt6.

Regan, Lesley. 2021. *Huaiyun Shengdian* 怀孕圣典 (*Your Pregnancy Week by Week: What to Expect from Conception to Birth*). Translated by Wang Xianzhe 王先哲. Beijing: China Women.

Schmalzbauer, Leah. 2004. "Searching for Wages and Mothering from Afar: The Case of Honduran Transnational Families." *Journal of Marriage and Family* 66, no. 5: 1317–31. https://doi.org/10.1111/j.0022-2445.2004.00095.x.

Sears, William, and Martha Sears. 2011. *Qinmi Yuer Fa* 亲密育儿法 (*The Attachment Parenting Book: A Commonsense Guide to Understanding and Nurturing Your Baby*). Translated by Jiarong Zhao. Nanjing: Jiangsu Literature and Art.

Sheller, Mimi. 2018. "Theorising Mobility Justice." *Tempo Social* 30, no. 2: 17–34.

Sheller, Mimi, and John Urry. 2006. "The New Mobilities Paradigm." *Environment and Planning A: Economy and Space* 38, no. 2: 207–26.

Shenzhenshi renmin zhengfu 深圳市人民政府 (Shenzhen Municipal Government). 2016. "Shenzhenshi renmin zhengfu guanyu fazhan shequ jiankang fuwu de shishi yijian" 深圳市人民政府关于发展社区健康服务的实施意见 ("Shenzhen Municipal Government's Implementation Suggestions on Developing Community Healthcare Services"). August 23. https://www.sz.gov.cn/zfgb/2006/gb513/content/post_4964352.html.

Shishang mabao 时尚妈宝 (Fashionable Mommy). 2015. "Xuehui dui baobao kuanrong, yexu huiyou xinde faxian" 学会对宝宝宽容, 也许会有新的发现 ("You Might Discover Something New If You Learn to Be More Tolerant to Your Child"). Sohu, last updated May 3. https://www.sohu.com/a/13396651_147967.

Stone, Pamela. 2007. *Opting Out? Why Women Really Quit Careers and Head Home.* Berkeley: University of California Press.

Sutherland, Jean-Anne. 2010. "Idealization of Motherhood." In *Encyclopedia of Motherhood*, edited by Andrea O'Reilly, 545–46. Thousand Oaks, CA: Sage.

To, Siu-ming, Yuk-yan So, and Ching-man Kwok. 2018. "Meaning-Making of Motherhood among Rural-to-Urban Migrant Chinese Mothers of Left-Behind Children." *Journal of Child and Family Studies* 27, no. 10: 3358–70.

Tungohan, Ethe. 2013. "Reconceptualizing Motherhood, Reconceptualizing Resistance: Migrant Domestic Workers, Transnational Hyper-maternalism and Activism." *International Feminist Journal of Politics* 15, no. 1: 39–57.

Tyldum, Guri. 2015. "Motherhood, Agency, and Sacrifice in Narratives on Female Migration for Care Work." *Sociology* 49, no. 1: 56–71. https://doi.org/10.1177/0038038514555427.

Wang, Haining, Fei Guo, and Zhiming Cheng. 2015. "Discrimination in Migrant Workers' Welfare Entitlements and Benefits in Urban Labour Market: Findings from a Four-City Study in China." *Population, Space, and Place* 21, no. 2: 124–39. https://doi.org/10.1002/psp.1810.

Weishengbu fushesi 卫生部妇社司 (Department of Women and Social Welfare, Ministry of Health). 2009. Zhonghua renmin gongheguo renmin zhengfu 中华人民共和国人民政府 (The Central People's Government of the People's Republic of China) (website), January 6. https://www.gov.cn/gzdt/2009-01/06/content_1197822.htm.

Yang, Ju Hua 杨菊华, and Chen Chuan Bo 陈传波. 2013. "Liudong renkou jiatinghua de xianzhuang yu tedian: Liudong guocheng tezheng fenxi" 流动人口家庭化的现状与特点 ("The Process of Familization of Migration in China"). *Renkou yu fazhan* 人口与发展 (*Population and Development*) 19, no. 3: 2–13.

Zhang, Liqiong 张丽琼, Zhu Yu 朱宇, and Lin Liyue 林李月. 2017. "Jiatinghua liudong dui liudong renkou jiuyelu he jiuyewending de yingxiang jiqi xingbie chayi: Jiyu 2013 nian quanguo liudongrenkou dongtai jiance shuju de fenxi" 家庭化流动对流动人口就业率和就业稳定性的影响及其性别差异—基于2013年全国流动人口动态监测数据的分析 ("The Impact of Family Migration on Employment Rate and Stability of Floating Population and Its Gender Differences: An Analysis of 2013 National Dynamic Monitoring Survey of Migrant Population"). *Nanfang renkou* 南方人口 (*South China Population*) 32, no. 2: 1–12.

Continuity and Disjuncture: The Translocal-Transnational Experiences of Chinese Skilled Trade Workers in Western Australia

Qian Gong and Huan Wu

Introduction

Over the past twenty-five years, scholars have explored multiple aspects of the cross-border ties that Chinese migrants have maintained with their home country after migrating to Australia. However, scant attention has been paid to the experiences of working-class Chinese migrants whose self-identities and migratory trajectories differ from the majority of skilled middle-class migrants. In this study, we look at a unique group of migrants: skilled trade workers who moved to the state of Western Australia (WA) from China. Most of our sample moved to Perth, the capital of WA, during the mining boom super cycle from the 2000s to the early 2010s. Our study showed that the case of Chinese skilled trade workers in WA provides a good model for studying the transformation of class identities in transnational migrations.

positions 32:4   DOI 10.1215/10679847-11306820
Copyright 2024 by Duke University Press

A notable feature of this group of migrants is that the majority of the cohort made two successive moves: from rural China to metropolitan cities and then from China to Australia. Through these travels, these workers have been inserted and reinserted into different economic, social, and cultural contexts. In her study on middle-class Chinese migrants' transnational subjectivities in Australia, Wanning Sun (2002: 80–87) compared their sentiments and experience of being "ethnicized" to those of rural migrants first encountering urban life, drawing an analogy between these two experiences. For those who left China and arrived in a foreign country in the 1980s and 1990s, the experience of arriving in the New World, or *chuguo* 出国 (going abroad), felt similar to villagers' *jincheng* 进城 (entering into the city). The new wave of skilled trade workers provides a chance to see these two experiences as part of a single continuum, reminding us of the significance of the "prehistory" of transnational migration.

Therefore, this study focuses on the nexus between urban-rural and transnational mobilities. We look for answers to the two primary questions: What are the changes affecting these workers' cultural and social status, economic status, and social networks during their internal and international migratory trajectories? And how do their translocal and transnational experiences impact each other? We argue that the Chinese skilled trade workers constantly negotiate their working-class and cultural identities during their two successive moves. These negotiations need to be understood within the context of their transitions from rural migrant subjectivity to postsocialist worker subjectivity in China and to transnational migrant identity in Australia. Their economic, social, and cultural capitals were preserved to some extent during the process of local and transnational migration, but they also experienced disjuncture and loss. In traversing multiple social spaces and class systems, their class identities constantly evolved and remained unstable. In each of the two phases of their mobility, Chinese migrant workers were subject to specific regimes of truth and power: family, capitalist workforce, and nation-states; each disciplined and controlled them in different ways, and engendered legible subjectivities (Ong and Nonini 1997: 23) such as *dagongzai* 打工仔 (laborer) "floating population," socialist "masters of the nation," skilled immigrants, and so on. Since the workers made both translocal and transnational moves, their transnational strategies for capital accumulation by making use of spatial disjunctures are extremely complex, with specific constraints and opportunities. They experience both continuity and disjuncture in their economic capital, cultural capital, and social capital during their two moves.

Context: New Forms of Mobility in China

Skilled trade workers are referred to as "unlikely settlers" (Stevens 2020) partly because their migration was possible only through more recent changes in the social contexts in both countries. While students, scholars, and middle-class migrants have moved in large numbers from China to Australia since the beginning of the reforms era in the late 1970s, and especially since the turn of the millennium, for China's rural population, such transnational mobility was out of reach both practically and in imagination. However, this same period witnessed even larger waves of mobility within China. Since the beginning of the reforms era, millions of peasants who used to be land-bound due to the inequitable *hukou* 户口 (household registration) system moved to cities to provide labor for urban expansion. In 2017, the number of rural-to-urban migrants reached 286 million, representing one of the largest migrations in human history (Qi 2019). Rural migrants got the training and skills to work as skilled workers but also faced various challenges (Qi 2019). Internal migration has at least two major impacts on this group of the working class. First, they acquired experience, training, and skills, which in turn enabled them to make the leap outward to a transnational move to Australia. Second, their second-class citizen status in the city left their social identities in a state of suspension. When they moved to Australia, driven by desires for upward social mobility, their various capitals once again went through a transformation.

The Translocal-Transnational Nexus

Although as distinguishing features of modern society, both internal and external migration have been studied extensively, they tend to be seen as two different mobilities. Jan Lucassen and Leo Lucassen (2017) see the separation of internal from transnational migration as unproductive and, in effect, privileging long-term settlement over temporary stays. Instead, they argue that internal is at least as important as transnational migration.

Meanwhile, since first appearing in the 1990s, a transnational perspective has similarly pushed the migration studies field to question the nation-state as the primary unit for analysis. The concept of transnationalism—the maintenance of long-term cross-border ties and structures after migration (Vertovec 1999)—challenges a state-centered approach, and challenges the assumption that emigration equals immigration (Boccagni 2017). The transnational perspective thus brings to the fore the cross-border connections of migrants' life trajectories. The key forms of ties and activities may be analyzed at two levels—identity-attitudinal ("bifocal" identifications and senses of belonging, pointing to both the home and the host society) and relational-behavioral (social relationships persisting at a distance; social practices creating systematic connections between origin and destination countries)—and across three domains: economic, political, and sociocultural (Boccagni 2012: 297).

In the Australian context, with an immigration policy that has for decades favored middle-class, professionally skilled migrants, literature using the transnational lens often focuses on international students (e.g., Gao 2001, 2006, 2009, 2011, 2013; Martin 2014, 2017), middle-class professional migrants (Sun 2002), and business migrants (Leong 2016). Researchers currently know relatively little about marginalized groups, such as the skilled trade workers who became transnational migrants and "unlikely settlers" thanks to the invisible hand of a globally connected capitalist economy (Stevens 2020). This group differs from the middle-class and elite migrants in that although the main impetus of their move is for economic accumulation, the practices of this group of migrants are very different from those of the consumption-based, lifestyle-oriented middle-class migrant population that has emerged along with the rise of China as an economic superpower.

Internal migration and transnational migration are generally dealt with in different academic fields. Extensive research has been done on rural migrants' declining material conditions in China (Solinger 1999; Pun and Lu 2010; Zhan 2015; Pun 2016) and the unequal and discriminatory discourse around this cohort (Sun 2009, 2014). For transnational migrants, scholars have discussed the characteristics of Chineseness in the context of diaspora and pointed out the important influence of local culture and interactions with the receiving society for the identification of Chinese migrants, as well as the flexibility and mobility of immigrants' identities (Ang 1998; Lin 2014; B. Wang 2018; Locher-Lo 2020). However, there is a need to examine the nexus between translocal and transnational migration experiences when these two mobilities are embodied by the same group of migrants. To bring these two closely related experiences into alignment is to pay attention to the multiple scales of analysis in transnational experiences. When we examine the ties and connections across national borders, we also need to look at translocal experiences, and their influence on migrants' sense of belonging and identification in the transnational settlement society.

Skilled Trade Workers in Western Australia

The arrival of Chinese skilled trade workers on the 457 Temporary Working Visa in WA is directly related to the mining boom in Western Australia. The "mining boom," which occurred between 2004 and 2014, enabled Western Australia to grow faster than any other state in Australia, in both population and economy. The neoliberal migration policy that emphasizes migration in the service of economic growth led to the introduction of skilled migrant workers to fill in gaps in the labor market. Even though the Australian immigration policy has mechanisms to restrict the settlement of temporary workers, labor market demands provided a window of opportunity for skilled trade workers to meet this demand and eventually acquire permanent residency. It is hard to pin down the exact number of skilled worker migrants, but since 2000, these workers and their families have accounted for almost one-seventh of the twenty thousand additions to Perth's China-born population (Stevens 2020: 66). Among our interviewees, most moved to Perth during this period, and economic benefits were among the most important motives that attracted them to work in Perth.

Catriona Stevens (2020) has undertaken a systematic study of Chinese skilled trade workers who migrated to WA during this period. Her study clarifies how capital-constrained skilled trade-worker migrants strategically manipulate various capitals to achieve migration goals. It also introduces "migration literacy" as a new term to express the lack of specific capital that affects Australian migrants' status. Stevens's research allows us to think about the changes in the economic, cultural, and political capital of Chinese skilled trade workers from the perspective of social class.

Social Class in the Age of Transnational Mobility: A Revised Analytical Framework

In understanding the translocal and transnational mobilities of these semi-skilled Chinese workers, we found Pierre Bourdieu's (1984) theorization of economic capital, cultural capital, and social capital useful. The richness of this conceptual framework helps us understand and interpret the multifaceted nature of trade workers' immigration experiences. Among the three types of capital, economic capital can be directly converted into money and expressed in the form of ownership of assets, while cultural capital, which can be transformed into economic capital under certain conditions, is expressed in the institutionalized form of educational qualifications and knowledge (Bourdieu 1984). Social capital is "the sum of the resources, actual or virtual, that accrue to an individual or a group by virtue of possessing a durable network of more or less institutionalised relationships of mutual acquaintance and recognition" (Bourdieu and Wacquant 1992: 14). Social capital can also, under some circumstances, be converted into economic capital. Although the concept of social capital has been criticized for being too broad, the concept is helpful to our analysis of the social networks of skilled trade workers in their homeland and host country. Social capital is a focus of our research because it links individual identity with the structural position of the individual in the group, which helps us understand the adaptation of skilled trade workers in the new society and the impact of mobility on individual identity. There are two general types of social capital: bonding social capital and bridging social capital. The concepts of bonding and bridging social capital are related to Mark Granovetter's (1983) notions of "strong ties" and "weak ties," respectively. Bonding social capital is usually found among strong ties such as family and close friends (Gittell and Vidal 1998; Putnam 2000). Bridging social capital is usually found among weak ties, such as distant acquaintances or friends from one's past. Previous studies have analyzed the relationship between immigrants' social capital and economic achievement and found that immigrants' bridging social capital can provide support for immigrants' economic upward mobility (Lancee 2016).

However, as Bourdieu's theory of class systems and individuals' location with them was confined within the boundary of the nation-state, it is inadequate for understanding international migrants (Rye 2019). Johan Fredrik Rye refers to this as "methodological nationalism." Rye's (2019: 40) study of Polish migrant workers in Norway illustrates "how transnational migrants occupy multilocal, inconsistent and unstable locations in the class structures in their host community." Moreover, "these contradictions produce several trajectories over time, which include both upward and downward social mobilities" (40). Rye's extension and amplification of Bourdieu's theories offer a more suitable framework for explicating the complex identities of the highly mobile cohort we examined in this study, given the multiscale mobilities in their life trajectories and the unstable and ever-shifting class positions they assume in different social contexts.

Our research involved semi-structured in-depth interviews with eleven Chinese skilled trade workers and their family members (see details in Appendix). Among them, there were five males and six females, and their average age was forty-eight. All of our interviewees were married and had children. Most of their children were adults, except for two of school age. On average, they had lived in Perth for sixteen years (up to 2023) and came from various provinces in China. We used the snowball sampling method and attempted to interview a diverse range of people by widening the profile of interviewees involved in the recruiting process. Some interviewees were encountered in our daily lives, and some recommended their friends to us. Each interview lasted about two hours. Although the interviews were mainly conducted in 2019 and 2021, the research also benefited from longitudinal ethnographic observations, as the lead author initiated the research project on 457 skilled trade workers living in Perth in 2016.

Continuity: Economic Capital as a Driver of Mobility

As noted above, the migration of Chinese skilled trade workers to Western Australia was largely a contingent measure to make up for the labor and skills shortages caused by the mining boom. The value of their human capital is highly dependent on the needs of Australia's economy, particularly the mining sector. Since the mining industry follows a boom-and-bust cycle, the need for their skills is often volatile and seasonal in nature.

This unstable, temporary sense of being was not new for this group of workers. As rural migrant workers seek a livelihood in urban areas, they had already been through a process of "unfinished proletarianization" (Pun and Lu 2010). Their experience in the major cities in China is best described as being stuck "in-between" statuses (Zhan 2015). Most peasant workers still own land in the villages where their parents live, whereas the cities, as the production center, provide them remittances in exchange for their labor and skills but exclude them from the urban welfare system. This precarious existence "in-between" creates a constant need for them to negotiate their identities between rural peasant and urban worker while identifying fully with neither.

Homeownership, for example, is one of the major obstacles that denies migrant workers in China a sense of city membership. Homeownership is highly prioritized in postsocialist Chinese society, with a private housing ownership rate of over 90 percent (Huang, He, and Gan 2021). However, many rural migrants, after a long time residing in the cities, remain unable to purchase a house due to their low income or policy restrictions, or both (Zhan 2015). The lack of home ownership serves as a constant reminder of their "peasant-worker" status and transient, "sojourner" identities in the city. Reflecting this, only one migrant among our interviewees had bought an apartment in a megacity in China. The rest were unable to purchase due to their lack of urban residential permits (*hukou*). In contrast, after moving to Australia, the workers' skills were highly in demand and transferable. These enabled the cohort to almost immediately get into the workforce and earn substantial salaries. The sense of loss common in their early migratory stage was offset or even obliterated by this new competitiveness in the Australian labor market. Many of them purchased properties and hence acquired a material "home" in Perth. Given that Chinese rural migrants' full citizenship in urban areas is defined through the purchasing of property (Y. Wang et al. 2020), it can be argued that their purchase of properties in Perth contributed significantly to the migrant workers' s "homemaking" process.

Apart from homeownership, another important factor that affects migrant workers' sense of security and upward social mobility in China is their children's education and employment prospects. Despite the fact that rural migrant workers made up the majority of China's urban unskilled labor market, social welfare entitlements for urbanites, such as free public education for children, have never been fully extended to this cohort. From the early 2000s, the central government implemented a number of policies to ensure rural migrant workers' children could access free education in government schools (*China Labour Bulletin* 2023). However, the implementation of these policies was resisted by the local governments of receiving cities, and the schooling of migrant workers' children remains more expensive, and the participation rate is a lot lower, than for children with urban *hukou* (*China Labour Bulletin* 2023). Either left behind or marginalized in the city, the second generation of migrant workers in China is filled with sentiments of "anger and resentment" (Pun and Lu 2010).

Whether their children could receive a good education and achieve better job prospects remained a preoccupation in the workers' minds. Children's education anchored their hopes and aspirations to transform their class identities as *dagongzai* 打工仔 or *dagongmei* 打工妹 (migrant laborers). When migrating from rural villages to cities, some of them had to leave their children with their grandparents or other relatives. Those who brought their children with them often had to make do with limited options in terms of schooling. However, when they moved to WA, these temporary sojourners' mentality usually led to an orientation toward a more permanent settlement. For example, welder LMY[1] bought a house in a top-ranking public school zone before a price hike in the property market. His son LZ was admitted to university as an engineering major. LMY's colleagues and friends all looked to LZ as a role model for the second generation of workers.

However, language plays an important role in the Chinese migrant workers' sense of belonging in Australia and poses a new challenge in their transnational migration. Lack of cultural capital with language at its core meant that the workers were often susceptible to exploitation, which translated into direct economic losses. Due to their low level of English proficiency, most workers had to rely on recruitment agents when finding or changing jobs.

Said the welder HM, "Because of our poor English, we can only get jobs through recruitment agencies. They charge very high fees and are responsible for negotiating the wages with the hiring company. We get the payment through recruitment agencies. Sometimes, the pay is miscalculated, and we have to go to them for compensation."

Nevertheless, even exploitative recruitment agencies often preferentially hire workers whose English proficiency is higher. The workers noted the role of language in the upward mobility of their peers and their own direct economic losses due to the lack of language proficiency. To most workers, those peers who joined the ranks of the recruitment agency because of their better language skills personified the conversion of cultural capital to economic and social capital.

To a large degree, confidence in language helped to determine whether they saw their life in Australia as transient or permanent. HM, for example, lamented that he made two fundamental mistakes after coming to Australia: the decision to acquire Australian citizenship, and the assumption that he did not need much English because he could simply rely on his son to interpret for him. At the time of our interview, he was trying to find a better job and was independently studying English. According to HM, these two mistakes left him in a conundrum: the decision to get citizenship eliminated his chance to go back to China, while his lack of competence in English denied him the chance to find better work opportunities and enjoy the local lifestyle in Australia.

Workers also mentioned how low English proficiency impacted their social relations both at work and in the community. Most of them worked for companies with other employees who were also new Chinese migrants of similar backgrounds. They understood simple work-related instructions in English, and their socializing at work was mostly confined to the Chinese migrant group. However, the ability to communicate came into the equation with more complicated social interactions. LMY was a very competent welder; however, with very limited English, he struggled at work, having to make guesses in some social situations. He got into strife with his supervisors and colleagues a few times on issues such as unfair job assignments and was frustrated by his inability to articulate his complaints.

From the migrants' narratives, one can see that it is not that migrants do not have the intention to learn English. In fact, the majority of them did make efforts to attend classes. However, most workers started working very soon after they arrived in WA. For some, the long working hours, extreme physical exertion, and the often fly-in/fly-out work schedule in remote locations made it difficult to commit to studying English. From the sociolinguistic point of view, the localizing processes of certain linguistic resources are uneven under globalizing conditions; these processes "are tied to the even distribution of the other resources—social, economic, cultural and spatial—which are in turn given meaning amongst specific social, ideological and historical circumstances" (Dovchin 2017). Although skilled trade workers had certain advantages in the distribution of economic resources after they came to Australia because they had the skills required by the local economy, they did not have an advantage in the distribution of social and cultural resources.

Disjuncture: The Hindered Flow of Cultural Capital

As a marginalized group under global capitalism, skilled trade workers experienced precarious conditions in both internal and transnational migration. However, while their initial culture shock is no less profound than that experienced by middle-class migrants, the migrant workers enjoyed certain advantages in adapting to their new environment. We found that there was a growing awareness of themselves as a collective entity and, at the same time, a strong desire for "gentrification."

The rural-to-urban outbound movement, to a certain extent, prepared the workers for transnational migration. Most of the welders, for example, acquired their skills through a family tradition or in an industry precinct in a big city such as Shenzhen, Xiamen, or Guangzhou. Some had worked for state-owned enterprises (SOEs) and benefited from the technical training provided by the SOEs. A few of them were technical experts and innovators and were clearly proud of their achievements and honors. The fifty-one-year-old HM, for example, was a welder in a defense industry company in Hubei Province. HM once came fifth in a national welding competition. This technical prowess enabled HM to transition into a private company employee in Shenzhen when the defense industry went into decline as the government stopped heavily subsidizing the sector.

Like HM, welders typically acquired their skills in the heavy industry sectors in the period when China was transforming itself from an agricultural economy into a manufacturing powerhouse. During this process, workers gained not only technical skills but also a whole new experience of sociality: a complex hybrid of kinship fraternity, socialist collectivity, and individualism. For example, welder LMY was admitted to the Jianghan Oilfield Technology Training College, a large SOE in China's central Hubei Province, through his uncle on April 25, 1988. He could recall this date precisely and immediately. He called this uncle his "second parent" because acquiring the trade skills he learned at the college was his first "life-changing experience." The training program was designed to train welders to work on a Chinese national project in Bangladesh. Even though he did not end up going to work on the project, it sowed the seed of the idea that his skills were part of a nation-building scheme and were much needed overseas.

This pattern of outbound movement to big cities and large enterprises also seemed consistent with migrant workers outside of heavy industries. The always-smiling seamstress LNH had been in the garment industry for over twenty years. She started learning tailoring in her hometown, Yangzhou, at eighteen and moved to Shanghai when the factory owner moved his business to Vietnam. Before coming to Australia, she worked in a garment factory in Shenzhen from 1998 to 2008. Her working hours in Shenzhen were 8:00 a.m. to 10:00 p.m., with a one-and-a-half-hour lunch break. She worked on weekends with only one day off per month. This intensive working experience and skills gained as part of the global production chain prepared LNH for her move to Australia. She was the one who encouraged her husband, a welder, to apply for the 457 visa to go to Australia. LNH found her own job in Perth through a work trial, which was sewing a zipper into a pair of pants. "It is easy-peasy for me," said LNH with pride in her skills.

However, although these skilled trade workers were confident that the human capital they brought was important for Australia and were proud of the quality of their work, there was a stronger sense of "skills for money" exchange relationships in their work in Australia. The "master of the nation" workers' subjectivity, promoted during China's socialist era, was never fully extended to migrant workers and was now completely lacking for transnational skilled trade workers. In their narratives, workers mentioned better health and safety measures in the working environment in Australia, but SLH, one of the female welders, said: "If we are afraid of heights, we can request a change of task. But here, men and women are treated the same because they get the same amount of pay. Companies in China will look after female workers more, and there is certain human touch [*renqingwei* 人情味]."

Denied urban citizenship in China, some of the rural migrant workers, particularly the second generation, demand their rights and entitlements from the Chinese state and, in doing so, have been in the process of acquiring a collective working-class identity (Pun and Lu 2010; Chan and Selden 2017; Siu 2015). Meanwhile, the first-generation migrant workers, particularly those with experience in SOEs, also maintained a residual socialist workers' identity. In Australia, however, the skilled workers mostly accepted the neoliberal market ethos, such as skills for money and every person for themselves. Furthermore, the conversion of human capital into other forms is experienced differently in the two migratory processes. In China, workers' human capital could be transformed into social capital, including leadership and symbolic capital, such as honors. But this was often hard to realize in WA. For example, LMY was promoted to a team leader in China as a result of his superb skills. In HM's house, the honor certificate he received in the Chinese national competition was conspicuously displayed. The sense of status loss was keenly felt in LMY and HM's cases, while welder TLJ, on the other hand, was pleased that he would be able to put his previously acquired managerial skills to use in Australia.

Research has shown that rural migrant workers in China's cities are often seen by middle-class, urban residents as the Other and *suzhi* 素质 (quality, or cultural civility) discourse is often utilized both to denigrate this migrant population's social status and to represent them as in need of "education" (Yan 2003; Sun 2009). The rural migrant workers were well aware of this social and status divide between the rural and the urban, which had been hammered institutionally by the urban residential permit system in China. For example, HM and his wife underlined that they had been hired *as urban residents* at the factory in Hubei and were, therefore, different from most of the other skilled trade workers who were hired as rural migrant workers.

This social status distinction in the national context, to a certain extent, reappeared in the transnational context (Stevens 2020). However, it was also disrupted and reorganized. The relative validation of the working-class culture, the egalitarian ethos, and the high incomes for trade workers in the Australian context meant that the skill sets of "tradies" were relatively highly valued in the wider society. During their internal migration in China, workers' manual skilled labor and mental work had been regarded as diametric opposites and mapped onto class relations, with the latter held in higher esteem. The workers were aware that this was reversed in Australian society, both in material terms and symbolically. Asked to compare life in China and Australia, CYQ, a carpenter who migrated from Fujian Province in 2007, replied, "Of course, it is better in Australia for us because manual labor is much more highly paid."

Apart from technical expertise, the other life skills they had acquired in rural living, such as organic gardening and fishing, were also in keeping with Australian middle-class leisure fads and often the envy of other migrants. However, discrimination against rural migrants still had a residual effect on the migrants. Despite years of friendship with the researchers, welder LMY still made a comment, "If we were not here (Australia), you people wouldn't want to deal with us." He saw the demarcations between classes (manual laborer versus intellectual) and was conscious that the migration experience had elevated his social status, or at least that the symbolic status was reorganized in Australia.

Coexisting Continuity and Disjuncture: The Mobility of Social Capital

When skilled trade workers encountered cultural discontinuity across borders due to language and cultural differences, their social networks underwent both disruption and continuity. This continuity was upheld not only through the use of social media to maintain connections to their home country but also by the workers preserving their prior social patterns in the destination country.

On the August 7, 2016, the lead author got a call from a friend, a welder migrant from Sichuan Province, inviting her to a party his fellow workers and colleagues had organized to celebrate the birth of the host's first grandchild. The party was organized as a typical rural Chinese-style "running

Figure 1 Chinese skilled trade workers at a gathering to celebrate the birth of a worker's granddaughter, August 7, 2016. Photograph by the authors.

banquet," with guests turning up and leaving freely as they saw fit. Over two hundred guests attended the event, nearly all welders and their relatives who had migrated to Perth during the mining boom. The gathering led to the realization that the format of Chinese skilled trade workers' social network in Perth resembles social networks in China's rural society.

In general, the social networks of skilled trade workers can be classified into three types: the family-oriented, virtual, and association membership (see fig. 2). The core part of the social network of skilled trade workers consists of family members and other workers from China. Following internal migration, the trade workers often acquired jobs or approached a migrant recruitment agency through kin and fellow villagers. Once they moved overseas, the same networks connecting apprentices and trainers, townsfolk, and ex-colleagues played a more significant role in their job seeking, presenting both a buffer in times of difficulty and access to opportunities. For example, LMY got his job in China through his kinship network and migrated to Perth with the help of his apprentice and trainer, who both migrated to Perth before him. The new migrants' social ties were often strengthened by ritual gatherings like the one discussed above over major events such as weddings, childbirth, birthdays, funerals, celebrations of the granting of permanent residency status, and traditional Chinese festivals. In the course of their conversations, they would naturally discuss which worker's child got married and which workers went fishing together during the holidays.

These everyday interactions, which occurred as frequently as nearly weekly before the COVID-19 pandemic, prevented the workers from leading isolated lives and formed an important part of acquiring a sense of belonging.

Although the second type of social network overlaps significantly with the first type, it is exclusively established and reinforced through social media. Mimi Sheller and John Urry (2006) point out that "mobility systems" (including transport and communication) facilitate "copresence" with key others (workmates, family, friends, and significant others). For skilled trade workers, WeChat, a Chinese instant messaging app launched in 2011, was the most important tool to help them maintain their personal networks. They not only relied primarily on WeChat to stay in touch with family and friends in Perth but also used this mobile app to communicate with family and friends in China. In follow-up interviews conducted in March 2023, it was revealed that as a result of travel restrictions during the COVID-19 pandemic, the workers were not only unable to travel back to China to reunite with friends and relatives but also had significantly fewer gatherings with friends in their local area. Instead, they increasingly relied on WeChat to sustain their social connections.

We found two key associations connecting the workers: one was a WeChat group called 457 Workers' Home, created in 2015, and the other was the WA Chinese Workers' Association, established in 2017. The founder of these two associations was TLJ, a welder from Fujian Province. He was one of the few who passed the immigration English exam (IELTS exam). Keenly aware of the problems trade workers face, after gaining experience with a recruitment company, TLJ set up his own recruitment agency. He established the 457 Visa WeChat group with the intention of enabling workers to assist each other and to ensure that future generations remember their origins. There were five hundred people in the group (the maximum number allowed). Daily posts included recruitment information, discussions of legal issues related to work, and advertisements for businesses and products.

TLJ also cofounded the WA Chinese Workers' Association (CWA) with seven other directors. The CWA organized gatherings and donations for fellow workers and disaster relief while providing an emotional anchor for the skilled trade workers. During the COVID-19 pandemic, the CWA organized a donation drive, with approximately 177 people responding and

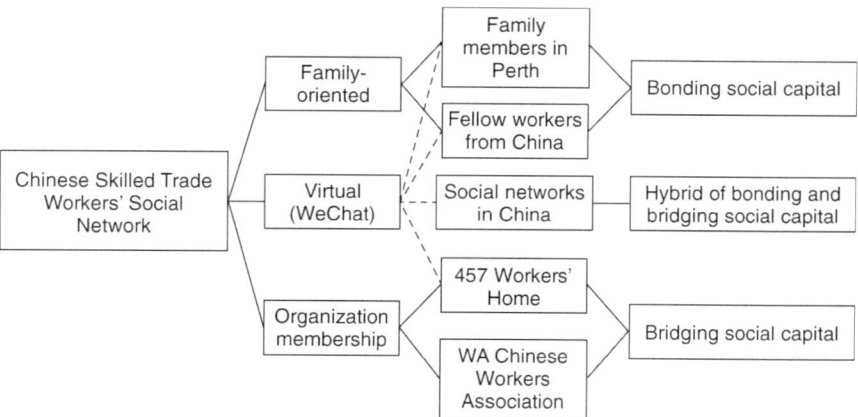

Figure 2 The three forms of social network maintained by Chinese skilled trade workers.

donating AUD 20,000. The association used the donations to purchase around two thousand sets of protective gear to donate to five hospitals in mainland China. They also purchased masks from China and sold them to migrant workers at cost, as well as donating some masks to local nursing homes in Perth.

The relationship between skilled trade workers and the above associations is relatively loose: They are not required to pay membership fees or participate in activities at set times. However, they did respond to calls from 457 Workers' Home and CWA to participate in activities that interested them and were able to access external information or seek assistance (e.g., finding work, legal aid) through the associations.

Social capital is of great significance to skilled trade workers. It was closely connected with research participants' material life, as social networks constituted a key resource in migrant adaptation, especially in seeking work or a place to live in the destination country (Łukaszewska-Bezulska 2020). It is also connected to their emotional life, affecting their individual identification and identification with the receiving society. Trade workers found it difficult to integrate into local social networks and build up bridging capital due to language barriers. Therefore, they relied more on their existing social relationships and the connections between other Chinese fellow workers from the same cohort (bonding social capital).

Both domestic and transnational migration had an impact on the social capital of skilled trade workers. Moving from rural areas to urban centers made clusters break down and transform into "personalised networking" (Hampton and Wellman 2001), while transnational migration further individualized relationships and created a reliance on their social media networks.

Although strong ties (bonding social capital) still play an important role in connecting skilled trade workers to their past and current lives, many of them also reflected on the drawbacks of these ties. This reflection came out of their mobility experiences. In Chinese society, *guanxi* 关系 (connection) plays an important role in people's daily lives. *Guanxi* largely consists of strong ties, and it is characterized by the dynamics of *mianzi* 面子 (social dignity) and *renqing* 人情 (human feeling) (Feng and Patulny 2021). As "floating populations" in urban areas, rural migrants are rarely able to access local social networks. During an interview, LNH commented that upon returning to China, she discovered that visiting a doctor in her hometown was costly, and individuals had to depend on their personal network to choose a preferred doctor. In contrast, this was not necessary in Australia. LMY, another interviewee, had a conflict with a colleague who was clearly in the wrong, but LMY was unable to argue back due to his limited English proficiency. The manager eventually intervened, and the coworker was terminated a few days later. LMY was surprised, as the coworker had been recommended by the boss's friend. This incident led LMY to contemplate Chinese social norms influenced by *guanxi*. Many interviewees expressed the view that Australia was a fairer society. At the same time, they also expressed nostalgia for the "human touch" in their hometowns and concerns about the fading of this personal connection within China as the society turned toward the prioritization of economic interests.

We found that skilled trade workers sometimes faced a rupture in social capital during transnational migration. They usually centered their strong social connections around family, which contributed to a type of social capital known as bonding social capital. However, over time, the attachment to their homeland tended to fade, and they struggled to establish new social connections outside of family and coworkers from China. This represented a rupture in social capital. Creating WeChat group and worker association was an attempt by the workers to break free from homogeneous social networks and connect with local communities in pursuit of more diverse social capital (bridging social capital). For example, TLJ mentioned the original intention of setting up this association: "The WeChat group (457 Workers Home) can only do small things. However, after registering the association, there will be an official platform that allows 457 workers to better integrate into local life in Australia."

Based on the founders' plan, the CWA aims to collaborate with local Chinese communities to unite skilled trade workers and their children and provide mutual aid while facilitating interaction between local Chinese businesspeople and skilled trade workers. While TLJ highlights the importance of helping workers resolve labor disputes, the association's actions have, in practice, been limited to offering suggestions and assistance. This has resulted in the association resembling a trade union within a Chinese state-owned enterprise rather than an Australian trade union that advocates for and represents workers' interests to employers and the government. In our most recent interview, TLJ discussed the challenges of managing the association, stating that it required a significant amount of time and energy to keep it running. The Chung Wah Association, the oldest local Chinese association, was teaching the initiators of CWA how to apply for government grants to offset this.

The social networks of the Chinese skilled trade workers in WA were highly homogeneous. Although they attempted to organize spontaneous gatherings, offer mutual support, and maintain connections with their home country through social media, these actions were not successful in increasing their social capital. Some workers recognized the significance of broadening their social networks to include diverse connections, as bridging social capital could provide access to a wider range of information and resources. Creating the WeChat group and worker association was a positive attempt to achieve this diversification, but their future development remains uncertain.

Conclusion

This article is based on a small-scale qualitative study of Chinese skilled worker migrants in Western Australia. This cohort has often been overlooked in studies on Chinese migrants, which focus on middle-class skilled migrants. Given Australia's increasingly selective and pragmatic migrant policy, which prioritizes economic, cultural, and social capital, this group of sojourners may be described as "unlikely settlers": different from unskilled and family migration on the one hand and skilled middle-class professional migrants on the other. Through semistructured in-depth interviews with skilled trade workers in Western Australia, this article has taken a closer look at their experience and the confluence of factors contributing to their circumstances in Australia.

We propose that the study of migration experiences, including those associated with transnational Chinese lives, should not be demarcated into two separate realms based on internal migration versus transnational experiences. A state-centered perspective tends to skew migrants' experiences, reinforcing the assumptions of stable and homogeneous national populations with long-term cultural and ethnic rootedness within the confines of the state (Lucassen and Lucassen 2017). Our study provides evidence that the Chinese migrant workers' dual migratory experiences are interconnected with both continuities and disjunctures across their different types of mobility experiences.

The implications of this research are at least twofold. First, to understand the negotiation of Chinese migrant identities, we must factor in prior economic processes. In the process of being recruited and trained for the Fordist period of socialist modernization, the skilled trade workers in our study acquired technical skills, a sense of citizenship, and national belonging to the Chinese nation as an imagined community. In the subsequent marketization of the reform era, the workers went through a partial individualization process. These experiences had a significant impact on their transnational movement and identity (re)formation in Australia.

Second, we found that class frames and hierarchy were no longer clear between the Chinese skilled workers and other Chinese immigrants. As Stevens (2020: iv) points out, "Nationally bounded homeland class frames are both repeated and challenged under the different economic and social conditions found in Perth." This cohort used their earlier internal migration experiences to adapt to the new overseas environment. However, unlike the highly transferable human capital that the migrant workers possessed, cultural capital was generally considered harder to acquire for them, even after they had successfully settled in Australia. As Katharyne Mitchell (1997: 229) puts it, "Although immigrants may become legal citizens through a prescribed, state-regulated path, immigrants become cultural citizens only through a reflexive set of formative and locally constructed processes." Chinese skilled workers' human capital became contextually strengthened through international migration. Although the sense of social status disparity in internal migration was reduced, the language barrier became more noticeable. The close, strong connections formed between the workers and their families and fellow workers serve as a source of mutual support but also, to some extent, limit their ability to expand their social networks with greater openness. While the Chinese transnationalism framework has led us to think about the intense and multiple interconnections of mobile people and media across borders, this study also shows that mobilities on different scales work in tandem to (re)constitute transnational migrants' identities and points to the importance of a translocal-transnational nexus in these migrants' life experiences.

Appendix

Table 1. Interviewees' basic details

Name of Interviewee	Gender, Age (2023)	Year Arrived in Australia	Former Career	Current Career	Interview Time (m/d/y)
LMY	M, 56	2007	welder	welder	3/30/19, 3/26/23
XJ	F, 51	2008	housewife	worker in a chicken factory	3/30/19
TLJ	M, 41	2006	welder	agent, private business owner	4/5/19, 10/30/21, 3/24/23
HM	M, 54	2005	welder	welder	6/2/19
CZY	F, 56	2005	quality inspector	worker in vegetable factory	6/2/19
YHP	M, 51	2008	welder	welder	6/16/19
SLH	F, 50	2007	welder	welder	6/16/19
TYH	F, 46	2005	welder	welder	6/16/19
LNH	F, 47	2008	worker in garment factory	worker in garment factory, ironing factory	8/4/19
A'ying	F, 43	2003	hairdresser	hairdresser	6/15/18, 11/18/18
CYQ	M, 47	2007	carpenter	carpenter	2/7/21, 6/29/21

Notes

We would like to thank the skilled trade workers who generously shared their stories over the long time when we collected the data for this article. Our gratitude also goes to this special issue editor, Fran Martin, whose dedication and support have made it possible for the migrant workers' voices to be heard.

1 All interviewees' names are coded using the acronyms of the pinyin spelling of their Chinese names.

References

Ang, Ien. 1998. "Can One Say No to Chineseness? Pushing the Limits of the Diasporic Paradigm." *boundary 2* 25, no. 3: 223–42. https://doi.org/10.2307/303595.

Boccagni, Paolo. 2012. "Revisiting the 'Transnational' in Migration Studies: A Sociological Understanding." *Revue européenne des migrations internationales* 28, no. 1: 33–50.

Boccagni, Paolo. 2017. "Transnationalism." In *The Wiley Blackwell Encyclopedia of Social Theory*, edited by Bryne S. Turner, 1–3. Hoboken, NJ: John Wiley and Sons.

Bourdieu, Pierre. 1984. *Distinction: A Social Critique of the Judgement of Taste*. London: Routledge.

Bourdieu, Pierre, and Loïc J. Wacquant. 1992. *An Invitation to Reflexive Sociology*. Chicago: University of Chicago Press.

Chan, Jenny, and Mark Selden. 2017. "The Labour Politics of China's Rural Migrant Workers." *Globalizations* 14, no. 2: 259–71. https://doi.org/10.1080/14747731.2016.1200263.

China Labour Bulletin. 2023. "Migrant Workers and Their Children." September 6. https://clb.org.hk/content/migrant-workers-and-their-children.

Dovchin, Sender. 2017. "Uneven Distribution of Resources in the Youth Linguascapes of Mongolia." *Multilingua* 36, no. 2: 147–79. https://doi.org/10.1515/multi-2015-0065.

Feng, Zhuqin, and Roger Patulny. 2021. "Should I Use My 'Weak' Social Capital or 'Strong' Guanxi? Reviewing and Critiquing Two Theories in the Context of Western-Chinese Migration." *Journal of Sociology* 57, no. 2: 464–82. https://doi.org/10.1177/1440783320925152.

Gao, Jia. 2001. "Chinese Students in Australia." In *The Australian People: An Encyclopedia of the Nation, Its People, and Their Origins*, edited by James Jupp, 222–25. Cambridge: Cambridge University Press.

Gao, Jia. 2006. "Migrant Transnationality and Its Evolving Nature: A Case Study of Mainland Chinese Migrants in Australia." *Journal of Chinese Overseas* 2, no. 2: 193–219. https://doi.org/10.1353/jco.2006.0012.

Gao, Jia. 2009. "Lobbying to Stay: The Chinese Students' Campaign to Stay in Australia." *International Migration* 47, no. 2: 127–54. https://doi.org/10.1111/j.1468-2435.2009.00515.x.

Gao, Jia. 2011. "Seeking Residency from the Courts: The Chinese Experience in the Post-White Australia Era." *Journal of Chinese Overseas* 7, no. 2: 187–210. https://doi.org/10.1163/179325411X595404.

Gao, Jia. 2013. *Chinese Activism of a Different Kind: The Chinese Students' Campaign to Stay in Australia*. Vol. 37 of *Social Science in Asia*. Edited by Vineeta Sinha, Syed Farid Alatas, and Kelvin Low. 44 vols. Leiden, Netherlands: Brill.

Gittell, Ross, and Avis Vidal. 1998. *Community Organizing: Building Social Capital as a Development Strategy.* Thousand Oaks, CA: Sage.

Granovetter, Mark. 1983. "The Strength of Weak Ties: A Network Theory Revisited." *Sociological Theory* 1: 201–33. https://doi.org/10.2307/202051.

Hampton, Keith, and Barry Wellman. 2001. "Long Distance Community in the Network Society." *American Behavioral Scientist* 45, no. 3: 476–95. https://doi.org/10.1177/0002764 0121957303.

Huang, Youqin, Shenjing He, and Li Gan. 2021. "Introduction to Special Issue: Unpacking the Chinese Dream of Homeownership." *Journal of Housing and the Built Environment* 36, no. 1: 1–7.

Lancee, Bram. 2016. "Job Search Methods and Immigrant Earnings: A Longitudinal Analysis of the Role of Bridging Social Capital." *Ethnicities* 16, no. 3: 349–67. https://doi .org/10.1177/1468796815581426.

Leong, Susan. 2016. "Provisional Business Migrants in Western Australia: Social Media and Conditional Belonging." In *Media and Communication in the Chinese Diaspora: Rethinking Transnationalism*, edited by Wanning Sun and John Sinclair, 184–202. London: Routledge.

Lin, Xia. 2014. "'Dance' of Chineseness: Negotiating Identities in London." PhD diss., Middlesex University.

Locher-Lo, Caroline Chung-Hsuan. 2020. "Chinese Heritage Maintenance: A Collective Case Study on Chineseness and Heritage Language in Contemporary British Columbia." PhD diss., University of British Columbia.

Lucassen, Jan, and Leo Lucassen. 2017. "Theorizing Cross-cultural Migrations: The Case of Eurasia since 1500." *Social Science History* 41, no. 3: 445–75. https://doi.org/10.1017/ssh .2017.19.

Łukaszewska-Bezulska, Justyna. 2021. "The Role of Social Capital in Labour-Related Migrations: The Polish Example." *Journal of International Migration and Integration* 22, no. 3: 949–66. https://doi.org/10.1007/s12134-020-00776-z.

Martin, Fran. 2014. "The Gender of Mobility: Chinese Women Students' Self-Making through Transnational Education." *Intersections: Gender and Sexuality in Asia and the Pacific*, no. 35. http://intersections.anu.edu.au/issue35/martin.htm.

Martin, Fran. 2017. "Mobile Self-Fashioning and Gendered Risk: Rethinking Chinese Students' Motivations for Overseas Education." *Globalisation, Societies, and Education* 15, no. 5: 706–20. https://doi.org/10.1080/14767724.2016.1264291.

Mitchell, Katharyne. 1997. "Transnational Subjects: Constituting the Cultural Citizenship in the Era of Pacific Rim Capital." In *Ungrounded Empires: The Cultural Politics of Modern*

Chinese Transnationalism, edited by Aihwa Ong and Donald Nonini, 228–56. New York: Routledge.

Ong, Aihwa, and Donald Nonini. 1997. "Introduction: Chinese Transnationalism as an Alternative Modernity." In *Ungrounded Empires: The Cultural Politics of Modern Chinese Transnationalism*, edited by Aihwa Ong and Donald Nonini, 3–36. New York: Routledge.

Pun, Ngai. 2016. *Migrant Labor in China: Post-socialist Transformations*. Cambridge: Cambridge University Press.

Pun, Ngai, and Huilin Lu. 2010. "Unfinished Proletarianization: Self, Anger, and Class Action among the Second Generation of Peasant-Workers in Present-Day China." *Modern China* 36, no. 5: 493–519. https://doi.org/10.1177/0097700410373576.

Putnam, Robert. 2000. *Bowling Alone: The Collapse and Revival of American Community*. New York: Simon and Schuster.

Qi, Ziwei. 2019. "An Overview of Rural to Urban Migration in China and Social Challenges." *Migration Letters* 16, no. 2: 273–82.

Rye, Johan Fredrik. 2018. "Transnational Spaces of Class: International Migrants' Multilocal, Inconsistent, and Instable Class Positions." *Current Sociology* 67, no. 1: 27–46. https://doi.org/10.1177/0011392118793676.

Sheller, Mimi, and John Urry. 2006. "The New Mobilities Paradigm." *Environment and Planning A: Economy and Space* 38, no. 2: 207–26. https://doi.org/10.1068/a37268.

Siu, Kaxton. 2015. "Continuity and Change in the Everyday Lives of Chinese Migrant Factory Workers." *China Journal*, no. 74: 43–65. https://doi.org/10.1086/681813.

Solinger, Dorothy. 1999. *Contesting Citizenship in Urban China: Peasant Migrants, the State, and the Logic of the Market*. Berkeley: University of California Press.

Stevens, Catriona. 2020. "Unlike Settlers in Exceptional Times: The Impact of Social Class and Selective Migration Policies on the Recent Migrations of Trade Skilled Workers and Their Families from China to Perth, Western Australia." PhD diss., University of Western Australia.

Sun, Wanning. 2002. *Leaving China: Media, Migration, and Transnational Imagination*. Lanham, MD: Rowman and Littlefield.

Sun, Wanning. 2009. "*Suzhi* on the Move: Body, Place, and Power." *positions: east asia cultures critique* 17, no. 3: 617–42. https://doi.org/10.1215/10679847-2009-017.

Sun, Wanning. 2014. *Subaltern China: Rural Migrants, Media, and Cultural Practices*. Lanham, MD: Rowman and Littlefield.

Vertovec, Steve. 1999. "Conceiving and Researching Transnationalism." *Ethnic and Racial Studies* 22, no. 2: 447–62. https://doi.org/10.1080/014198799329558.

Wang, Bingyu. 2018. "Becoming a Rooted Cosmopolitan? The Case Study of 1.5 Generation New Chinese Migrants in New Zealand." *Journal of Chinese Overseas* 14, no. 2: 244–67. https://doi.org/10.1163/17932548-12341381.

Wang, Yuqu, Zehong Wang, Chunshan Zhou, Ying Liu, and Song Liu. 2020. "On the Settlement of the Floating Population in the Pearl River Delta: Understanding the Factors of Permanent Settlement Intention versus Housing Purchase Actions." *Sustainability* 12, no. 22: 9771. https://doi.org/10.3390/su12229771.

Yan, Hairong. 2003. "Neoliberal Governmentality and Neohumanism: Organising Suzhi/Value Flow through Labor Recruitment." *Cultural Anthropology* 18, no. 4: 493–523.

Zhan, Yang. 2015. "'My Life Is Elsewhere': Social Exclusion and Rural Migrants' Consumption of Homeownership in Contemporary China." *Dialectical Anthropology* 39, no. 4: 405–22. http://www.jstor.org/stable/43895167.

Caught between Two Transnationalisms:

Mainland Chinese Students' Emotional Conflicts in Recent Hong Kong Protests

Lin Song and Shih-Diing Liu

Hong Kong: A Zone of Suspension

In June 2019, a series of large-scale protests broke out in Hong Kong, a former British colony handed over to China in 1997 under a "one country, two systems" disposition that grants the city a high degree of autonomy. The protests began in opposition to a proposed extradition law allowing the transfer of suspects from the Special Administrative Region to the Chinese mainland. They then escalated to an unprecedentedly wide and prolonged anti-government movement with frequent and increasingly violent clashes between protesters and the police. At the time of writing (March 2023), despite Beijing's implementation of a wide-ranging national security law in Hong Kong designed to curtail opposition, social unrest is still ongoing in various forms (Ho 2021; Su and Cheung 2021).

positions 32:4   DOI 10.1215/10679847-11306832

The protests are the latest manifestation of Hong Kong's tensions with mainland China. The widespread anxiety in Hong Kong over the mainland's growing presence corresponds to a wider, global uneasiness with China's rising geopolitical power and the accompanying cross-border mobilities of Chinese capital and people (Goodman 2017; Zeng and Li 2019). The protests, in this sense, are symptomatic of a newly expanded Chinese transnationalism in the "global China" era. Hong Kong has conventionally been theorized as a node of Chinese transnationalism that cuts across national borders while "not contained by a single nation-state or subject to its influence" (Ong and Nonini 1997: 323). But the state-led economic and political integration of Hong Kong and mainland China is giving rise to new ties, flows, and interactions of people across the border. As a liminal territory located *at once* inside and outside China, Hong Kong provides an ideal vantage point through which to examine the dynamics of this new form of Chinese transnationalism. In this article, we follow the "new mobilities paradigm" (Sheller and Urry 2006) in unpacking Chinese transnationalism's cultural dynamics. As Mimi Sheller and John Urry (2006: 211) point out, mobility is "not a question of privileging a 'mobile subjectivity,' but rather of tracking the power of discourses and practices of mobility in creating both movement and stasis." We are interested in how the newly expanded, Sino-centric form of Chinese transnationalism is mediated and lived out through everyday affective practices. For this reason, we focus on a group that arguably best embodies the quandaries of Chinese transnationalisms today—mainland Chinese students in Hong Kong. Fran Martin (2018) argues for the distinctness of student migrants, since their cross-border experiences afford a "zone of suspension" through which students unlearn and renegotiate normative life scripts and ideological expectations from their home societies. These experiences became highly visible and contested during the recent Hong Kong protests. In exploring mainland students' experiences in Hong Kong, we ask: What emotional experiences has the new Chinese transnationalism produced in Hong Kong? How do mainland students negotiate emotional boundaries between nationalism and transnationalism in Hong Kong? What are the consequences of their reworkings of Chinese identity?

We take emotions as our focus of analysis because they flesh out in a wide range of cultural practices of embodied meaning-making (Burkitt 2014: 14). Emotions create a connection with as well as alienation from collective bodies such as the nation (Harding and Pribram 2002; Gorski 2013; Faria 2014). They constitute a distinctive domain where transnational subjectivities are negotiated. We argue that as cross-border subjects, mainland students are caught in growing tensions generated by the new Chinese transnationalism in Hong Kong. As a result, they are constructed by both Hong Kong and mainland media along the lines of dis/identification with nationalism as an "emotional regime" (Zembylas 2016). Reflecting on mainland students' negotiation with and defiance of the emotional norms of nationalism, we suggest that "minor transnationalism" (Lionnet and Shih 2005) is a useful conceptual tool through which to displace the conventional center/margin and majority/minority conceptions and think through the entrenched nationalism/localism dichotomy. In their theorization, Françoise Lionnet and Shu-Mei Shih (2005: 5) argue that the transnational should be "conceived as a space of exchange and participation wherever processes of hybridization occur and where it is still possible for cultures to be produced and performed without necessary mediation by the center." We argue that during the student protests, Hong Kong was temporarily turned into a minor transnational space of grassroots exchange between different groups of students. This space nurtures contradictory emotional experiences and enables mainland students to produce forms of affective mobility in unpredictable ways.

In what follows, we start by situating mainland students in relation to two competing transnationalisms in Hong Kong. After outlining our methods, we examine how both Hong Kong and mainland media's representations of mainland students, though driven by disparate political imaginaries, invariably frame them along the lines of Chinese nationalism and China-centrism. Then we explain how a minor transnational position could emerge by reflecting on the ways in which mainland students negotiate divisive, binary positions in diverse and sometimes subversive ways. We conclude by discussing the broader implications of minor transnationalism in the context of antagonistic affective attachments to nations and places.

One City, Two Transnationalisms

As a capitalist outpost during China's years of high socialism, Hong Kong has historically played a pivotal role in Chinese transnationalism. The "in-between" space the territory occupied enabled it to function as "a node of unique networks" during the Cold War (Hamilton 2021: 7–10). Hong Kong provided a space on the doorstep of the Maoist revolution for Chinese elites to develop transnational linkages and business strategies. During China's Reform era, it was the linchpin of the country's integration into the US-led global capitalist economy. By the 1990s, it handled 40–45 percent of China's foreign trade (3). It is therefore not surprising that Hong Kong has been conceived as a center of Chinese transnationalism. Donald M. Nonini and Aihwa Ong (1997: 23–26), for instance, in conceptualizing Chinese transnationalism as "an alternative modernity," saw Hong Kong as a hub of mobility for Chinese diasporic communities, whose trajectories exceed nation-state-based transnationalism. This view was shared by many other scholars in the 1990s and 2000s, who positioned Chinese transnationalism as outside the Chinese mainland and manifested by geographically "peripheral" Chinese societies. A good example is Tu Wei-ming's (1991) provocative assertion that since the PRC experienced a significant rupture from traditional Chinese culture, capitalist societies such as Hong Kong and Taiwan would eventually replace mainland China as the center of a transnational cultural China. Similarly, in her influential conceptualization of the Sinophone, Shih (2007: 4) champions "a network of places of cultural production outside China and on the margins of Chineseness." In such a line of thinking, Hong Kong becomes a nodal point in Chinese transnationalism because of its liminal status, and mainly because it is imagined as the *outside* of the PRC.

Such an imagination of Hong Kong as a transnational city outside the Chinese border (*jingwai* 境外) still holds sway today. The recent influx of migrants, talents, and students from mainland China testifies to Hong Kong's appeal as a global city. The mainland Chinese student population in Hong Kong has tripled over the last decade and makes up almost 70 percent of the city's nonlocal students (University Grants Committee 2019). With worsening Sino-US relations and growing geopolitical tensions worldwide, Hong Kong is becoming an even more popular destination for mainland students pursuing education outside the Chinese mainland (Sharma 2022). But the situation has changed significantly when compared to that of the 1990s. Iam-chong Ip (2020: 4) describes mainland Chinese youth in Hong Kong as embodying a type of "Sino-centric transnationalism," which manifests in two ways: first, Hong Kong is positioned in the "Sino-centric" world of cities due to its geographical and cultural proximity, serving only as "a transitory place for navigating across the cosmopolitan world" (5–6); second, the mainland migrants in Hong Kong also display "subjectivity, practices, and desires in compliance with China's political calculations and flexible capitalism" (4). With the phenomenal growth of mainland students, Hong Kong's role is changing from a center for diasporic Chinese communities to a springboard for mainland Chinese elites.

Arguably, then, two competing Chinese transnationalisms coexist in Hong Kong. The first is rooted in Hong Kong's geohistoric legacies. This transnationalism functions as a centrifugal force that characterizes Hong Kong as an exceptional free market different from communist China and connected to the capitalist West. The second transnationalism is driven by the PRC's growing economic and geopolitical power and its proactive recentering of itself on the world stage. This version of transnationalism is centripetal, in the sense that Hong Kong is increasingly assimilated into Beijing's state-building project (Fong 2017). Beijing's policies such as the 2003 Closer Economic Partnership Arrangement (CEPA) between Hong Kong and mainland China strategically positioned Hong Kong as an offshore financial center for the PRC (Hung 2022: 45). More recently, mainland Chinese companies have overtaken foreign corporations as the biggest presence of outside business in Hong Kong (101). The "mainlandization" of Hong Kong's economy led to the political ascendancy of the mainland business elite (83), further tilting Hong Kong's transnationalism toward the mainland Chinese side.

As cross-border subjects, mainland students are the product of these two transnationalisms. On the one hand, their presence in Hong Kong is a direct result of the growing reliance of Hong Kong's higher education sector on mainland applicants, which is itself part of a larger plan for regional integration (Chao 2012). On the other, they also perceive their cross-border mobility in Hong Kong as integral to an imagined cosmopolitanism that enables them to move beyond China and Chinese state power (Ip 2020: 4). Mainland students in Hong Kong are also inevitably caught in between the tensions produced by these competing Chinese transnationalisms. As Ling Tang (2021: 37) points out, during the recent Hong Kong protests, mainland students were typically understood through "the assumed dichotomy between authoritarian, illiberal China and the democratic liberal West." In other words, they were frequently seen as agents of Sino-centric transnationalism, and therefore threatening Hong Kong's liberal values. Scholarly discussions of mainland students in Hong Kong tend to focus on their adaptation strategies (Xu 2015; Yu and Zhang 2016) or understand them as aspiring subjects pursuing an elitist "Hong Kong dream" while detached from local political struggles (Ip 2020). But these perspectives fail to fully account for how mainland students negotiate their positions as transnational subjects—in particular, the emergence of political sympathies with their Hong Kong student peers and the complex and conflicted positioning of some mainland students inside/outside the protest movement. To better understand mainland students' physical and emotional mobilities in Hong Kong, we combine qualitative methods of textual analysis with in-depth interviews to analyze both media construction of mainland students as an emotional signifier and their own emotional experiences.

Data collection for this research was carried out in two stages. The first stage of online observation lasted for five months from September 2019 to January 2020 at the height of the protests. During this time, we gathered textual and visual materials from various online archives from both Hong Kong and mainland China, including major news outlets like China Central Television (henceforth CCTV), *Apple Daily*, and *Stand News*, and social networking sites such as Facebook and WeChat. Based on viewing statistics as well as the material's relevance to ongoing emotional tensions, we classified, selected, and analyzed key media events related to mainland students. In the second stage (August to September 2020), we conducted semistructured interviews with ten mainland students. The participants were recruited through personal networks.[1] While their durations of stay in Hong Kong vary from one year to nine years, all of them lived in Hong Kong from September 2019 to January 2020 and experienced the protests firsthand. Their educational backgrounds differ from master ($n=7$) and PhD students ($n=2$)

to PhD graduate (*n*=1). Based on our prior knowledge of the participants, we purposely selected those with different attitudes toward the protests, from supportive (*n*=4) to neutral (*n*=3) to averse (*n*=3). The interviews were conducted in Mandarin Chinese (Putonghua), the participants' mother tongue, although some participants (*n*=4) also know how to speak Cantonese. The interviews lasted from sixty to ninety minutes and were loosely structured with a set of questions revolving around the events we selected. Conducted in a flexible and open manner, our interviews also encouraged the participants to share their opinions and experiences about the protests in particular and mainland–Hong Kong relations in general. Due to social distancing restrictions imposed by the COVID-19 pandemic, all interviews were carried out virtually on Zoom, a synchronous platform found to bring the benefits of convenience, interactivity, and ease of use for data collection (Archibald et al. 2019). All names cited in this article are pseudonyms.

Dis/identifying "Mainland Student" and the Politics of Fear

The making of "mainland students" as an identity category in Hong Kong is charged with contradictory emotional experiences. Emotions function as a key element in the re/production of subjectivity, culture, and power relations (Harding and Pribram 2002: 408). In a world of movement, emotions constitute the central aspects of individuals' positionings of themselves vis-à-vis others (Svašek 2012: 3). The migrant experience, in particular, foregrounds the interaction between different ways of cultivating and managing emotions as affected by different societal backgrounds through disembedding, translocating, and reembedding (Boccagni and Baldassar 2015: 75). Through our interviews, we found that "mainland student" as an identity registers a contradictory field of emotional relations shaped by Hong Kong's long-standing stereotypes about as well as new tensions with mainland China. The most outstanding tensions emanate from the two "emotional regimes" (Reddy 2001: 129) of mainland China and Hong Kong that establish disparate sets of normative emotions. On the one hand, the high tides of nationalism in mainland China, fueled by the country's economic growth and state-orchestrated "Chinese Dream" narratives (Guo 2019; Shi and Liu 2019), continue to reinforce the "brainwashed patriot" stereotype of mainland students in Hong Kong. On the other, mainland students are also confronted by local protests that are antagonistic and averse to the top-down, centralizing Chinese identity (Lowe and Tsang 2017: 140; Dupré 2020: 19). Regardless of their own political leanings or beliefs, mainland students in Hong Kong are pre-framed by these stereotypes. The tensions between the national and the local illustrate the difficulties in realizing a minor transnational position that could exceed the parameters of *both* the Chinese national as an overarching, assimilationist framework *and* the Hong Kong local as a romanticized site of resistance (see Lionnet and Shih 2005: 6). The highly binarized and charged pattern of emotional conflicts points to the fixity and complexity of "mainland students" as an identity category and the laborious process of self-making and remaking for cross-border subjects.

Felix was a twenty-seven-year-old PhD student who, prior to coming to Hong Kong, completed his undergraduate studies in the United States and worked both in China and overseas. He told us that he initially rejected seeing himself as a "mainland student" because despite being born and raised in mainland China, he left since high school and felt more affinity with international students. However, as the protests escalated, he started to self-identify as a mainland student as well: "It all became very personal. You would be treated differently if you spoke Putonghua. At the height of the protests on campus, our dorm was surrounded by radical protesters. It was very scary." Felix's sentiments are echoed by Alex, twenty-two years old and finishing his one-year master's program at a Hong Kong University at the time of the interview. He confessed that during his stay, he increasingly felt a "sense of shame" associated with mainland students as the protests escalated. Such contradictory identificatory experiences were common among Hong Kong's mainland students during the protests. They reflect the actual complexity of mainland students as a group and how they (re)negotiate their original identity positions as cross-border subjects. This process of remaking self-identities is associated with the coexistence of two types of transnationalism in Hong Kong and was intensified by the protests against Chinese authorities.

In our observation, such a remaking of mainland students' identity is a dynamic process involving Hong Kong people's emotional perceptions of mainland China. While narratives of migrants as a perceived threat are common in transnational migration (Svašek 2010; Zembylas 2012; Esses, Medianu, and Lawson 2013), Hong Kong's discontent and antagonism toward mainlanders are more complexly intertwined with its shifting status in relation to competing regimes of Chinese transnationalism. The increasing presence and influence of mainland China in Hong Kong has been seen as "a humiliating setback" and even "a form of internal colonization" by Hong Kong nativists (Ip 2015: 415). A native Hong Kong identity is thus "solidified in opposition to mainland China" through "psychical processes of (dis)identifications" (Lowe and Tsang 2017: 140), especially amid continued failures of local struggles for political change.

In September 2019, Hong Kong tabloid *Apple Daily* covered a story entitled "red-shirted Putonghua-speaking mainland student storming protest rally." It was the first day of a new term in Hong Kong tertiary institutions. Thousands of students gathered in a rally to kick off a two-week class boycott protesting against the government's continued inaction on their demands. A stage, decorated with protest banners reading "Boycott for Freedom," was set up for public speeches. Right before the rally started, a young male mainland student in a red T-shirt rushed onto the stage. In an attempt to disrupt the rally, he angrily tore apart a protest banner, unplugged the loudspeakers, and yelled at the crowd: "I am Chinese! I support the Hong Kong police! You don't deserve to be university students!" while waving his Chinese passport (*Apple Daily* 2019). The report soon went viral in local news outlets and social media platforms together with the footage. On *Apple Daily*'s website, negative responses flooded the comments zone. Some of these comments are milder, such as "this is Hong Kong, not China." Some are harsher—for example, "They are so brainwashed that they cannot think straight!" and "Fuck off mainland pricks!" (*Apple Daily* 2019).

The *Apple Daily* report is an example of a series of emotionally charged portrayals of mainland students in local media, which is itself a product of the tension between the two transnationalisms and their respective emotional regimes. In November 2019, local news portal *Stand News* also released a story about the "fleeing" of mainland students over clashes between protesters and the police on university campuses. Despite the fact that the decision to temporarily leave Hong Kong amid campus turmoil was common among all nonlocal students (Leung and Sharma 2019), mainland students' "fleeing" was depicted in a particularly sensationalist fashion, with the report quoting some mainland students as saying "our country will ensure our safety" (*Stand News* 2019). Local media coverage like this offers a way of illustrating the emotional construction of mainland students as an object of fear. Existing scholarship has indicated that emotions not only impact what kind of media message gains visibility and currency but also influence how people feel about, understand, and act on social realities (Nabi 2009; Barlett and Gentile 2012). What stands out in the reports is how they portray mainland students as an embodiment of Chinese state nationalism and, further, an object of fear. Take the *Apple Daily* report as an example: the striking visual cue of the mainland student's red shirt, which matches the color of the Chinese national flag, and his waving the Chinese passport made him a conspicuous and easily generalizable symbol for all mainland students, portrayed as blindly nationalistic. Despite the fact that, as a heterogeneous group, mainland students in fact hold very diverse views about the protests, this narrative evokes an essentialist politics of fear by constructing the mainland student as more than just an outsider—he is a violent "other" and an embodiment of China-centrism. As Ip (2015) argues, Hong Kong's various brands of localism are an emotional response to "an anxiety over Hong Kong as a collective form of life" (410), which envelops the local society with an "apocalyptic future fear" (415). In order to cope with fear, people contain it within an object from which they turn away. This "turning away" enables the construction of a "fellowship": it allows individual bodies to defend themselves against fear through the protection of in-groups or "people like me" and the alienation of out-groups or "others" (Ahmed 2004: 74–75).

Local media's negative portrayals of mainland students, therefore, deny their plurality and heterogeneity and evoke a politics of fear as part of the broader discursive formation where Hong Kong is constructed as a victimized subject under the threat of mainland China. This discursive formation corresponds to Hong Kong people's anxiety, distrust, and insecurity as the city is increasingly incorporated into the Sino-centric global China project. Whereas such fear-based identity politics open up space for local resistance (see Chow, Fu, and Ng 2019), they also paradoxically reinforce a dichotomous and antagonistic structure of feeling. This problem is clear from Felix's everyday experiences. Despite spending years in the United States, he was labeled a "CCP (Chinese Communist Party) spy" by his peers because of his origin: "I found out that I was excluded from a WhatsApp group for PhD students in my cohort, because a local student and an international student apparently decided that I was a CCP spy and didn't want to add me in. . . . Maybe this was some kind of joke for them, but I took it seriously because it hurt me both socially and professionally."

Such an experience of discrimination and exclusion illustrates mainland students' dilemma of being caught in between the two transnationalisms. Maruška Svašek (2010: 872) argues that migrants' emotional interactions with the locals "help to construct de-territorialized and re-territorialized identities." The collapse between the signs of "mainland student" and "CCP spy" thus points to a political articulation where mainland student identities—regardless of their actual political stances and intentions—are reterritorialized, associated with "China" as a fearful entity. Under these conditions, living beyond the local/national binary became difficult, if not impossible.

Winnie, who attended CUHK because of its established tradition of social activism and was an active participant in the protests, compared being a mainland student to "staying in the closet": "Because I speak Cantonese, I have never 'come out' [as a mainland student] in the protests, because this label comes with too many negative implications. Local students will assume that you are brainwashed and that you cannot understand Hong Kong." Winnie's experiences of stigma despite her sympathetic attitude toward the protests complicate assumptions based on the politics of fear. They also shed light on the difficulty of formulating cross-border dialogue and solidarity. Since the city's fear-based identity politics is locked into the binary opposition of Hong Kong versus mainland China, local imaginations fail to move beyond Chinese nationalism as a framework of reference. In other words, despite localism's claim of autonomy and resistance, its allegedly decentering disposition remains bound by a "national versus local" binary where "the center"—the Chinese state in this case—in fact remains dominant (as the power to be resisted). Here we see how China-centrism is inadvertently reproduced by its opponents. But this does not imply that there are no subversive potentials inherent in transnational engagement. Paradoxically, the coexistence of two transnationalisms seems to have both reinforced *and* displaced the national as an ideological and emotional framework, as a result of increased cross-border movements and interactions. Below, we discuss how a minor transnational position could emerge from these interactions.

The National as a Site of Emotional Dis/investment

In August 2019, China's official mouthpiece, CCTV, posted an article via its WeChat account about how the Chinese national flag has been desecrated by Hong Kong protesters. Accompanied by pictures of the national flag in the sea in Tsim Sha Tsui, the article told a story of how "hysterical rioters," amid clashes with the police, took down the national flag from a flagpole and threw it into the sea while "letting out vicious laughter." It also stressed that shortly after the incident, "patriotic citizens who love China and Hong Kong" raised a new flag at the pole. Showing pictures of the flag flying in the wind, the article concluded with the sentences "The National Flag Shall Not Be Desecrated! Five-Star Red Flag, You Are My Pride! Five-Star Red Flag, I Am Proud of You!" in large red font (CCTV News 2019). Later that month, CCTV started a social media campaign on Weibo, where it claimed that "China's national flag has 1.4 billion flag bearers" with a picture of the five-star red flag, and encouraged netizens to share and affirm "I am a flag bearer." With many celebrities answering the call, the post was reposted over ten million times (Linder 2019).

Krzysztof Jaskulowski (2016: 571) points out that the national flag is not only "a specific part of everyday reality that allows access to the abstract notion of the nation" but is also treated "as physically and causally related to the nation." Desacralization of the flag, therefore, is often believed to have direct consequences for the nation and threatens its existence (557). During the Hong Kong protests, Chinese state media repeatedly used the national flag as a nodal point of "affective epidemics": empty and highly mobile sites that redistribute and disperse emotional investments to establish ideological structures of identification and belonging (Grossberg 1992: 284). The image of an endangered national flag is fundamental to state-orchestrated affective epidemics that organize, discipline, and mobilize people's attention, volition, mood, and passion, placing them in the service of nationalism as a political agenda (255).

Yet such a pattern of emotional investment has limitations and could entail contention and resistance. As Lawrence Grossberg (1992: 284) points out, the nodal point of an affective epidemic functions as a fetishized site "invested with values disproportionate to [its] actual worth." This indeterminate status of the national flag as a fetishized emotional symbol became the basis for critical reflections on state nationalism among mainland students in Hong Kong. Svašek (2012: 13) argues that mobilities open up new "'affective possibilities' in current places of residence that also influence the ideas [migrants] hold about their own identity and the way they experience the world." This is true for our interviewees, many of whom drew on their cross-border experiences to negotiate the passionate attachment summoned by the national flag and came up with alternative feelings that framed the Hong Kong protests in different ways. Their mobility enabled them to engage in ongoing processes of identity remaking. Debby, a PhD graduate who spent nearly a decade studying in Hong Kong before recently returning to mainland China, shared her thoughts on the national flag incidents:

> This might be difficult for Hong Kongers to understand, but as mainlanders we know propaganda when we see it, and we don't really buy into what's in the news. . . . Although I do love my homeland since it's where I was born and raised, I don't feel like the national flag is a part of myself. It's common in countries like the US for people to burn national flags during protests. It reflects deeper layers of social problems.

Debby's response is characterized by a dual sense of dissociation: she not only dissociated national symbols from her sense of belonging but also decoupled her emotional investment from her place of origin. In doing so, she claimed attachment to multiple places to strategically displace and complicate, while also retaining, her mainland student identity. Her strategies demonstrate "the complexities of multiple identification and emotional attachment" (Svašek 2010: 868) that underlie practices of transnationality. Drawing on this transnationalist outlook, Debby took an ambivalent stance that was neither nationalist nor localist. She shared, for example, that although she sympathized with protesters' demands at the start of the movement and could even understand violence during confrontations between protesters and the police, she found it hard to agree with militant protesters and their vandalism. These reflections reveal the complexity and heterogeneity of mainland students' sentiments, which cannot be fully contained by an essentialist, reified national/local binary. When we asked Debby how she understood the status of mainland students in Hong Kong, she concluded: "I think it is important not to take sides. You need to listen to both sides' stories and come up with your own judgment. . . . For example, people appear to understand nationalism as absolute loyalty toward official ideology. I don't think that is right."

The comments signify an attempt to transcend and transform the fixity, normativity, and closure of Chinese identity as a coherent and unitary category. While state nationalism seeks to normalize mainland students' emotional subjectivities (Shi and Liu 2019), then, there has never been a lack of defiance against and renegotiation of its emotional expectations. Mia, who pursued a master's degree during the protests, told us that she found Hong Kong a very welcoming place even though she was not good at Cantonese or English. She also shared that although she received calls from the police from her hometown warning her not to participate in the protests, she still did what she could to understand Hong Kong's social movements. She said:

> I think desacralizing the flag is just the protesters' tactic for expressing resistance and dissent. And I think what's important is not to fly the flag to declare our own stance. This is not the way to solve the problem. . . . We need to look at this from a Hong Kong perspective. . . . Will local students understand what the mainland student did, or will they see it as provocative and threatening? There's a lot at stake if we keep misunderstanding each other.

Mia's experiences demonstrate the enabling and delimiting effects of becoming a transnational subject in Hong Kong. Her cross-border experiences make it possible for her to temporarily evade discipline by the CCP and resist nationalism's emotional reach and even take political risks in supporting social movements in Hong Kong. But her observation of the difficulty of mutual understanding also raises questions about the limitations of Hong

Kong's transnationalism: could mainland students truly see things from a "Hong Kong perspective," if such a perspective is already a by-product of the parochial identity politics, which often expresses itself in the form of prejudice and exclusion? How could mainland students overcome the emotional impasse that pins them in restricted political presumptions and social spaces? These questions point to the essentializing effects of Hong Kong–mainland hostilities that shape the emotional structure (Liu and Shi 2021) of Hong Kongers and mainlanders, whose multiple emotional experiences seldom intersect.

Toward a Minor Transnationalism

The analysis presented in this article illustrates how transnational engagements by Chinese nonstate actors (the students) produce contradictory emotional experiences and hybrid identities in multiple ways. By addressing the emotional aspects of Chinese border-crossing practices, our research shows how the PRC's mobility regime has nurtured subversive potentials inherent in migrant students' everyday experiences in Hong Kong. The expansion of cross-border flows of people to and from mainland China has paradoxically *both* unsettled *and* reinforced China-centrism in the era of President Xi's Chinese dream.

We propose that minor transnationalism is a useful concept through which to address the emotional quandaries and the micro level of people's everyday experiences of the new Chinese transnationalism in Hong Kong in the global China era. As we have demonstrated through our analysis of mainland students' affective attachments, the city's changing status in Chinese transnationalism has produced complex emotional dynamics that revolve around a persistent national/local binary and accompanying emotional boundaries. Such a binary motivates antagonistic feelings and politics of belonging, demarcating between an assimilationist "national" subject and a resistant "local" one. The paradoxical result of this binary, however, is the reinforcement of the Chinese state as a center that mediates the logic of dis/identification. What is lacking in this binary model, in the words of Lionnet and Shih (2005: 7), is "an awareness and recognition of the creative interventions that networks of minoritized cultures produce within and across national boundaries." Whereas mainland students in Hong Kong are not "minor" in a strict socioeconomic sense, the "double marginalization" they face between the PRC nationalism and Hong Kong localism (Tang 2021: 36) means that they could become agents of "minor expressivity" that is "necessarily mixed and transnational" (Lionnet and Shih 2005: 9). Indeed, mainland students' rejection and transgression of *both* Chinese nationalist *and* Hong Kong localist politics demonstrates how they "fall upon cultural resources outside the dominant ones . . . that pretend to singularity and authenticity" (9). This simultaneous suspension of nationalist and localist preoccupations also constitutes the prerequisite for challenging structural divisions and seeking alliances outside one's own limited frame (Chen 2010: 99–102).

The case of mainland students in Hong Kong illuminates how a hybridized political subject could emerge even amid the new, Sino-centric version of Chinese transnationalism, which is fueled by China's growing economic power and imbued with nationalist sentiments. As we have shown, whereas Chinese state nationalism's intensified structures of belonging may form a cardinal part of one's subjectivity, the mobility regime gives rise to an unstable site of contestation and disruption, through which mobile subjects renegotiate senses of belonging and statist configurations of identity. A nonessentialist understanding of these fragmented experiences could become the first step in reshaping and decentering Chinese transnationalism today.

Appendix

Table 1. Participant Demographics

Pseudonym	Age	Gender	Educational level	Number of years in Hong Kong
Debby	31	F	PhD	9
Oliver	28	M	PhD student	3
Felix	27	M	PhD student	2
Linda	24	F	Master's	1.5
Emily	24	F	Master's	1.5
Winnie	23	F	Master's	1.5
Fred	23	M	Master's	1
Alex	22	M	Master's	1
Mia	23	F	Master's	1
Howard	23	M	Master's	1

Notes

1 One of the authors of this article used to be a mainland student in Hong Kong; the other works in Macau. Although both have extensive social networks in Hong Kong, due to the sensitivity of the topic many declined the invitation to be interviewed.

References

Ahmed, Sara. 2004. *Cultural Politics of Emotion*. Edinburgh: Edinburgh University Press.

Apple Daily. 2019. "Zhongda neidisheng caichang si hengfu, shai qiangguo huzhao, bei bao luo tai hou tao qu" 中大內地生踩場撕橫額 晒強國護照 被抱落台後逃去 ("CUHK Mainland Student Storms the Stage, Shows His Chinese Passport, and Flees after Taken Down the Stage"). September 2. https://hk.news.appledaily.com/local/20190902/Z7EVHG 2BXVPV2H5ZEJKUS27QSY/.

Archibald, Mandy M., Rachel C. Ambagtsheer, Mavourneen G. Casey, and Michael Lawless. 2019. "Using Zoom Videoconferencing for Qualitative Data Collection: Perceptions and Experiences of Researchers and Participants." *International Journal of Qualitative Methods* 18. https://doi.org/10.1177/1609406919874596.

Barlett, Christopher P., and Douglas A. Gentile. 2012. "Attacking Others Online: The Formation of Cyberbullying in Late Adolescence." *Psychology of Popular Media Culture* 1, no. 2: 123–35. https://doi.org/10.1037/a0028113.

Boccagni, Paolo, and Loretta Baldassar. 2015. "Emotions on the Move: Mapping the Emergent Field of Emotion and Migration." *Emotion, Space, and Society*, no. 16: 73–80. https://doi.org/10.1016/j.emospa.2015.06.009.

Burkitt, Ian. 2014. *Emotions and Social Relations*. Thousand Oaks, CA: SAGE.

CCTV News. 2019. "Baotu jiang guoqi diuru haizhong, aiguo aigang renshi lingchen jiang guoqi chongxin shengqi!" 暴徒将国旗丢入海中,爱国爱港人士凌晨将国旗重新升起! ("Rioters Threw the National Flag into the Sea. Patriotic and Hong Kong-loving People Raised the Flag Again in the Early Morning"). WeChat Official Accounts Platform, August 9. https://mp.weixin.qq.com/s/nkNr1TgSX2tctvtI2conYQ.

Chao, Roger Y. 2012. "Intra-Nationalization of Higher Education: The Hong Kong Case." *Frontiers of Education in China* 7, no. 4: 508–33. https://doi.org/10.1007/BF03396952.

Chen, Kuan-Hsing. 2010. *Asia as Method: Toward Deimperialization*. Durham, NC: Duke University Press.

Chow, Siu-lun, King-wa Fu, and Yu-Leung Ng. 2019. "Development of the Hong Kong Identity Scale: Differentiation between Hong Kong 'Locals' and Mainland Chinese in Cultural and Civic Domains." *Journal of Contemporary China*, no. 124: 568–84. https://doi.org/10.1080/10670564.2019.1677365.

Dupré, Jean-François. 2020. "Making Hong Kong Chinese: State Nationalism and Its Blowbacks in a Recalcitrant City." *Nationalism and Ethnic Politics* 26, no. 1: 8–26. https://doi.org/10.1080/13537113.2020.1716436.

Esses, Victoria M., Stelian Medianu, and Andrea S. Lawson. 2013. "Uncertainty, Threat, and the Role of the Media in Promoting the Dehumanization of Immigrants and Refugees." *Journal of Social Issues* 69, no. 3: 518–36. https://doi.org/10.1111/josi.12027.

Faria, Caroline. 2014. "Styling the Nation: Fear and Desire in the South Sudanese Beauty Trade." *Transactions of the Institute of British Geographers* 39, no. 2: 318–30. https://doi.org/10.1111/tran.12027.

Fong, Brian C. H. 2017. "One Country, Two Nationalisms: Center-Periphery Relations between Mainland China and Hong Kong, 1997–2016." *Modern China* 43, no. 5: 523–56. https://doi.org/10.1177/0097700417691470.

Goodman, David S. 2017. "Australia and the China Threat: Managing Ambiguity." *Pacific Review* 30, no. 5: 769–82. https://doi.org/10.1080/09512748.2017.1339118.

Gorski, Philip S. 2013. "Nation-ization Struggles: A Bourdieusian Theory of Nationalism." In *Bourdieu and Historical Analysis*, edited by Philip S. Gorski, 242–65. Durham, NC: Duke University Press.

Grossberg, Lawrence. 1992. *We Gotta Get Out of This Place: Popular Conservatism and Postmodern Culture*. London: Routledge.

Guo, Yingjie. 2019. "From Marxism to Nationalism: The Chinese Communist Party's Discursive Shift in the Post-Mao Era." *Communist and Post-Communist Studies* 52, no. 4: 355–65. https://doi.org/10.1016/j.postcomstud.2019.10.004.

Hamilton, Peter E. 2021. *Made in Hong Kong: Transpacific Networks and a New History of Globalization*. New York: Columbia University Press.

Harding, Jennifer, and E. D. Pribram. 2002. "The Power of Feeling: Locating Emotions in Culture." *European Journal of Cultural Studies* 5, no. 4: 407–26. https://doi.org/10.1177/1364942002005004294.

Ho, Kelly. 2021. "Hong Kong Activists Stage Demonstrations Worldwide during China's National Day." *Hong Kong Free Press*, October 4. https://hongkongfp.com/2021/10/04/hong-kong-activists-stage-demonstration-worldwide-on-chinas-national-day/.

Hung, Ho-fung. 2022. *City on the Edge: Hong Kong under Chinese Rule*. Cambridge: Cambridge University Press.

Ip, Iam-chong. 2015. "Politics of Belonging: A Study of the Campaign against Mainland Visitors in Hong Kong." *Inter-Asia Cultural Studies* 16, no. 3: 410–21. https://doi.org/10.1080/14649373.2015.1069054.

Ip, Iam-chong. 2020. *Hong Kong's New Identity Politics: Longing for the Local in the Shadow of China*. London: Routledge.

Jaskulowski, Krzysztof. 2015. "The Magic of the National Flag." *Ethnic and Racial Studies* 39, no. 4: 557–73. https://doi.org/10.1080/01419870.2015.1078482.

Leung, Mimi, and Yojana Sharma. 2019. "Foreign Governments Urge Students to Leave Hong Kong." *University World News*, November 14. https://www.universityworldnews.com/post.php?story=20191114230210708.

Lionnet, Françoise, and Shu-Mei Shih. 2005. "Introduction: Thinking through the Minor, Transnationally." In *Minor Transnationalism*, edited by Françoise Lionnet and Shu-mei Shih, 1–23. Durham, NC: Duke University Press.

Liu, Shih-Diing, and Wei Shi. 2021. "Why Is Reconciliation Impossible?" *Made in China Journal* 6, no. 3: 127–32. http://doi.org/10.22459/MIC.06.03.2021.15.

Lowe, John, and Eileen Y. Tsang. 2017. "Disunited in Ethnicity: The Racialization of Chinese Mainlanders in Hong Kong." *Patterns of Prejudice* 51, no. 2: 137–58. https://doi.org/10.1080/0031322x.2017.1304349.

Martin, Fran. 2018. "Overseas Study as Zone of Suspension: Chinese Students Renegotiating Youth, Gender, and Intimacy." *Journal of Intercultural Studies* 39, no. 6: 688–703. https://doi.org/10.1080/07256868.2018.1533538.

Nabi, Robin L. 2009. "Emotion and Media Effects." In *The SAGE Handbook of Media Processes and Effects*, edited by Robin L. Nabi and Mary B. Oliver, 205–22. Thousand Oaks, CA: SAGE.

Nonini, Donald M., and Aihwa Ong. 1997. "Chinese Transnationalism as an Alternative Modernity." In *Ungrounded Empires: The Cultural Politics of Modern Chinese Transnationalism*, edited by Aihwa Ong and Donald M. Nonini, 13–24. New York: Routledge.

Ong, Aihwa, and Donald M. Nonini. 1997. "Afterword to *Ungrounded Empires: The Cultural Politics of Modern Chinese Transnationalism*, edited by Aihwa Ong and Donald M. Nonini, 323–32. New York: Routledge.

Reddy, William M. 2001. *The Navigation of Feeling: A Framework for the History of Emotions*. Cambridge: Cambridge University Press.

Sharma, Yojana. 2022. "Mainland China Students Shun the West, Turn to Hong Kong." *University World News*, October 7. https://www.universityworldnews.com/post.php?story =20221007083431939.

Sheller, Mimi, and John Urry. 2006. "The New Mobilities Paradigm." *Environment and Planning A: Economy and Space* 38, no. 2: 207–26.

Shi, Wei, and Shih-Diing Liu. 2019. "Pride as Structure of Feeling: *Wolf Warrior II* and the National Subject of the Chinese Dream." *Chinese Journal of Communication* 13, no. 3: 329–43. https://doi.org/10.1080/17544750.2019.1635509.

Shih, Shu-mei. 2007. *Visuality and Identity: Sinophone Articulations across the Pacific*. Los Angeles: University of California Press.

Stand News. 2019. "Duojian daxue neidisheng ji li gang, shuijing zhu zhongda lushing cheli, wangchuan zhonglianban yisi neng zou jiu zou" 多間大學內地生急離港-水警助中大陸生撤離-網傳-中聯辦意思能走就走 ("Mainland students from Several Universities Left Hong Kong in Haste. Marine Police Assisted CUHK Mainland Students in Evacuating. Online Rumors State that the Liaison Office Advised Mainland Students to Leave if They Could"). Last updated November 13. https://www.thestandnews.com/politics/多間大學內地生急離港-水警助中大陸生撤離-網傳-中聯辦意思能走就走/.

Su, Alice, and Rachel Cheung. 2021. "Police Raids on Movie Screenings. Censors Closing In. Hong Kong's Filmmakers Fight to Stay Free." *Los Angeles Times*, September 16. https://www.latimes.com/world-nation/story/2021-09-16/china-hong-kong-movies-censorship.

Svašek, Maruška. 2010. "On the Move: Emotions and Human Mobility." *Journal of Ethnic and Migration Studies* 36, no. 6: 865–80. https://doi.org/10.1080/13691831003643322.

Svašek, Maruška. 2012. "Affective Moves: Transit, Transition, and Transformation." In *Moving Subjects, Moving Objects: Transnationalism, Cultural Production, and Emotions*, edited by Maruška Svašek, 1–40. New York: Berghahn Books.

Tang, Ling. 2021. "Guarding the Space In-Between: The Quandary of Being a Liberal Mainland Student Migrant in Hong Kong." *British Journal of Chinese Studies* 11: 36–52. https://bjocs .site/index.php/bjocs/article/view/71.

Tu, Wei-ming. 1991. "Cultural China: The Periphery as the Center." *Daedalus* 134, no. 4: 145–67.

University Grants Committee. 2019. *UGC Annual Report, 2018–19*. https://www.ugc.edu.hk /eng/ugc/about/publications/report/AnnualRpt_2018-19.html.

Xu, Cora Lingling. 2015. "When the Hong Kong Dream Meets the Anti-mainlandisation Discourse: Mainland Chinese Students in Hong Kong." *Journal of Current Chinese Affairs* 44, no. 3: 15–47. https://doi.org/10.1177/186810261504400030.

Yu, Baohua, and Kun Zhang. 2016. "'It's More Foreign Than a Foreign Country': Adaptation and Experience of Mainland Chinese Students in Hong Kong." *Tertiary Education and Management* 22, no. 4: 300–315. https://doi.org/10.1080/13583883.2016.1226944.

Zembylas, Michalinos. 2012. "The Politics of Fear and Empathy: Emotional Ambivalence in 'Host' Children and Youth Discourses about Migrants in Cyprus." *Intercultural Education* 23, no. 3: 195–208. https://doi.org/10.1080/14675986.2012.701426.

Zembylas, Michalinos. 2016. "The Therapisation of Social Justice as an Emotional Regime: Implications for Critical Education." *Journal of Professional Capital and Community* 1, no. 4: 286–301. https://doi.org/10.1108/jpcc-05-2016-0015.

Zeng, Ka, and Xiaojun Li. 2019. "Geopolitics, Nationalism, and Foreign Direct Investment: Perceptions of the China Threat and American Public Attitudes toward Chinese FDI." *Chinese Journal of International Politics* 12, no. 4: 495–518. https://doi.org/10.1093/cjip/poz016.

From *Golden Venture* to Golden Visas:

The Reenchantment of Culture and Flexible Citizenship in a Nativist World

Pál Nyíri and Fanni Beck

Introduction

The quest for a better life that drives global migration flows is usually understood as driven by economic accumulation. Although theories of migration have become more nuanced, migrants are still seen primarily as rational economic actors aiming to maximize their incomes. In particular, Chinese migrants have been seen as paragons of flexible accumulation and resource maximization through "flexible citizenship" and "ethnic entrepreneurship" throughout modern history (Ong 1999; Zhou 2010) and often have been associated with the concept of "trading diasporas" (Cohen 2008; see also Tagliacozzo and Chang 2011). These notions suggest an ethnic network that has developed special skills to navigate various legal and social systems to their advantage while utilizing social and cultural capital to minimize

positions 32:4   DOI 10.1215/10679847-11306844

risks and maximize profits. This perception has been strengthened since the 1980s by the popular business-school literature on the role of the Chinese diaspora in the economic success of the "Asian Tigers" (e.g., Weidenbaum and Hughes 1996; Redding 1993) and the influential theoretical work of Aihwa Ong (1999).

Other forms of migration—lifestyle migration, marriage migration, educational migration—are acknowledged but not taken very seriously in conceptualizing what migration is. Xiang Biao (2021) has recently suggested that we see these as a shift from "production migration" aimed at capital accumulation to "*reproduction* migration" intended to maintain and enhance life. Utilizing the Engelsian distinction between "the production and reproduction of the immediate essentials of life," Xiang argues that reproduction is not only one of "the determining factor[s] in history" (Engels 1884; cited in Xiang 2021: 34), but in international migration as well. The growing number of Chinese people who migrate not for higher incomes or advancing careers but for benefiting from better education, care, lifestyle, and quality of food, air, and water in the destination attests to the emergence of reproduction as an increasingly influential determinant in migration. This trend reflects China's changing position within the global system of production and reproduction: these migrants leave China not because they need money but precisely because they have it.

From *Golden Venture* to Golden Visas

When mainland China reemerged onto the global migration scene in the 1990s, it was at a time of global neoliberal transformation and relative economic deregulation in China itself. This was a time of rags-to-riches stories, when starting a small business (known as *xiahai* 下海 [jumping into the sea]) was the most popular path to upward mobility, when Jack Ma started his English-teaching business, and when "selling tea-pickled eggs pays more than developing a nuclear bomb" (*kaifa yuanzidan buru mai chayedan* 開發原子彈不如賣茶葉蛋) was a popular saying among academics. The first migration flows from a reopened China were of contract workers (mostly in construction carried out by state companies in Africa and Asia), students (at first mostly graduate students in North America, Australia, and Japan) and small entrepreneurs, many of whom had been laid off by state enterprises and were now selling Chinese-made consumer goods in Eastern Europe and elsewhere (Nyíri 2011). All of these flows can be seen as aiming at accumulation. (Accumulation need not be directed at economic capital; it can also work via the conversion of different forms of capital [Bourdieu 1986], such as the translation of university degrees into better-paying jobs.) Entrepreneurial migration, though overwhelmingly legal, attracted public attention through tragedies involving illegal migrants, such as the shipwreck of the *Golden Venture* in New York Harbor in 1993 and the discovery of fifty-eight corpses in a refrigerator truck in Dover in 2000.

The "emigration gold rush" (*chuguo taojin re* 出國淘金熱), as it was called, captured the public imagination in China. It became the subject of fiction (e.g., Chen D. and Chen M. 1997) and numerous TV dramas set in Moscow, Paris, New York, and Tokyo, the first and best-known being *Pekingers in New York* (1994), based on Glen Cao's autobiographically inspired 1992 novel *The Chinese Woman of Manhattan*. A lurid romanticism of the frontier characterized this genre. Typically, its heroes were solitary men who found their way to the global city, and after many misadventures and much *chiku* 吃苦 (eating bitterness), outwitted "whitey" (*laowai* 老外) on his own turf and struck it rich. As Geremie Barmé (1999) shows in his analysis of *Pekingers in New York*, the theme of upending racial hierarchies was an important one in the genre (cf. Nyíri 2006). This was also a period of rising popular nationalism marked by the popularity of books such as *China Can Say No* (*Zhongguo keyi shuo bu*), published in 1996 (Song, Zhang, and Qiao 1996). The West, in this genre, was a rather generic backdrop of modernity, marked by skyscrapers and fast cars, which often contrasted with the squalor endured by the protagonists. Struggling to make their way from rags to riches, they had no time to pause on a café terrace.

While this fantasy was projected onto global cities, a more typical reality—arguably the most distinct artifact of this migration wave—was the Chinese market, which began its global career in Eastern Europe but was soon found across Africa, Southeast Asia, and South America. At the Chinese market, the migrant entrepreneurs—initially itinerant peddlers known as *daoye* 倒爺—who sold consumer goods included villagers from southern China but also many former employees—from state-owned trade enterprises, factories, and even banks—who had been laid off or just preferred taking the risks of entrepreneurship. At the time, *middle class* was not yet a term widely applied to Chinese society, but many market traders came from middling positions as midrange state employees or minor cadres with higher or secondary educations. The life stories told at the market were mostly stories of separation from family and sacrifice endured in order to make money to make life better for the children—these featured in purportedly documentary literature that included books such as *Chinese in Eastern Europe: A Chronicle of the 1990s New Gold Rush Emigration* (*Zhongguoren zai Dongou: 1990 niandai chuguo taojin re jishi* [Mao 1992]) or *Tearful Danube* (*Leisa Duonaohe* [Li 1993]). As with migrant workers inside China, the same logic of economic accumulation meant that children were often left behind.

The life stories of the 1990s are unimaginable today. Although people continue to go abroad in the name of sacrifice and *chiku* for the sake of a more secure future (Driessen and Xiang 2021), rags-to-riches is no longer a believable scenario. Thirty years' economic growth coupled with decreasing upward mobility has raised incomes but produced a more stratified society. On the one hand, people have more money. They are better educated. Many lead middle-class lives, own real estate and cars, and travel abroad for leisure. On the other hand, they have no faith that they will do better in the future. On the contrary, they are afraid of losing what they have, or that their children or child will lose what they have. The risk-taking of the 1990s has given way to risk minimization. If the operative term of the 1990s was *xiahai*, the operative terms of the 2020s are *neijuan* 内捲 (involution), referring to increased efforts without improved social status (Q. Wang and Ge 2020), and *tangping* 躺平 (lying flat), or refusing to participate in the rat race (Sun 2021).

And yet the sort of middle-class people whose predecessors were found in the Chinese markets in Eastern Europe in 1990s are still leaving. They are not leaving to make more money. In fact, they usually don't make money abroad at all; sometimes they make some, but their main source of income remains in China. It is such migrants who make up the bulk of Chinese migrants taking advantage of the so-called "golden visa," or immigration-for-investment schemes in Southern and Eastern Europe. Most of these schemes were started after the 2008 recession and required a relatively modest investment on the scale of several hundred thousand euros, though amounts and conditions varied. The most popular schemes have been those operated by Greece, Hungary, Portugal, and Spain. In total, these have attracted some fifty thousand Chinese migrants to Europe (Beck and Nyíri 2022; see Surak and Tsuzuki 2021 for an overview).

A Global Stage for the Chinese Middle Class—and Its Children

What, then, do we mean by middle class in China? Lu Xueyi (2002) famously defined it in terms of a combination of occupational categories, income, consumption, and ethos (cf. Nathan 2016). Our approach builds on Lu's, but, twenty years later, it requires modification because the class and income structure of Chinese society have undergone significant changes at both ends. At one end, the rich, including both private entrepreneurs and rentier members of the high echelons of bureaucracy, have become richer and more numerous; at the other end, blue-collar work in the private sector has become more precarious. We consider "the middle class" to be a useful category that can be distinguished both from "the rich" and the precariat, best defined not through income, property, occupation, education, relation to the party-state system (*tizhi* 體制), or even a combination of these, but rather through the structure of consumption, aspirations, and social duties. By drawing attention to the centrality of children in middle-class aspirations, Barbara Ehrenreich (1990) makes a compelling argument for including it in the definition. The reason for this is that unlike in other classes, where membership is transmitted by simple inheritance (for people at the extremes of the social spectrum, class position is inherited along with money or the lack of it), the middle class needs to reproduce each generation through the careful molding of its children. Thus, individuals who own real estate and cars; spend substantial parts of their income on optional services broadly related to social reproduction, such as extracurricular classes for children, leisure activities, and paid care for the elderly; *and* whose incomes or social position are not so high as to free them from worries about their reproduction in the next generation are, for us, living middle-class lives.

As Luigi Tomba (2009) has pointed out, the middle class in China is the product of meticulous reformist social engineering rather than a "natural" outcome of the country's transition to socialist market economy. It has been effectively imagined into being through policies facilitating private property acquisition and increasing leisure time and salaries for professionals in the public sector. The middle class is a crucial strategic tool for capitalist transition: it provides the consumer basis for domestic production; it carries out the professional intellectual labor new modes of production require; it provides a source of aspiration to lower classes; and last but not least, by embodying the imaginary of social mobility through open-ended meritocracy, it is the perfect ideological construct to justify rising inequality (Heiman, Freeman, and Liechty 2012). Indeed, Stephanie Donald and Yi Zheng (2009: 5) have argued that "middle-class-making [was] the foundational project for post-reform affluent China." In identifying the new model citizen as middle class, with high cultural/educational capital and the capacity to consume, the CCP legitimized material comfort while encouraging the poor to pursue the middle-class ideology of investment-driven self-determination. Marked as "the most important actors in China's civilizing project" or the "backbone of the advanced forces of production," the middle class is assigned an important role not only as consumers but also as spiritual prefects: as "the object, inspiration, and exemplary yardstick for contemporary governmental discourses of self-improvement" (Tomba 2009: 592).

While other post–World War II states, in East Asia and elsewhere, have played an active role in the conjuring-up of a middle class, this array of instruments deployed in a compressed time, coupled with relentless ideological shepherding in the form of "quality education" (*suzhi jiaoyu* 素質教育) campaigns, has few if any parallels, and it makes for a tense and ambivalent relationship between the middle class and the state. Although the usual predictions that the rise of the middle class would signal greater public resistance to authoritarian domination have proved wrong (Nathan 2016), nor do this class's aspirations entirely fit the Party's bill. As our research among middle-class Chinese migrants in Hungary shows, the better-educated and higher-aspiring middle class thus produced has embarked on a career of its own. This departure from the state project is probably best captured by the popularity of the discussion on *neijuan* and *tangping*, which reveals a fundamental middle-class unease and a capacity to act on it. Bingchun Meng (2018: 157) suggests that "middle-class identity, agenda, positionality and aspiration are all distilled into parents' anxiety over bringing about a good life for their children." Indeed, anxieties about maintaining class status, securing a healthy environment, and having some breathing space under China's increasingly all-encompassing surveillance regime are all projected onto one's children. It is for this reason that children are central in justifying middle-class emigration, which functions as an externalization of risks and anxieties onto a global stage.

Gracia Liu-Farrer (2016) has argued that the emigration of the wealthy is another form of accumulation through the acquisition of a particular kind of asset: overseas life experience. This might make sense in countries that are the centers of global modernity, where education, jobs, networks, or simply real estate in San Francisco or London offer symbolic capital that is convertible to class advantage in China. But if we look at the case of Hungary, or Southern European countries that have recently received middle-class Chinese migrants, we get a different picture. Middle-class Chinese leave the world cities of Shanghai, Peking, and Canton to settle in Hungary—where not only don't they make money but they also don't have access to globally convertible education or desirable jobs for the children—in order to alleviate more immediate anxieties.

From "Gold Digging" to "Lying Flat"

In the research we have been conducting among "golden visa" immigrants in Hungary, one interlocutor told us: "Our expectations are quite simple: a good enough life in a good enough environment, where the kid can be happy. However simple this sounds, we could not realize that in China." Overwhelmingly, and almost uniformly, migrants name their reasons to migrate as clean air, safe food, a green environment, a relaxed lifestyle, and most of all an escape from "involution" in a society they see as polluted, expensive, ruthlessly competitive, and overly materialistic. A conscious rejection of this competition is a striking element of migrants' narratives. It is often described as an escape from an overwhelming pressure to perform—projected onto one's children but perhaps, in an unacknowledged way, relating to oneself. As one of our interlocutors put it: "In China, expectations are very high, you have to paint, you have to swim, you have to play the piano, and speak English, of course.... You must do everything professionally, go to training classes all the time. Our salary is not enough to pay for all the classes for the kid." As the quotation suggests, expectations on children directly translate into immense expectations on their parents in terms of energy, time, and money—and it is exactly this pressure they seek to leave behind.

Unlike twenty years ago, these migrants are not aiming to move from a semiperiphery to a center of world modernity—or at least they say they do not. (In reality, some had applied to the EB-5 investor immigrant program in the United States, or wanted to move to Canada under the Business Immigration Program, which required an investment of C$800,000, but when their US application was rejected or the Canadian program was abruptly canceled in 2014, they quickly had to choose another destination after having already made arrangements to leave.) Instead, they are moving *away from* global cities *to* a semiperiphery; they are *downscaling* rather than upscaling (Beck and Nyíri 2022). In the imagination of these middle-class migrants, Europe is no longer a proxy for the generic West but is cast in contradistinction to *both* China and the Anglo-American world that are understood as excessively competitive (Nyíri 2017). The dream in these stories is not modern life among skyscrapers but slow life in a green, culturally and historically rich, infrastructurally amenable, and—as we will discuss below—racially white urban setting that is seen as distinct from North American and Australian modernity (Nyíri and Beck 2020). The protagonists are not heroes or villains who struggle and sacrifice, but happy nuclear families. This is a sort of overseas *tangping* dream that rejects the imperative of constant development and getting ahead in the name of staying still and enjoying the moment.

One of our informants told us that he and his wife do not like high-rises and had not been to either North America or Australia; instead, they "yearned" for European culture and architecture. After moving to Hungary, he took a wine-tasting course, bought an espresso machine, and is experimenting with different sorts of coffee. They took two three-week driving holidays in Italy, including a detour to the vineyards of Barolo. Another couple say they rejected the idea of moving to the United States because of the proliferation of guns and drugs there—not good for raising a boy.

A young mother whose husband works in the United States said she was reluctant to move to America, a country founded, she says, by unpatriotic people. Rather, she wanted to expose her four-year-old daughter to European culture before their eventual move to the United States. She takes her daughter to museums and on trips to Western Europe; at home, she has her listen to Peking opera and recite classical Chinese poetry. Many migrants emphasize Hungary's "rich cultural environment" as something that compensates for its "poverty and shabbiness." As one mother told us, "You've got to have culture."

The centrality of the child in these migrant narratives is remarkable, especially if we compare them to the 1990s, in which the *present* of the child was absent, although its future often loomed explicitly or implicitly behind the narratives of sacrifice. Not only did all of our interlocutors (bar one) move to Hungary with their children, but most of them explicitly named their child's needs and the necessity to provide a suitable physical, social, and educational environment for them as the primary reason behind relocation. Whereas for 1990s migrants, the family meant the more or less extended kin whose *material* welfare was presented as the purpose of (mostly male) migration (whether or not they actually ended up benefiting), for today's middle-class migrants the family is the nuclear family whose primary function is *emotional* care, and which constitutes the ideal form of child-rearing.

As Ehrenreich suggests, what defines the middle class is its children, and more particularly its specific ideas and practices about child-rearing. One of the proxies for middle-class status is what Ehrenreich (1990: 83) sees as professionalism (which Bourdieu would call habitus) that is acquired through investment in long-term education: "All that parents can do is attempt, through careful molding and psychological pressure, to predispose each child to retrace the same long road they themselves once took." Similarly, Annette Lareau (2003) observes that "concerted cultivation"—as opposed to working-class "natural growth parenting"—defines middle-class child-rearing. These observations can be applied to China's middle class in equal measure.

However, the popularity of "intensive parenting," or parents' hands-on involvement with their children's daily lives, among today's Chinese middle class has had ambivalent consequences. Widely seen as making parents responsible for securing their child's competitiveness through the cultivation of their talents, it has exacerbated an ultracompetitive environment for children, in which money and time became increasingly coveted—yet inherently limited—resources, an environment migrant parents say they fled from (Yang X. 2021).

Moreover, because in practice it is usually mothers who attend to the child's emotional needs and shuttle them from one extracurricular activity to the next, "intensive parenting," despite its foreign origins, has contributed to what Yan Yunxiang (2021: 223–52) sees as the revival of the Confucian ideal of the "virtuous womanhood" under a state-led ideology of "neo-familism." Indeed, in some cases—as with Hong Kong "astronauts" in 1990s Canada (Ong 1999)—it is the mother who stays with the child in Hungary and becomes a full-time housewife, usually having quit a white-collar job in China, while the husband stays in China and continues to earn an income. Quitting one's career in order to relocate to the other side of the world and provide one's child with the best environment—less stress, less studying, more time, and blue skies—has emerged as a new pattern of motherly sacrifice. But in other cases, both parents move to Hungary and take care of the child together, living in semiretirement off income that continues to accrue from property or business in China. Many parents are vocally opposed to their own parents' participation in raising their children and prefer to have them a continent away in a way that rather goes against China's revived discourse of filial piety. A third scenario—though certainly on a smaller scale—is enacted by stay-at-home fathers who decide to quit the rat race in order to devote their time to their child and to support their wife's career.

Ken is one such person embodying this emerging ethos of fatherly sacrifice. A biological engineering and marketing graduate, he decided to take a break from his highly paid career in order to take his son to Hungary before school age and devote all his time and energy to smoothening his transition to the new country. Rather than waiting until his late thirties or early forties, as most middle-class Chinese men do, he opted to have a child early on, already planning to leave China for a less stressful and cleaner environment for child-rearing. Soon after his son was born, he submitted a US immigrant investor visa application, which was rejected after a three-year wait. At this point Dan, his son, had only one year left before having to start school, and Ken and his wife felt they had to find a quick way out. "Both my wife and I have studied in China, and we think education is not going in the right direction . . . I think you can learn only if you enjoy studying. In the Chinese education system that's simply impossible." Ken made his peace with Hungary because "the country might be small, but at the end of the day, the only thing that matters is that Dan is happy and is growing up enjoying life and developing his own personality."

At least initially, then, these parents do not look for the utility of educational outcomes in terms of their convertibility to global careers by moving to places associated with global wealth and power (Liu 1996), which may lead to upward mobility for children (Woronov 2008), but rather they seek less stress and more free time, indicating that they are less concerned with future social mobility and more with the present, affective quality of life (Beck and Nyíri 2022). Instead of attempting to compete by conforming to the prescribed models of achievement and trajectories for social mobility, the families in our study utilize the capital they already accumulated to opt out of that competition early on and open up new opportunities in the transnational sphere, thereby creating "a room for maneuvering, and for altering the trajectories that were seemingly laid out at birth" (Orellana et al. 2001: 587).

Interestingly, many of these parents choose ordinary public schools for their child's education in Hungary. As one of our interlocutors mentioned, the agency that introduced the Hungarian immigration scheme to her advertised the country as having "excellent free education." She recited the internalized idea that even though Hungary was a small country, "it's a nation that loves studying." This claim is usually supported not by test results or state spending on education—both would locate Hungarian education in the bottom segment of the region—but by the number of Nobel Prize winners. In the opinion of these Chinese parents, free access, in contrast to the overt commodification of education in China, is part of what "good education" means. A young single mother in Budapest who manages a translation company in Wuhan described her process of school selection in the following way: "My primary objective when choosing a school for my son was not really an educational standard, but to find teachers who are not only kind and devoted to children but are also unconditionally welcoming toward immigrant children." Keeping to her word, instead of opting for a private international school in Budapest's upper-class districts, she chose a relatively run-down public school in the heart of an ill-reputed inner-city district of Budapest that is famous for its inclusiveness. But why would she need to move to the other side of the world to find a school that does not discriminate against Chinese students? As this reasoning suggests, what our interlocutors were looking for was really anything that was different from Chinese education (Beck and Nyíri 2022).

Over time, however, parents tend to become more ambivalent about the wisdom of such a choice, and anxiety about losing out begins to cast a shadow on the ideal of a carefree and happy childhood. Indeed, one group on the WeChat social media app catering to some three hundred Chinese parents in Budapest, where members initially shared leisure tips, gradually evolved into a high-pressure environment where members give each other tips about more efficient studying habits and extracurricular classes. As one remorseful but ambivalent confession in the group read, "I am an extremely lazy mother. I got so tired under the high pressure of education back home, so after we came to B[udapest] I just let go [*laughing-crying face emoji*]; apart from making sure there's enough to eat, drink, and use, I feel I have been far too careless about her studies, I regret it so much, I have to focus more [*sorry face emoji*]." Still, the initial rationale is an important departure from the utility-driven transnational educational choices familiar from the Chinese context (Hansen and Thøgersen 2015) that are generally understood as the direct outcome of what Andrew Kipnis (2011) has identified as the pervasive "educational desire" that has become a determining force in Chinese society. This is so even if parents who explicitly endorse freedom and try to reintroduce free time into the vocabulary—and practice—of child-rearing may rationalize their choices by believing that enabling a child to develop their inner propensities might make him or her more competitive in the long run.

If we want to look for a pop culture representation of this migration, it may be *Where Are We Going Daddy?*, a hugely popular reality show in which fans can vicariously participate in the family lives of China's most popular celebrities. In each episode, a celebrity "daddy" goes on a trip with his child, within China or abroad. The destination is kept secret from the child, who has to figure it out after arrival. Because the concept is to show fathers taking care of their children in an unfamiliar environment while their wives, back in China, watch and comment, Chinese authorities have praised the series for its *zheng nengliang* 正能量 (positive energy), as it putatively promotes progressive family values (Keane and Zhang 2017; Hird 2018). Several episodes of *Daddy* were filmed in Hungary in 2018, and although their direct—intended—effect was to promote tourism rather than migration to Hungary (Sherry Snow Pear 2018), the show's images of consuming wholesome food in the Hungarian countryside combined with father-child bonding reflects the fantasies of many migrant parents.

Looking for the Pure Land

Europe—in contradistinction to the global cities of liquid, hybrid ultra-modernity—has long been a purveyor of slowness, luxury, "authenticity," and purity in such things as food, cosmetics, or "culture" to the global middle and upper classes. In the past twenty years, we have seen the rise of a middle-class pursuit of authenticity in China as well. Authenticity and purity can be related to safety when it comes to food, baby formula, or cosmetics. We know how powerful the fears of contamination and adulteration are in contemporary China; Yan (2012), among others, has written about the centrality of such fears in debates about morality. But authenticity has also become prized when it comes to architecture, dwellings, and antiques: here, state-backed neotraditionalism has coalesced with the rising middle-class quest for consumable culture to produce the heritage fever that has been much written about (Silverman and Blumenfield 2013; Zhu and Maags 2020). Even the countryside has been remarkably resignified in this recent period, from the locus of backwardness to the location of genuine Chinese culture, from the location of dirt to the location of purity.

And as the Chinese middle class laments that there is little left of the authentic self to be consumed, Europe becomes the unadulterated Other still available for consumption (Nyíri and Beck 2020). This has been reflected in dramatic changes in the preferences of Chinese tourists in Europe. In the 1990s, they were mostly looking for urban modernity—and were disappointed by the lack of skyscrapers, broad avenues, and high-tech rail networks (Nyíri 2006: 99–108). But in the 2010s, the focus of increasingly sophisticated middle-class travelers shifted to the delights of nature and the terroir: many were visiting the hot springs in Iceland or taking road trips to French wineries. By the end of the decade, Balkan countries like Serbia and Montenegro were among the European destinations with the steepest increases in Chinese tourist numbers (European Travel Commission 2020).

Middle-class desire for authenticity and rootedness has also manifested itself in the rising popularity of rural "communes" (X. Wang 2021). However, this desire cannot be satisfied in China, as actually moving to such a commune, or to another form of countryside living made amenable for consumption, is often prohibitively expensive (such as the much-publicized Aranya Commune in Hebei [C. Yang 2021]). Even more importantly, it means cutting one's children off from good schools and potentially attracting unwanted attention as nonconformists: discussions of *tangping* on social media have been deleted by government censors (E. Chen 2021). It is, therefore, cheaper, safer, and more convenient to search for this pastoral utopia elsewhere, and migrants project a feeling akin to nostalgia for a simpler life and more meaningful human relations onto Europe. Middle-class Chinese migrants remain flexible citizens in the sense that their transnational lives are enabled by a form of arbitrage of differing and unequal economic and social regimes. They benefit from wider access to such flexible citizenship made possible by the expansion of "golden visas" and other selective immigration schemes. Yet for those seeking refuge in the groundedness of *terroir*, flexible citizenship may have lost much of its emotional appeal. Middle-class migrants may be flexible citizens, but they want to achieve or recover—for themselves or their children—a sense of tangible cultural citizenship they feel they have lost or never had.

In this optics, lifestyle migrations may intersect in unexpected ways with currents of ideologies of environmental, cultural, and racial purity. And this is the final twist we would like to highlight. Since Max Weber, we have associated modernity with disenchantment. Ong (2005) points out how postcolonial developmentalist governments like Singapore's or Malaysia's developed discourses of cultural uniqueness meant to "reenchant" citizens in order to differentiate and legitimize their modernizing projects vis-à-vis those of the former colonial powers. Increasingly, reenchantment with culture has become a global trend in the repertoire of authoritarian populism (Mishra 2017). The new non-Euro-American consumer class emerges against the backdrop of a world racked by a populist backlash against the "liquid" and the "hybrid" celebrated by postmodern theorists, searching for something solid amid constant flux. And Hungary, because of the nativist ideology championed by its government, has a particular appeal here.

To be sure, Hungary offers middle-class Chinese migrants a quickly attainable, discounted version of Europe. But the Hungarian government's militant anti-immigration rhetoric since 2015 has made global headlines. This is an apparent paradox. Yet it seems precisely this nativism that strikes a chord with Chinese migrants. State-controlled Chinese media has portrayed Europe as failing to contain the wave of refugees bringing crime and disorder (Shi-Kupfer, Gong, and Lang 2016). This official narrative coalesced with a popular antiliberal discourse in Chinese social media, which, like the American alt-right or Hungary's prime minister Viktor Orbán, accuses liberals of betraying the interests of their countries and their historical values (Zhang 2019). In this narrative, hard-working Chinese migrants are victims of *baizuo* 白左 ("libtards") who embrace undeserving queue-jumpers and undermine the values that made Europe great in the past (Zhang 2018; cf. Lin 2020). In contrast, Prime Minister Orbán (2017), while firmly rejecting immigration in general, has said that "real refugees," who flee political correctness in Western Europe, were welcome in the country. This stance resonates with many of our interlocutors. The mother of a twelve-year-old boy who moved to Hungary from Shanghai in 2015 told us: "I like Orbán. Because he managed to keep out the riffraff. Because he knew that if he let bad people in, good people like us wouldn't come."

In part, this is linked to a perception of safety and order: several migrants said Hungary was safer than Western European countries because it had fewer African and Muslim immigrants. After an Austrian-born ethnic Albanian man shot four people in Vienna in November 2020, the consensus on social media groups formed by Chinese "golden visa" immigrants in Hungary was that the lack of refugees in Hungary makes such an attack unlikely. A young man who graduated from a Scottish university and worked as a researcher for a Communist Party think tank but decided to move to Europe as it was "free" from the "lies of the Chinese government" mentioned the small number of Africans as the main reason for his choice of Budapest over Scotland. Similarly, when Ken had to make a quick decision about moving abroad and faced a choice between Greece, Portugal, Spain, and Hungary, he rejected the first three because of what he thought were their unstable governments and poor economy, but most importantly, the massive presence of Muslim immigrants. A country that was "relatively traditional, relatively religious," as he assumed Hungary to be, was a safer environment for Chinese immigrants like him. Probably following Hungarian government discourse conveyed by Chinese media—but disregarding actual levels of church attendance or influence—he considered Hungary a genuinely Christian country in a way other European countries were not, and it was this feature that made the country more welcoming and inclusive in his eyes. Although initially they considered moving on to Vienna, after his son encountered what he saw as xenophobic behavior at a Vienna playground he changed his mind, saying this was not the sort of environment he wanted the child to grow up in: "I don't want him ever to be told by anyone to go back to his country." He attributed their more positive experience in Hungary to the Christian nature of its society.

But, in addition to safety, there is another layer of meaning associated with whiteness and Christianity that has to do with purity. Worries about contamination of consumer goods (food, drugs, cosmetics) are ubiquitous in China (Yan 2012), but here suspicions of cultural contamination have a racial undertone. Just as milk powder can be trusted as genuine if it has been canned in Holland or New Zealand, Europe can be trusted as genuine if it is white. In *Vice China*, a youth magazine, a Chinese student in England wrote, "Europe is someone's luxurious and beautiful living room; we have come a long way to this land of manners and brought our money. . . . Suddenly, a bunch of uninvited guests break down the door, have no appreciation for the display in the living room, and pay no heed to us, who are sitting with stiff backs on the sofa" (Ji 2019). In these migrant stories, the adversary is no longer the white man who must be defeated in order to attain wealth, but the colored poor who might spoil its enjoyment.

Long Live Being Happy

Kaixin wan sui 開心萬歲 (long live being happy) is the motto of one of our interlocutors' profile on her social media account. Such phrases are the stock of Chinese social media user profiles, yet in the context of migration to Hungary it acquires a new, programmatic significance. The migration we describe in this article is limited to a small number of people. Yet it is significant, first, because it reflects new ways in which Chinese people relate to and remake the world as the balance of economic power continues to shift. One aspect of this is the remaking of global racial and class hierarchies, which produces new ideological alliances and oppositions. While reconceptualizations of the good life and deterritorialized strategies for attaining it are broader and more varied global processes, they intersect with these ideological and racial shifts.

Second, our case suggests that, for a rising global middle class, migration cannot be reduced to an accumulation strategy for upward mobility or a way of hedging against risks: it can also be a strategy of resistance against pressures produced by social and educational involution. Simultaneously, it can provide a lens onto shifting family ideologies. It shows that we need to widen the usual focus on economic accumulation in migration—even in the broader sense that includes education—to consider a broader variety of what it means to seek a better life. Xiang's (2021) formulation of "reproduction migration" is helpful in capturing the tectonic shifts in the global political economy of migration if we think of the West as becoming a site of reproduction.

Yet this classification is too limiting for two reasons. First, it implies a separation between the economic and the social, but productive and reproductive activities are much harder to separate from each other. Second, reproduction implies preservation—for example, preserving class status across generations (through the conversion of forms of capital or the securing of wealth). This captures part of the phenomenon but not the rejection of one's existing lifestyle and status, the opting out of a circuit of capital conversion, and the aspirations for an imagined different life. These raise complex questions that cannot be answered within a purely political-economy framework. Xiang writes that the root cause of reproduction migration is the monetization of reproduction needs such as health care and education, and people migrate to be able to *keep up* with that monetization. But our research suggests that they may also migrate to *opt out* of it—if they have the luxury of that choice. Elsewhere, writing about Chinese workers and engineers abroad, Miriam Driessen and Biao Xiang (2021: 205) observe that "Chinese migration is no longer about American or Japanese dreams. . . . Chinese migrants pursue Chinese dreams." This observation holds for much migration throughout history, but in our case, migrants do seem to pursue European dreams.

References

Barmé, Geremie. 1999. *In the Red*. New York: Columbia University Press.

Beck, Fanni, and Nyíri Pál. 2022. "'It's All for the Child': The Discontents of Middle-class Chinese Parenting and Migration to Europe." *China Quarterly*, no. 251: 913–34. https://doi .org/10.1017/S0305741022000169.

Bourdieu, Pierre. 1986. "The Forms of Capital." In *Handbook of Theory and Research for the Sociology of Education*, edited by J. Richardson, 46–58. New York: Greenwood.

Chen, Dian, and Chen Mei. 1997. *Sheng He* 聖河 (*Holy River*). Peking: Wenhua Yishu Chubanshe.

Chen, Elsie. 2021. "These Chinese Millennials Are 'Chilling,' and Beijing Isn't Happy." *New York Times*, July 3.

Cohen, Robin. 2008. *Diasporas: An Introduction*. London: Routledge.

Donald, Stephanie Hemelryk, and Yi Zheng. 2009. "Introduction: Post-Mao, Post-Bourdieu: Class Culture in Contemporary China." *Portal Journal of Multidisciplinary International Studies* 6, no. 2. https://doi.org/10.5130/portal.v6i2.1390.

Driessen, Miriam, and Biao Xiang. 2021. "Chinese Labor Migrants in Asia and Africa." In *Global East Asia: Into the Twenty-First Century*, edited by Frank Pieke and Koichi Iwabuchi, 199–208. Berkeley: University of California Press.

Ehrenreich, Barbara. 1990. *Fear of Falling: The Inner Life of the Middle Class*. New York: Harper Perennial.

Engels, Friedrich. 1884. *Origin of the Family, Private Property, and the State*. Marxists Internet Archive, 2010. https://www.marxists.org/archive/marx/works/download/pdf/origin_family .pdf.

European Travel Commission. 2020. *European Tourism 2019—Trends and Prospects (Q4/2019)*. Brussels: European Travel Commission. https://etc-corporate.org/reports/european-tourism -2019-trends-prospects-q4-2019/.

Hansen, Anders Sybrandt, and Stig Thøgersen. 2015. "Chinese Transnational Students and the Global Education Hierarchy." *Learning and Teaching* 8, no. 3: 1–12. https://doi.org /10.3167/latiss.2015.080301.

Heiman, Rachel, Carla Freeman, and Mark Liechty. 2012. *The Global Middle Classes: Theorizing through Ethnography*. Santa Fe: School for Advanced Research Press.

Hird, Derek. 2018. "Smile Yourself Happy: Zheng Nengliang and the Discursive Construction of Happy Subjects in China." In *Chinese Discourses on Happiness*, edited by Gerda Wielander and Derek Hird, 106–28. Hong Kong: Hong Kong University Press.

Ji, Cai. 2019. "Wo yi ge zai guonei bei ma 'baizuo' de liuxuesheng, chu le guo zenme jiu biancheng 'youpai'" 我一个在国内被骂"白左"的留学生，出了国怎么就变成"右派"了 ("How I, a Student Who Used to Be Derided as 'White Leftie' in China, Became a 'Rightist' Abroad"). *Vice China*, January 30. http://www.vice.cn/read/i-am-not-left-or-right-i-am-chinese.

Keane, Michael, and Joy Danjing Zhang. 2017. "Where Are We Going? Parent–Child Television Reality Programmes in China." *Media, Culture, and Society* 39, no. 5: 630–43. https:// doi.org/10.1177/0163443716663641.

Kipnis, Andrew B. 2011. *Governing Educational Desire: Culture, Politics, and Schooling in China*. Chicago: University of Chicago Press.

Lareau, Annette. 2003. *Unequal Childhoods: Class, Race, and Family Life*. Berkeley: University of California Press.

Li, Zhongqiang. 1993. *Leisa Duonaohe: Zhongguoren zai Xiongyali* 淚灑多瑙河:中國人在匈牙利 (*Tearful Danube: Chinese in Hungary*). Peking: Zhongguo Wuzi Chubanshe.

Lin, Yao. 2020. "Beaconism and the Trumpian Metamorphosis of Chinese Liberal Intellectuals." *Journal of Contemporary China* 30, no. 127: 85–101. https://doi.org/10.1080/10670564 .2020.1766911.

Liu, Xin. 1996. "Space, Mobility, and Flexibility: Chinese Villagers and Scholars Negotiate Power at Home and Abroad." In *Ungrounded Empires: The Cultural Politics of Modern Chinese Transnationalism*, edited by Aihwa Ong and Donald Nonini, 91–114. New York: Routledge.

Liu-Farrer, Gracia. 2016. "Migration as Class-Based Consumption: The Emigration of the Rich in Contemporary China." *China Quarterly*, no. 226: 499–518. https://doi.org/10.1017 /S0305741016000333.

Lu, Xueyi. 2002. *Dangdai Zhongguo shehui jieceng yanjiu baogao* 當代中國社會階層研究報告 (*Research Report on Social Strata in Contemporary China*). Peking: Shehui kexue wenxian chubanshe.

Mao Chun. 1992. *Zhongguoren zai Dongou: 90 niandai xin rechao chuguo taojin jishi* 中國人在東歐:90年代新熱潮出國淘金記事 (*Chinese in Hungary: A Chronicle of the New Emigration Gold Fever of the 90s*). Peking: Zhongguo Lüyou Chubanshe.

Meng, Bingchun. 2018. *The Politics of Chinese Media*. New York: Palgrave Macmillan.

Mishra, Pankaj. 2017. *Age of Anger: A History of the Present*. London: Farrar, Straus and Giroux.

Nathan, Andrew. 2016. "The Puzzle of the Chinese Middle Class." *Journal of Democracy* 27, no. 2: 5–19. https://doi.org/10.1353/jod.2016.0027.

Nyíri, Pál. 2006. "The Yellow Man's Burden: Chinese Migrants on a Civilizing Mission." *China Journal*, no. 56: 83–106. https://doi.org/10.2307/20066187.

Nyíri, Pál. 2011. "Chinese Entrepreneurs in Poor Countries: A Transnational 'Middleman Minority' and Its Futures." *Inter-Asia Cultural Studies* 12, no. 1: 145–53.

Nyíri, Pál. 2017. *Reporting for China: How Chinese Correspondents Work with the World*. Seattle: University of Washington Press.

Nyíri, Pál, and Fanni Beck. 2020. "Europe's New Bildungsbürger? Chinese Migrants in Search of a Pure Land." *Diaspora* 20, no. 3: 305–26.

Ong, Aihwa. 1999. *Flexible Citizenship: The Cultural Logics of Transnationality*. Durham, NC: Duke University Press.

Ong, Aihwa. 2005. "(Re)Articulations of Citizenship." *PS: Political Science and Politics* 38, no. 4: 697–99. https://doi.org/10.1017/S1049096505050377.

Orbán, Viktor. 2017. "Nineteenth Annual Address." Budapest, February 10. https://2015-2022 .miniszterelnok.hu/orban-viktor-19-evertekelo-beszede/.

Orellana, Marjorie Faulstich, Barrie Thorne, Anna Chee, and Wan Shun Eva Lam. 2001. "Transnational Childhoods: The Participation of Children in Processes of Family Migration." *Social Problems* 48, no. 4: 572–91. https://doi.org/10.1525/sp.2001.48.4.572.

Redding, S. Gordon. 1993. *The Spirit of Chinese Capitalism*. Berlin: Walter de Gruyter.

Sherry Snow Pear. 2018. "Tanfang 'Qizi de langman lüxing' qujingdi, shechi de Ouzhou hai cangzhe gao xingjiabi de wanfa" 探访《妻子的浪漫旅行》取景地,奢侈的欧洲还藏 高性价比的玩法 ("A Visit to the Location of 'Wives' Romantic Trip:' Luxurious Europe Hides More Value-for-Money Ways to Play"). *zhihu.com*, September 10. https://zhuanlan.zhihu .com/p/44216505.

Shi-Kupfer, Kristin, Jasmine Gong, and Bertram Lang. 2016. "Questioning Not the EU, but the 'Western System.'" *MERICS China Monitor*, July 12. https://merics.org/en/report/questioning-not-eu-western-system.

Silverman, Helaine, and Tami Blumenfield. 2013. "Cultural Heritage Politics in China: An Introduction." In *Cultural Heritage Politics in China*, edited by Tami Blumenfield and Helaine Silverman, 3–22. New York: Springer.

Song, Qiang, Zhang Zangzang, and Qiao Bian. 1996. *Zhongguo keyi shuo bu* 中国可以说不 (*China Can Say No*). Peking: Zhongguo Wenlian Chubanshe.

Sun, Liping. 2021. "Tangping jue fei jinjin fasheng zai diceng" 躺平绝非仅仅发生在底层 ("Lying Flat Is Definitely Not Confined to the Bottom of Society"). *Sun Liping Social Observation* (blog), May 31. https://mp.weixin.qq.com/s/mZ48KoCESTZXmWQCMiAhHA.

Surak, Kristin, and Yusuke Tsuzuki. 2021. "Are Golden Visas a Golden Opportunity? Assessing the Economic Origins and Outcomes of Residence by Investment Programmes in the EU." LSE Research Online Documents on Economics. London: London School of Economics and Political Science. https://econpapers.repec.org/paper/ehllserod/110458.htm.

Tagliacozzo, Eric, and Wen-Chin Chang, eds. 2011. *Chinese Circulations*. Durham, NC: Duke University Press.

Tomba, Luigi. 2009. "Of Quality, Harmony, and Community: Civilization and the Middle Class in Urban China." *positions: east asia cultures critique* 17, no. 3: 591–616. https://doi.org/10.1215/10679847-2009-016.

Wang, Qianni, and Shifan Ge. 2020. "How One Obscure Word Captures Urban China's Unhappiness." *Sixth Tone*, November 4. https://www.sixthtone.com/news/1006391/how-one-obscure-word-captures-urban-chinas-unhappiness.

Wang, Xuandi. 2021. "In China's New Age Communes, Burned-Out Millennials Go Back to Nature." *Sixth Tone*, January 15. https://www.sixthtone.com/news/1006694/in-chinas-new-age-communes%252C-burned-out-millennials-go-back-to-nature.

Weidenbaum, Murray L., and Samuel Hughes. 1996. *The Bamboo Network: How Expatriate Chinese Entrepreneurs Are Creating a New Economic Superpower in Asia*. New York: Simon and Schuster.

Woronov, T. E. 2008. "Raising Quality, Fostering 'Creativity': Ideologies and Practices of Education Reform in Beijing." *Anthropology and Education Quarterly* 39, no. 4: 401–22. https://doi.org/10.1111/j.1548-1492.2008.00030.x.

Xiang, Biao. 2021. "Reproduction-Driven Labor Migration from China" *Georgetown Journal of Asian Affairs* 7: 34–43.

Yan, Yunxiang. 2012. "Food Safety and Social Risk in Contemporary China." *Journal of Asian Studies* 71, no. 3: 705–29. https://doi.org/10.1017/S0021911812000678.

Yan, Yunxiang. 2021. *Chinese Families Upside Down: Intergenerational Dynamics and Neofamilism in the Early Twenty-First Century.* Leiden, Netherlands: Brill.

Yang, Carol. 2021. "Inside Aranya, China's Exclusionary Paradise." *Sixth Tone*, July 21. https://www.sixthtone.com/news/1008052/inside-aranya%252C-chinas-exclusionary-paradise.

Yang, Xiong. 2021. "The Roots of and Solution to 'Education Involution' in the Age of Artificial Intelligence." *Reading the China Dream* (blog). https://www.readingthechinadream.com/yang-xiong-on-educational-involution.html (accessed November 1).

Zhang, Chenchen. 2018. "Governing Neoliberal Authoritarian Citizenship: Theorizing *Hukou* and the Changing Mobility Regime in China." *Citizenship Studies* 22, no. 8: 855–81. https://doi.org/10.1080/13621025.2018.1531824.

Zhang, Chenchen. 2019. "Right-Wing Populist Discourse on Chinese Social Media: Identity, Otherness, and Global Imaginaries." Brussels Working Papers 3/2019. SSRN, February 24. https://doi.org/10.2139/ssrn.3325917.

Zhou, Min. 2010. *Chinatown: The Socioeconomic Potential of an Urban Enclave.* Philadelphia: Temple University Press

Zhu, Yujie, and Christina Maags. 2020. *Heritage Politics in China: The Power of the Past.* London: Routledge.

China Anxiety: Deracializing Debates about Housing and Education

Christina Ho, Dallas Rogers, and Jacqueline Nelson

Introduction: China Anxiety

The rise of China and the rapid expansion of its middle class are having far-reaching impacts on societies around the world, creating anxieties about the growing mobility of Chinese people and capital. In Australia, for whom China is the largest trading partner, public debates about not just trade but all manner of economic, social, and political issues are now infused with an anxiety about Chinese influence. While headlines about "political interference" and "trade wars" have proliferated in recent years, this article explores two arenas that have arguably received less public attention—namely, the role of Chinese migrants and Chinese capital in Australian housing and education.

As Fran Martin suggests in the introduction to this special issue, one emerging line of intellectual inquiry in China studies focuses on the global

positions 32:4 DOI 10.1215/10679847-11306856

mobility and new assemblages of people, culture, capital, and expertise throughout the region. This is a complex geographical, political, and cultural landscape that involves new types of movement of people and capital across national borders, and new networks of people, capital, and knowledge to allow this mobility to occur. Citing Ching Kwan Lee's notion of "global China," Martin "draws attention to these developments, highlighting those 'outward flows of investment, loans, infrastructure, migrants, media, cultural programmes and international and civil society engagement' that have so markedly intensified since the beginning of this century" (Martin, this issue; quoting Lee 2022: 313). These new mobilities and assemblages are operative from global (e.g., regional, transnational, and geopolitical) down to local levels (e.g., biographical, translocal, and ethnographic). In this article, we are interested in what it is like to live in a culturally, materially, and geopolitically shifting Asia-Pacific region, in an era that is being defined by a more globally focused China.

China's diaspora is increasingly mobile throughout the Asia-Pacific region. Not only are the "new Chinese" living more transnational lives and establishing homes in multiple locations, but they are developing new global and hybrid Chinese identities, through international study and migration (Chan and Koh 2018: 2). They are a significant force in global real estate markets as property consumers (Ma 2020), and some work in the global real estate industry as investment lawyers, accountants, and real estate agents to facilitate the movement of people and money from Asia to Australia (Ma, Rogers, and Troy 2023). These new Chinese investors and migrants have complicated cultural identities and nation-state allegiances and are engaged in international real estate and education practices that transcend static cultural stereotypes (Robertson 2021). As Xiao Ma et al. (2022) write,

> Looking at how families combine real estate, migration and foreign education, provides a critical insight into how and why immigrants create, form or sustain socio-cultural and financial relations in multiple places. Transnational families are not simply settlers in a new country. They are, rather, networks of people engaged in *transnational lives* that typically integrate different physical sites, cultural spheres, and political and regulatory environments.

This article documents how the growth of new Chinese mobilities, in the form of people and capital, has been enabled by Australian government policies attempting to engage with a rising China. In the process, these new mobilities have generated anxieties about "locals" being left behind. These anxieties reflect larger-scale concerns about the shifting world order, with China's ascension threatening the dominance of Western powers, as well as concerns about new class formations locally, as nonwhite migrants arrive in Australia as well-resourced, highly educated, upper-middle-class professionals. Unlike previous generations of migrants, the economic resources of the new migrants from China causes them to be seen as a threat to preexisting relations of power in Australia.

An important context for considering these developments is the fact that in Australia as elsewhere, there is growing competition for desirable places in both the housing and education "markets." In this competition, "Chinese" individuals are often seen as being "too successful." In housing, the "Chinese" are successful in making strategic real estate purchases, including for investment purposes.[1] In education, Chinese migrants' children dominate enrollments in high-performing selective schools and classes, and perform disproportionately well in standardized tests. In relation to both housing and education, public debates have included expressions of anxiety and resentment at "others" taking up valuable positions in these increasingly competitive markets. Concerns about being left behind or left out have become racialized, with Chinese individuals blamed for crowding out more deserving "local" people.

However, a key point that often disappears from public discussion of these issues is that inbound movements of Chinese people and capital are in fact the product of Australian government policies that have often directly sought greater engagement with an economically growing Asian region, particularly China. In recent decades, government policies have encouraged greater commercialization of housing and education, growing foreign investment, and increased entry of people from Asia into Australia through the skilled migration program. Despite this extensive courting by the Australian government, popular anxieties have often focused on blaming "the Chinese" for their perceived competitive advantage, and/or for bending the rules of Australia's education and housing systems.

Such concerns about "the Chinese" must be analyzed within the context of Australian racism. The anxieties outlined above reflect long-standing concerns about the "yellow peril" that predate white Australian nationhood. Nineteenth-century Australian history is replete with moral panics and fears of an "Asian invasion" or "Chinese takeover" (Jayasuriya and Pookong 1999). Indeed, one of the first acts of the newly federated Australian nation was to pass legislation banning Chinese immigration, encompassed in the Immigration Restriction Act in 1901, better known as the White Australia policy. This act institutionalized the racism that characterized Australia from invasion onward.

Prior to this immigration ban, large numbers of immigrants from China were attracted to goldfields in New South Wales and Victoria from the 1850s, and the Chinese population in Australia grew from a very few in 1841 to 38,000 in 1861 (Choi 1975: 22). Questions about moving Asian labor and capital into Australia have been central to the resistance to Chinese migrants in Australia ever since (Rogers 2017). This history illustrates that a racial politics seeking to change the way Chinese migrants move and use their labor and capital through and on Australia's colonized land—land first stolen from Indigenous peoples—has long been central to white nationhood in Australia (Rogers 2017).

However, despite periodic revivals of all-too-familiar anti-Asian "invasion" or "takeover" discourses, Australia's immigration program has welcomed significant numbers of new arrivals from China since the early 2000s. More than three-quarters (75.8 percent) of all China-born immigrants in Australia arrived between 2001 and 2021, and in 2021 there were more than a half million (549,614) people born in China living in Australia, accounting for 2.2 percent of the country's total population. Meanwhile, 5.5 percent of Australian residents reported a Chinese ancestry (ABS 2021). Australia's skilled migration and foreign student programs have been important drivers of these developments, with many Chinese international students gaining permanent residency in Australia following their tertiary studies (Hugo 2008; Robertson 2021). As a result of this, Australian residents born in China tend to be highly educated. Among Australian residents born in China, 50 percent have a university degree and 45.6 percent are employed as managers or professionals. In both cases these figures are substantially higher than the national average (ABS 2021).

This increased immigration into Australia of well-resourced, upper-middle-class Chinese individuals has coincided with the dramatic economic rise of China, and the growing political assertiveness of its one-party state. This potent combination has reignited "invasion" or "takeover" anxieties within Australia (Rogers, Wong, and Nelson 2017). These anxieties, in turn, have framed the way many Australians have viewed perceived imbalances or inequalities in national housing and education markets (Ho 2020; Robertson 2021; Rogers and Koh 2017). We argue here that closely following the push to marketize housing and education in Australia has been Chinese, and indeed Chinese Australian, success at navigating these marketized spaces. In line with Australian racism, this success has been racialized. Our argument in this article is that critical attention must be paid to the *policy structures* that set up the housing and education markets in the first place. Current public anxieties focus excessively on one group of individuals who are drawn into and then operate within these structures. These individuals are persistently framed as "foreign," and their behavior and apparent success within national housing and education markets are understood in racialized ways.

Racializing and Marketizing Housing and Education

In making the argument outlined above, we deploy two key concepts in our analysis of housing and education: "racialization" and "marketization."

The idea of racialization has a long history, though the term itself emerged more recently (Meer and Modood 2019). Influential race scholar Robert Miles elaborated on the concept of racialization in a number of works in the 1980s. Racialization describes the way biological or cultural characteristics are seen to "define and construct differentiated social collectivities" (Miles and Brown 2003: 101). Racialized groups are seen to have a cultural core: a uniform and static way of life (Modood 2005). Although racialization is distinct from racism, given that racialization typically has the effect of constructing a group of people as problematic or inferior, we argue that it is built on and made possible by underlying societal racism toward the target group.

The concept of racialization has been usefully deployed to examine intercultural relations in a variety of social settings. In Aotearoa, or New Zealand, Francis Collins (2006) examines the racialization of Asian students by the media. In this case racialization serves to fix "a diverse group of individuals within a singular racial identity that is known by stereotypical economic, cultural and social characteristics" (Collins 2006: 217). That is, Asian students in Auckland are represented by the media as economically, culturally, and socially Other. Collins describes "a fantasy of the geographical origin of Asian student" and the way that young New Zealanders with "Asian" heritage, or permanent residents with similar ancestry, also become implicated in this Othering (218). One important implication of the racialization Collins describes is the creation of "a racial category, Asian, that can be known and controlled in the New Zealand context" (221). Within this imaginary, particular individuals and particular behaviors are racialized as "Asian" or "Chinese." In the Australian context, as we explain below, this includes behaviors such as particular forms of investment property purchasing and the use of private tutoring.

We argue that the racialization of "the Chinese" in Australia is a key conditioning context for the public response to Chinese "success" in Australian housing and education. Furthermore, within this housing and education context, those seen as Chinese in Australia are also marketized; that is, they are treated as racialized consumers in housing and education markets. The idea of marketization we are drawing on is loosely informed by the work of Karl Polanyi (1975). Polanyi argues that before the advent of "market society," the economy was embedded within social structures and relations. Social norms placed "redistributive" and "reciprocity" limits on the penetration of markets into social life. But the rise of capitalism was underwritten by a "great transformation" of this relationship. The creation of markets in land (nature), labor (people), and money (capital) each removed important social limits on the market, eventually leading to the marketization of almost every facet of our lives.

While the concept of racialization is useful for analyzing intercultural relations in housing and education, the concept of marketization is useful for analyzing the creation of foreign real estate and education markets by government through public policy. Bringing some racial consideration to Polanyi's class analysis of marketization, we contend that foreign real estate investment and education markets are racialized in Australia. As detailed below, decades of neoliberal government policies have transformed the way Australians view housing and education, such that they are now viewed primarily as commodities to be bought and sold, and people engaging in these markets are viewed primarily as consumers. As Caitlin Neuwelt-Kearns et al. (2021: 4) note, in the neoliberal context of society today, "marketization processes—privatization, corporatization, commodification, competition"— have profoundly shaped how society is organized along race, class, and other lines.

Once a group of people is racialized, their participation in a social arena can effectively be racialized as well (El-Enany 2020). In our cases, while many groups participate in activities such as buying and selling real estate, or using private tutors, concerns about competition and inequality are disproportionately racialized in relation to Chinese families engaging with these practices, such that public debates have increasingly framed Australian housing and education controversies in racial terms, ignoring the broader state-driven policy structures that have facilitated controversial outcomes.

The next section of this article sets out the policy structures that have created the current housing and education systems in Australia. This is followed by two sections that take housing and education in turn, detailing some of the ways in which Chinese nationals and Chinese Australians have been racialized in popular understandings of the housing and education systems in Australia and, in turn, how controversies in these systems have become defined in the public imagination as racial ones. The article's final section examines how alternative frameworks for understanding these two markets may provide a more useful foundation for productive public debate.

Housing and Education Policy in Australia

The policy structures that underlie the current housing and education systems in Australia play a key role in governing the way that individuals operate as racialized subjects within these systems—or markets, as they have become. Looking first at housing policy, we must consider the housing market as a whole. The various policy settings shaping housing practices are clearly demarcated along domestic and foreign lines.

The domestic policy settings shaping housing are complex and have a range of aims, some of which conflict with each other. There exists an intersecting suite of housing supply-and-demand-side policy levers, taxation incentives for developers and investors, cash handouts for first home buyers, bank regulation, and federal funding programs for social and public housing (Pawson, Milligan, and Yates 2020). A key aim of these policies is to drive productivity and economic growth. Following a strong federal funding program for public housing in the immediate postwar period, official support for public housing has been steadily declining since at least the 1970s. This has been coupled with a focus on moving the Australian population into housing ownership, supported by a new set of taxation settings (such as negative gearing) and land-use policies that encouraged housing ownership and investment. In the late 1990s, homeownership peaked at about 70 percent of households (Pawson, Milligan, and Yates 2020). The first decade of the 2000s saw an increasing commodification of the housing system with more investors in the market, income-to-housing-cost ratios blowing out, and more younger people renting, for longer. By 2020, the rate of homeownership had fallen to about 65 percent and housing affordability in major Australian cities was in crisis. The treatment of housing as an investment vehicle for wealth creation has been heralded as a new "asset economy" era in housing (Adkins, Cooper, and Konings 2020).

Policies governing individual foreign real estate investment add an extra layer on top of the domestic policies discussed above. Australia's federal government developed its foreign real estate investment rules to direct foreign capital into new dwelling construction in order to support construction jobs and economic growth and improve housing affordability (Rogers and Dufty-Jones 2015). As such, and with some exceptions, nonresident foreign nationals are typically restricted from buying established properties. The government's argument that increasing housing supply might address housing affordability pressures has been widely criticized in Australia, including by the country's leading housing researchers (Phibbs and Gurran 2021). Critics argue that injection of foreign capital adds to, rather than decreases, domestic housing affordability pressures (Pawson, Milligan, and Yates 2020; Phibbs and Gurran 2021). Yet these policies have led to an influx of foreign investment in Australian housing over the last two decades, on top of an acceleration of domestic property purchases for investment purposes (Ma, Rogers, and Troy 2023).

Education policy settings similarly shape the way that individuals operate within them. Since the 1980s, federal and state governments in Australia have set out to enhance competition and choice in the education system. Key policy reforms include establishing more selective and specialist government schools; increasing funding to nongovernment schools; relaxing school catchment zone policies to enable families to apply to nonlocal government schools; expanding standardized testing (for example, with the institution of NAPLAN, or the National Assessment Program—Literacy and Numeracy); and creating the MySchool website that contains statistical academic and socioeconomic information on all schools in Australia (Windle 2015; Campbell, Proctor, and Sherington 2009; Ho 2020).

All these changes have been implemented in the name of providing more choice for families, either by increasing the types of schools families can apply to or by providing more information about schools' performance, funding, and student cohorts. Not only has school choice been presented as a democratic right for citizens, but in accordance with neoliberal ideology, greater choice is viewed as promoting competition in education, in turn lifting the quality of the "service" provided, as families are empowered to reject schools perceived as substandard in favor of perceived high-quality schools.

In these ways, families have been encouraged to take a market-oriented approach to education, comparing schools and engaging in strategies to maximize their children's chances of being accepted into a "desirable" school. Such strategies include moving into the catchment zone of a desirable school, undertaking private tutoring to prepare children for admissions and scholarship tests, and enrolling children into extracurricular activities to enhance their enrollment competitiveness for top-performing schools. This has created additional anxiety for families of school-age children, who in previous generations were more likely to simply send their children to the local comprehensive public school.

Race and Real Estate

In the context of the housing policy settings outlined above, this section documents the racialization of Chinese nationals and Asian Australians in Australia through their actual or perceived engagement with foreign real estate investment. Several key changes to the foreign investment housing market occurred between 2010 and 2020. Foreign investment in Australian real estate grew rapidly from A$6 billion in 2010 to A$29 billion in 2016 on the back of a significant injection of Chinese capital, before a spectacular fall back to A$5 billion in 2019. This period is known as "the foreign investment 'boom and bust'" (Ma, Rogers, and Troy 2023: 5).

The cultural politics of foreign real estate investment was highly visible when the federal government's geopolitical commitment to Asia (Australian Government 2012) became entangled with a media discourse linking Chinese foreign investors with increasing property prices and corruption. This was particularly evident in the commentary associated with the 2014 Parliamentary Inquiry into Individual Foreign Investment in Residential Real Estate (HRSCE 2014). However, although the inquiry's chairperson, then opposition MP Kelly O'Dwyer, associated a large proportion of the growth in residential real estate approvals with nonresident Chinese investors, evidence from the Australian Treasury and others indicated that Chinese purchases accounted for only 2 to 4 percent of the real estate market (McCarthy and Song 2018: 329).

In the Australian housing system, the politics of nonwhite citizens purchasing real estate is a highly charged issue linked to national housing identities such as the so-called Great Australian Dream of homeownership. At a time when housing affordability is at an all-time low in every Australian city, there is widespread concern at the prospect of younger generations being locked out of homeownership, in addition to worries about the housing stress being felt by many, across the generation divide. Concerns about unequal access to housing increasingly focus on the role of foreign investors, who between 2010 and 2020 were seen as too dominant in Australian real estate markets.

Chinese investment, in particular, has been "constructed ontologically and ideologically as a threat" (McCarthy and Song 2018: 325). Compared to foreign investment from "friendly" (read: white) Euro-American sources, Chinese investment is viewed as threatening not only because of racial difference but also due to suspicions about Chinese communism representing an alien and hostile economic and political force—an authoritarian "China Inc" (Nyland, Forbes-Mewett, and Thomson 2011: 616). Despite bipartisan support for foreign investment in residential real estate, media reporting suggests that popular anxiety ran high during the foreign investment boom-and-bust period, with allegations that foreign investors were driving up property prices, locking out "local" buyers and owner-occupiers (Wong 2017).

Within this context, two of the authors' research explored Sydneysiders' perceptions of foreign investors in Sydney, with a particular emphasis on Chinese investors (Rogers, Wong, and Nelson 2017). While there was an assumption in public policy and media rhetoric in the mid-2010s that there existed a high level of public concern about foreign investment, there was surprisingly little data that examined public perceptions. Our study examined whether the dominant voices in this debate represented broad public views about this issue.

We conducted a survey of 899 Sydney residents in November 2015, just prior to the 2016/17 high-water mark of the Chinese foreign investment boom. Our study found high levels of concern and discontent about foreign investment. Participants were asked to identify factors that they felt contributed to rising house prices in Sydney. Foreign investment was the factor identified most frequently by participants and was twice as likely to be selected than domestic factors such as the purchase of a home to live in and the negative gearing policy, which enables local taxpayers to offset losses on investment properties through the tax system. This was despite the reality that Australian government policies actively encourage both foreign and domestic property investment. More than three in four agreed that foreign investment was driving up house prices. In line with this, almost two-thirds did not think foreign investment should be encouraged, more than half believed that the government was not effectively regulating foreign investment, and a majority did not believe foreign investment should even be permitted in Sydney.

But in what ways might we say that the debate about foreign real estate investment is racialized? The high volume of foreign capital coming from China at the time of our study, together with the dominant media frames discussed above, meant that "foreign investment" effectively operated as a proxy for "Chinese investor" in our survey. In participating in Australia's foreign investment market—a market that was created by the Australia federal government for exactly this purpose (to attract foreign investors)—Chinese nationals were racialized by the Australian media and in broader public debate. As Xiao Ma, Dallas Rogers, and Laurence Troy (2023: 3) show, "Land acquisition and property investment by European foreigners are rarely mentioned in the mainstream media in Australia.... The activities of Asian investors, by comparison, have featured prominently in media discussions about foreign real estate investment since at least the 1980s" (also see Wong 2017).

Another way of exploring the racialization of the federal government's foreign real estate investment market is to look at the boundaries constructed between "foreign" and "domestic" investors in debates about Chinese foreign real estate investors. In another study, we found that members of the public in Australia misidentified "Australian-Chinese" people (i.e., Australian citizens) who were buying Australian real estate as being "Chinese bidders" and "Chinese nationals" (Rogers, Lee, and Yan 2015: 736). Australians often assume that all individuals who they perceive as ethnically Chinese are foreigners, discounting the possibility that many may be long-term residents or Australian citizens of various ethnic backgrounds (736).

The racialized tensions between "foreign" and "domestic" investors in Australia's housing markets, and particularly public discontent with the rise of Chinese real estate investment, exposes a dilemma for the federal government's attempts to build a foreign real estate market in Australia within the context of the geopolitical aspirations to foster an economically beneficial relationship with China. The government's policy settings and public rhetoric encouraged foreign investment, including Chinese investment. And yet intercultural relations on the ground in Australian cities were tense around Chinese real estate investment, since Chinese nationals and Australian Chinese were racialized as foreign housing consumers and competitors in the housing market.

To add further detail to this finding, participants in our 2015 survey research were given the opportunity to provide comments about housing costs and foreign investment in Sydney. The characterization of "Chinese" through these comments revealed the racialization of Chinese people living in Australia, as well as Australians with Chinese heritage. For example, one of the most frequent comments made was around the supposed failure of "the Chinese" to integrate socially.

Along these lines one respondent wrote that Chinese immigrants "don't integrate[,] create Chinese communities and only buy goods and services from their Chinese communities" (survey respondent 3). Chinese foreign investors, and by implication Chinese Australians, were also seen as rule benders whose motivation for purchasing housing was purely for financial gain:

> I think there is far too much bending of the rules—particularly by foreign investors. They buy large properties as a bolt hole for their money, pricing people who actually live and work here out of their neighbourhoods, and then do not live in the property, leaving it vacant. . . . I was told reliably by a friend that out of a block of 8 houses in her area, only one was occupied. I can see the same thing along our street too. One house was built and sold for 2.45 million, (which was already overpriced) and 8 months later was sold for 3.5 million to a foreign investor, without anything being done to it. It stands empty, just like so many others round here. (survey respondent 278)

These comments indicate an explicit *Othering* at play, which occurs in at least two ways.

First, the racialization of "the Chinese" depicts a group that pushes deserving Australians out of the housing market. We see this clearly in the following quote: "My family sold a house in Chatswood, three years ago to Chinese. They lived in it for three months. It now sits empty and neglected. This house [was] sold by my family for $2.7 million. Some young Australian family could be living in that house" (survey respondent 452). In these excerpts, respondents (re)articulate a racialized set of assumptions about the negative effects of Chinese foreign investors on the domestic housing system. European and North American foreign investors are rarely positioned as absentee investors who are pushing "Australians" out of the housing market. Yet Chinese immigrants are positioned in this way regardless of their actual behavior or motivations.

Second, the Australasian real estate industry is in fact key to promoting the Australian government's foreign investment policies (Rogers, Lee, and Yan 2015; Wong 2017), and actively promotes itself to Asian investors as part of its transnational business model (Dal Maso, Robertson, and Rogers 2021). One foreign investment entrepreneur described this business model as follows: "One of the founding principles [of his foreign real estate investment] company, was; it wasn't about real estate, it was about educating the Chinese consumer about the [foreign investment] opportunity that existed in the world. Our target audience was high-net-worth, affluent Chinese consumers who had the means and ability to travel internationally" (Dal Maso, Robertson, and Rogers 2021: 569). Thus, the model focused on "teaching" Chinese foreign buyers about Australia's foreign investment policies, rules, and laws is key to this business model, but operates on essentialized racial categories (Dal Maso, Robertson, and Rogers 2021; Rogers, Lee, and Yan 2015). This model positions "the 'other culture as risky' to fuel wary attitudes between buyers and developers, and to subsequently develop its mediating role therein" (Dal Maso, Robertson, and Rogers 2021: 572).

In summary, Australian government policies have in recent years facilitated and encouraged the inflow of "Chinese" capital into Australian real estate markets in the form of foreign investment. While the scale of these property purchases has both dramatically escalated and then fallen spectacularly over the last ten years, overall "Chinese" foreign investment remains a small fraction of total property purchases. Although popular anxieties about housing affordability often blame "Chinese" investors, the reality is much more complex. We propose that legitimate concerns about housing inequality need to be refocused to examine how public policies have facilitated this inequality—with policies about foreign investment just one small part of the picture. Resentment at "Chinese" property investors, which is part of broader geopolitical and economic concerns about an increasingly dominant China, undermines community relations in Australia.

Race and Educational Success

Just as "Chinese" property investors are seen as "too" successful in the real estate market, in the arena of education, there is growing anxiety about the success of children of Chinese migrants in Australian schools. In this case, we focus on perceptions about Chinese Australian students in the education system in the state of New South Wales (NSW). The majority of these students were born in Australia with parents who are first-generation migrants from China. A smaller number are from longer-established Chinese migrant families (from China and other source countries).

The state of NSW has arguably the most hierarchical education system in Australia, with almost fifty academically selective high schools that routinely outperform all others in standardized tests, including in the all-important Higher School Certificate (HSC) exams that determine students' university entrance opportunities. Although selective schools are public (government-funded) schools that enroll students on the basis of their results in a centralized admissions test, there is much public disquiet about Chinese and other Asian Australian families allegedly "gaming" the system in order to gain a place. Concerns have focused on these migrant families' use of private tutoring in particular, and on allegedly authoritarian "Chinese" parenting practices symbolized in the figure of the "tiger parent" (Chua 2011).

It is not difficult to see why these concerns exist. Among fully selective high schools in NSW, enrollments are dominated by students from Language Backgrounds Other Than English (LBOTE). In Sydney, LBOTE students make up 80 percent or more of enrollments in all but two fully selective high schools (Ho 2019). In NSW's top-performing school, James Ruse Agricultural High School, LBOTE students constitute 97 percent of enrollments.[2] There is qualitative evidence that LBOTE students are also overrepresented in primary school Opportunity Classes (Ho 2020), which are specialized classes for gifted and talented students and are unofficial "feeders" for selective high schools.

Asian Australians comprise the vast majority of these LBOTE students. Children of migrants from China are typically the largest cohort within the selective schools, joined by students from an array of other Asian backgrounds, including Korean, Vietnamese, Indian, Sri Lankan, and Bangla-deshi. In the popular imaginary, the identity of these students tends to be simplified into the category "Asian" or "Chinese." This conflation is also often deployed by Asian Australian students themselves. For example, in Christina Ho's (2020) research on Asian Australian families and selective schools, a Chinese Australian respondent remarked about her selective school, "It's like a mini-Chinatown."

In public debates, commenters have often argued that selective schools have become dominated by Chinese and other Asian Australians because "their culture" suits the cutthroat competitive process of gaining admission. "Selectives are skewed Asian because what it takes to pass the test suits their culture," argued one parent in an article published in the high-circulation *Good Weekend* newspaper magazine. Another parent in the same article explained, "The Chinese are very savvy at working the system" (Broinowski 2015).

In the popular imagination, "Chinese culture" includes a willingness by parents to subject their children to punishing weekly routines consisting of hours of after-school tutoring and home study as well as tight restric-tions on leisure activities such as playdates with friends. This "culture," it is argued, relegates childhood to a relentless pursuit of academic success, with the target of achieving a top HSC ranking, enabling admission into the most prestigious university courses.

This interpretation of Asian or Chinese "culture" fuels anxiety and resent-ment on the part of middle-class Anglo-Australians, who perceive themselves, self-flatteringly, as relaxed and liberal parents. Their self-perceived parenting style cannot countenance the type of authoritarian and demanding parenting they associate with Chinese migrants. As a result, they fear their children will never be able to compete with the children of migrants. In the words of Liz, one of Ho's Anglo-Australian parent respondents whose primary school-age children attended a high-performing opportunity class:

> Both my kids play string instruments. The Asian kids whip them. They practice an hour a day.... The kids in Year 3 come in and already play in the school orchestra. It's not just music. Every super star child at the swim-ming carnival is Asian. They're doing hours a day, going up and down

the pool, perfecting. Anything that has a technique involved, that you can perfect, like swimming, violin, that's where they're going, and doing at a high level.

The "Asian" practice of private tutoring is a particular touchpoint of racialized resentment. While traditionally, in Australia, it is low-achieving students who have engaged in private tutoring for remedial purposes—to "catch up"—many Asian Australian students who are already academically high-achieving engage in private tutoring to "get ahead," or specifically to prepare for tests, including the selective school admissions test. In the last decade, commercial tutoring centers have proliferated in cities such as Sydney, concentrated in areas where large numbers of Asian migrants have settled. Students spend months or sometimes years preparing for admissions tests, doing weekly practice tests and refining their test-taking skills.

* * *

In the eyes of many non-Asians, test preparation tutoring is tantamount to "gaming" the system. One of Ho's Anglo-Australian student respondents, Robert, labeled tutoring as "that cheating system," arguing that it distorted the outcomes of selective school admissions, excluding intelligent applicants who had not been tutored. Meanwhile, Robert's father likened tutoring to "doping" in sport.

It is not surprising that such perceptions have arisen in relation to Asian Australians' approach to education. They build on long-standing stereotypes of Asian migrants, and particularly the Chinese, as the "model minority" (Fong 2008; Li and Wang 2008). As the "model minority," Chinese and other Asian migrants have been lauded for their hard work and self-reliance. However, there has always been a dark side to the stereotype—namely, that Asians' industriousness poses an ever-present threat to others. There is always a threat that the model minority could become "too successful" and "take over" particular arenas within their hosts' society, whether this is jobs, school places, or real estate. As described above, this is particularly pertinent in an era where changes in the global order threaten the taken for granted predominance of white-dominant Euro-American countries. And in the Australian setting, the changing profile of recent migrants, who are now overwhelmingly skilled professionals, threatens the taken-for-granted social and cultural dominance of Anglo-Australians.

Of course, the model minority stereotype has always hidden the diversity of experiences and practices within Asian migrant communities. Not every Asian Australian student is successful in school, and not every Asian migrant parent is a pushy "tiger parent." In fact, the stereotype of the smart, successful Asian student can be extremely detrimental. Unrealistic expectations create mental health problems for many Asian migrant children, for example (Qin 2008). And assumptions that Asian migrant students are high achievers may prevent many from getting the support they need.

Alongside these social risks, another of the dangers of the model minority stereotype is the cultural essentialism embedded within it. Within the stereotype, Chinese and other Asian migrants' behavior is viewed as an inexorable product of their deeply rooted "culture." Traits such as industriousness and accumulative materialism are viewed as "cultural." Resentment at such traits, as we have shown, then becomes racialized resentment. This resentment fuels forms of racism that claim "cultural incompatibility" between Asians and Westerners, leading to a questioning of multiculturalism as a basis for social cohesion.

Indeed, some commentators have used the success of Chinese and other Asian migrants in Australia to repudiate the policies of multiculturalism and immigration policy that is not racially discriminatory. For instance, in 2019, then NSW Labor Party leader Michael Daley expressed concern about "Asians with PhDs" taking local jobs and driving young people out of Sydney (Australian Associated Press 2019). "Culture" is not only a dangerous explanation for Chinese Australians' and Asian Australians' success in the education system; it is also inaccurate. These students' educational performance cannot be explained simply by reference to cultural factors. There are social and political factors that play as great, if not greater, a role. These factors revolve around Asian Australians' status as migrants.

First, as noted above, Chinese and other Asian migrants in Australia are a "hyper-selected" group (Lee and Zhou 2015). In the last two decades, they have overwhelmingly arrived as skilled migrants, reflecting Australian policy settings since the 1990s that have prioritized applicants' educational qualifications and occupational skills. Skilled migrants now comprise 70 percent of the overall permanent migration intake (Australian Government 2019). Australia has seen a dramatic shift in the profile of its migrants, from the "working class ethnics" of the postwar period to the current "multicultural middle class" (Colic-Peisker 2011). As highly skilled individuals who have benefited from education, Chinese and other Asian migrants naturally value schooling. Their emphasis on education therefore is not just a "cultural" phenomenon but a direct product of their class status and the fact that they were selected by the Australian government for admission as skilled migrants.

Second, Chinese and other Asian migrants in Australia are responding logically to a competitive education system. Coming from some of the most fiercely competitive education systems in the world—for example, in China—Asian migrants understand how to strategically navigate education systems. Again, their success can be seen as a product of government policy.

As described above, over the last two decades, Australian governments have systematically created a market in schooling, with reforms that have created greater hierarchies between schools and heightened competition for places in "desirable" schools. As in the realm of migration, these policies in education benefit well-resourced middle-class families. Chinese and other Asian migrants are particularly well positioned to benefit because of their class status and overseas experience with competitive schooling systems.

So while many view Chinese Australian and Asian Australian educational or real estate success as a product of "Asian" or "Chinese" culture, this perspective fails to account for the crucial role played by Australian government policies. In many ways, the stereotypical successful Asian Australian student or real estate investor is a product of decades of neoliberal policies in immigration, education, and foreign investment. In all of these arenas, Australian government policy has become more selective, more elitist, and more geared toward picking winners.

Conclusion: The New Chinese Mobilities and Australian Housing and Education

In this article, we have tried to illustrate how, over recent decades, successive Australian governments, like many other governments worldwide, have instituted policies encouraging the inbound mobility of Chinese people and capital. Seeking to engage with a rising China, Australian governments have pursued policy programs incentivizing migration and investment from Chinese individuals. These programs have worked in tandem with policies that have led to the marketization of housing and education in Australia, such that these arenas are characterized as "markets" within which "consumers" participate. As the marketization of housing and education in Australia have occurred alongside the growth of the new P. R. Chinese mobilities, activity within these "markets" has become racialized, with anxiety over the role of "the Chinese" in these increasingly competitive arenas.

This article has shown that Australian anxiety that focuses on "Chinese" individuals, reflecting global anxiety about the rise of China, fails to recognize the role played by the Australian government in facilitating the mobility of Chinese migrants and capital. Although Chinese migrants have often been beneficiaries of neoliberal policies in housing and education in Australia, they played no part in creating these policies. They simply act within the rules set by government policies. The marketization of Australian housing, where housing becomes a repository for capital and associated capital gain, operating alongside government policies allowing—even encouraging—foreign investment in housing, has created a market whereby investors gain financially from the buying and selling of housing. Chinese investors, or Asian Australians as the case may be, have simply been successful operators within this system, as have many domestic investors. Similarly, many of Ho's Chinese Australian respondents acknowledged the anxiety about their dominance in selective schools but emphasized that migrants had fairly earned their places within a system set by governments. As one recent selective school graduate said, "We feel like we've worked in the system. We've done nothing wrong to get to where we are. . . . It's not our fault that things are a particular way." Another remarked, "If you want your kid to go to a selective school, there's a system. . . . It's like, the world is how it is. You've just got to adjust to it."

As such, anxiety about increasing competition or inequality in Australia's housing and education systems should lead to a questioning of the policies that encourage such trends. In Australia as in other societies where these anxieties arise (e.g., Ley 2010), blaming Chinese or Asian migrants for benefiting from the system is unfair and futile. If governments reversed some of the marketization of housing and education that has occurred over the last two decades, many of the strategies used by Chinese migrant families would bear less fruit. Private tutoring to prepare for the selective schools admissions test would be useless if there were no selective schools, for instance. Reducing the tax incentives designed to encourage investment property purchases, and increasing capital gains taxation, would render property investments a less attractive proposition.

Equally important is the fact that anxiety about "the Chinese" in Australian housing and education occurs within the structures of Australian racism. This means that legitimate concerns about housing affordability and equitable access to high-quality education become uncomfortably mixed with racism. A much more productive public debate could be had with less of an emphasis on culture and race, and more attention on public policy. This might also take some of the heat out of current debates. For example, the association of Chinese Australian students with selective schools means that some now feel prevented from criticizing the selective system for fear of being labeled racist. Communities need to be able to critique national and state education systems without becoming derailed by a focus on the *occupants* of that system. Similarly, communities need to be able to have a frank public discussion about the purpose and desirability of foreign (and domestic) investment in real estate without becoming fixated on the perceived racial identity of property buyers.

Ultimately, these case studies of housing and education in Australia reveal a great deal about intercultural relations, and in particular, the longstanding underlying anti-Chinese racism in Australia that enables racialized resentment against the "too successful Chinese." As we have argued, not all players active in these markets are identified as problematic. Neither white foreign investors nor white families using private tutoring are rendered visible, despite engaging in the same "problematic" behaviors as "the Chinese."

More broadly, in relation to the theme of this special issue, our case studies of Australian housing and education provide an account of the local social consequences of the changing global order caused by the rise of China. Like many governments, successive Australian governments of all political persuasions have sought to benefit from Chinese economic development by implementing policies to attract Chinese human and financial capital.

As we have shown, this has in turn altered local class and ethnic relations within Australian society, an effect we see especially starkly in the arenas of housing and education. The anxiety generated by these shifting relations of power demonstrates at a local level the far-reaching consequences of a rising China and the new Chinese mobilities.

Notes

1 We place "Chinese" in quotation marks because the national and cultural identity of these individuals can be ambiguous and unstable, as will be explained in this article. But in popular parlance, this ambiguity contributes to an essentializing understanding of "Chinese" individuals as inherently foreign (see Fitzgerald 2019).
2 My School (website), ACARA (Australian Curriculum, Assessment and Reporting Authority), https://myschool.edu.au (accessed January 22, 2023).

References

Adkins, Lisa, Melinda Cooper, and Martjin Konings. 2020. *The Asset Economy: Property Ownership and the New Logic of Inequality*. Cambridge: Polity.

Australian Associated Press. 2019. "Michael Daley Claims Asian Workers Taking Young People's Jobs in Sydney." *Guardian*, March 19.

Australian Bureau of Statistics (ABS). 2021. "People in Australia Who Were Born in China (Excludes SARs and Taiwan): 2021 Census Country of Birth QuickStats." https://www.abs.gov.au/census/find-census-data/quickstats/2021/6101_AUS (accessed March 8, 2023).

Australian Department of Home Affairs. 2019. *Australia's 2019–20 Migration Program*. Australian Government. https://www.homeaffairs.gov.au/research-and-stats/files/report-migration-program-2019-20.pdf.

Australian Government. 2012. *Australia in the Asian Century*. http://asiancentury.dpmc.gov.au/white-paper.

Broinowski, Anna. 2015. "Unnatural Selection." *Sydney Morning Herald Good Weekend Magazine*, January 24.

Campbell, Craig, Helen Proctor, and Geoffrey Sherington. 2009. *School Choice: How Parents Negotiate the New School Market in Australia*. Sydney: Allen & Unwin.

Chan, Yuk Wah, and Sin Yee Koh. 2018. *New Chinese Migrations: Mobility, Home, and Inspirations*. New York: Routledge.

Choi, C. Y. 1975. *Chinese Migration and Settlement in Australia*. Sydney: Sydney University Press.

Chua, Amy. 2011. *Battle Hymn of the Tiger Mother*. New York: Penguin Books.

Colic-Peisker, Val. 2011. "A New Era in Australian Multiculturalism? From Working-Class 'Ethnics' to a 'Multicultural Middle-Class.'" *International Migration Review* 45, no. 3: 562–87.

Collins, Francis Leo. 2006. "Making Asian Students, Making Students Asian: The Racialisation of Export Education in Auckland, New Zealand." *Asia Pacific Viewpoint* 47, no. 2: 217–34.

Dal Maso, Giulia, Shanthi Robertson, and Dallas Rogers. 2021. "Cultural Platform Capitalism: Extracting Value from Cultural Asymmetries in RealTech." *Social and Cultural Geography* 22, no. 4: 565–80.

El-Enany, Nadine. 2020. *(B)ordering Britain: Law, Race, and Empire*. Manchester: Manchester University Press.

Fitzgerald, John. 2019. "Mind Your Tongue: Language, Diplomacy and Community in Australia-China Relations." *The Strategist*, October 2. https://www.aspistrategist.org.au /mind-your-tongue-language-diplomacy-and-community-in-australia-china-relations/.

Fong, Timothy. 2008. *The Contemporary Asian American Experience: Beyond the Model Minority*. 3rd ed. London: Pearson.

Ho, Christina. 2019. *Ethnic Divides in Schooling*. https://cpd.org.au/work/ethnic-divides -in-schooling-discussion-paper/.

Ho, Christina. 2020. *Aspiration and Anxiety: Asian Migrants and Australian Schooling*. Melbourne: Melbourne University Publishing.

HRSCE (House of Representatives Standing Committee on Economics). 2014. *Report on Foreign Investment in Residential Real Estate*. Australian Government.

Hugo, Graeme. 2008. "In and Out of Australia: Rethinking Chinese and Indian Skilled Migration to Australia." *Asian Population Studies* 4, no. 3: 267–91.

Jayasuriya, Laksiri, and Kee Pookong. 1999. *The Asianisation of Australia?: Some Facts about the Myths*. Melbourne: Melbourne University Press.

Lee, Ching Kwan. 2022. "Global China at Twenty: Why, How, and So What?" *China Quarterly*, no. 250: 313–31.

Lee, Jennifer, and Min Zhou. 2015. *The Asian American Achievement Paradox*. New York: Russell Sage Foundation.

Ley, David. 2010. *Millionaire Migrants: Trans-Pacific Life Lines*. Malden, MA: Wiley Blackwell.

Li, Guofang, and Lihshing Wang. 2008. "Introduction: The Old Myth in a New Time." In *Model Minority Myth Revisited: An Interdisciplinary Approach to Demystifying Asian American Educational Experiences*, edited by Guofang Li and Lihshing Wang, 1–18. Charlotte, NC: Information Age.

Ma, Xiao. 2020. "Chinese Housing Policy, Capital Switching, and the Foreign Real Estate Investment 'Boom and Bust' in Australia." *International Journal of Housing Policy* 21, no. 3: 451–63.

Ma, Xiao, Dallas Rogers, Jacqueline Nelson, and Y. Yingfei Wang. 2022. "Foreign Real Estate Investment and International Education as a Family Wealth Strategy." In *Families, Housing, and Property Wealth in a Neoliberal World*, edited by Richard Roland and Rowan Arundel, 155–73. London: Routledge.

Ma, Xiao, Dallas Rogers, and Laurence Troy. 2023. "Chinese Property Developers after the Decline in Foreign Real Estate Investment in Sydney, Australia." *Housing Studies* 38, no. 7: 1284–1303.

McCarthy, Greg, and Xianlin Song. 2018. "China in Australia: The Discourses of Changst." *Asian Studies Review* 42, no. 2: 323–41.

Meer, Nasar, and Tariq Modood. 2019. "Islamophobia as the Racialisation of Muslims." In *The Routledge International Handbook of Islamophobia*, edited by Irene Zempi and Imran Awan, 18–31. New York: Routledge.

Miles, Robert, and Malcolm Brown. 2003. *Racism*. New York: Routledge.

Modood, Tariq. 2005. *Multicultural Politics: Racism, Ethnicity, and Muslims in Britain*. Minneapolis: Minnesota University Press.

Neuwelt-Kearns, Caitlin, Tom Baker, Octavia Calder-Dawe, Ann E. Bartos, and Susan Wardell. 2021. "Getting the Crowd to Care: Marketing Illness through Health-Related Crowdfunding in Aotearoa New Zealand." *Environment and Planning A: Economy and Space* 56, no. 1: 541–56.

Nyland, Chris, Helen Forbes-Mewett, and S. Bruce Thomson. 2011. "Sinophobia as Corporate Tactic and the Response of Host Communities." *Journal of Contemporary Asia* 41, no. 4: 610–31.

Pawson, Hal, Vivienne Milligan, and Judith Yates. 2020. *Housing Policy in Australia: A Case for System Reform*. Singapore: Palgrave Macmillan.

Phibbs, Peter, and Nicole Gurran. 2021. "The Role and Significance of Planning in the Determination of House Prices in Australia: Recent Policy Debates." *Environment and Planning A: Economy and Space* 53, no. 3: 457–79.

Polanyi, Karl. 1975. *The Great Transformation: The Political and Economic Origins of Our Time*. 2nd ed. Boston: Beacon.

Qin, Desiree B. 2008. "Doing Well vs. Feeling Well: Understanding Family Dynamics and the Psychological Adjustment of Chinese Immigrant Adolescents." *Journal of Youth and Adolescence* 37, no. 1: 22–35.

Robertson, Shanthi. 2021. *Temporality in Mobile Lives: Contemporary Asia-Australia Migration and Everyday Time*. Bristol, UK: Bristol University Press.

Rogers, Dallas. 2017. *The Geopolitics of Real Estate: Reconfiguring Property, Capital, and Rights*. Lanham, MD: Rowman and Littlefield.

Rogers, Dallas, and Rae Dufty-Jones. 2015. "Twenty-First-Century Australian Housing: New Frontiers in the Asia-Pacific." In *Housing in Twenty-First-Century Australia*, edited by Dallas Rogers and Rae Dufty-Jones, 221–36. London: Routledge.

Rogers, Dallas, and Sin Yee Koh. 2017. "The Globalisation of Real Estate: The Politics and Practice of Foreign Real Estate Investment." In *The Globalisation of Local Real Estate: The Politics and Practice of Foreign Real Estate Investment*, edited by Dallas Rogers and Sin Yee Koh. Special issue, *International Journal of Housing Policy* 17, no. 1: 1–14.

Rogers, Dallas, Chyi Lin Lee, and Ding Yan. 2015. "The Politics of Foreign Investment in Australian Housing: Chinese Investors, Translocal Sales Agents, and Local Resistance." *Housing Studies* 30, no. 5: 730–48.

Rogers, Dallas, Alexandra Wong, and Jacqueline Nelson. 2017. "Public Perceptions of Foreign and Chinese Real Estate Investment: Intercultural Relations in Global Sydney." *Australian Geographer* 48, no. 4: 437–55.

Windle, Joel A. 2016. *Making Sense of School Choice: Politics, Policies, and Practice under Conditions of Cultural Diversity*. New York: Palgrave Macmillan.

Wong, Alexandra. 2017. "Transnational Real Estate in Australia: New Chinese Diaspora, Media Representation, and Urban Transformation in Sydney's Chinatown." In *The Globalisation of Local Real Estate: The Politics and Practice of Foreign Real Estate Investment*, edited by Dallas Rogers and Sin Yee Koh. Special issue, *International Journal of Housing Policy* 17, no. 1: 97–119.

The Sinophone as an Uneven Experience of Time and Place: Translocal Media Consumption in Chinese-Speaking Malaysia

Ting-Fai Yu

Introduction

In Chinese-speaking Malaysia, media consumption is necessarily both trans-local and transnational. On one hand, Chinese cultural practices including language use differ quite widely from one state to another, leading to diverse, geographically specific media preferences and consumption patterns. On the other, the Sinophone cultural products consumed are predominantly produced outside Malaysia, arriving multidirectionally from other parts of the Chinese-speaking world. While the fields of Asian media and cultural studies have provided useful perspectives on transnational media flows and their cultural impacts, these studies have tended to focus on relationships *between* different nation-states (e.g., Chua 2012; Chua and Iwabuchi 2008; Hong and Jin 2021; Iwabuchi, Muecke, and Thomas 2004; Martin et al.

positions 32:4 DOI 10.1215/10679847-11306868
Copyright 2024 by Duke University Press

2020; Kawashima and Lee 2018), rather than the local complexities *within* them, or the connections between localities across and beyond the nation. To challenge this privileging of the national over the local, this article proposes that Malaysia needs to be brought into the discussion to illustrate how overseas Chinese identity formation through media consumption can be as much a translocal as a transnational phenomenon. Specifically, it demonstrates how Chinese-speaking Malaysia has been unevenly affected by Sinophone media flows across generations and regions, resulting in divergent cultural practices and aspirations, and it highlights intraethnic complexities that are determined by both temporal and spatial contexts.

In its attempt to engage theorizations of translocality and transnationality in productive tension with each other, this article presents two observations on how Chinese Malaysians' media use exemplifies translocal practices in relation to other Sinophone locations, especially Hong Kong and Singapore, since the 1990s, as well as highlighting the implications of the present dominance of PRC (People's Republic of China) media in Malaysia. First, it examines Chinese Malaysians' consumption of Chinese-language media as an intergenerational experience, vis-à-vis the general shift from the popularity of Hong Kong media before 2000 toward media from the PRC in the present. For example, the broadcasting of TVB dramas on national television once made Hong Kong an ideal reference point for being (overseas) Chinese and produced a generation of Cantonese speakers, despite many Malaysian viewers not being ethnically Cantonese. This exemplifies the persistent presence of Hong Kong's past in Malaysian everyday life, resulting in temporally displaced, nostalgic investments in a collectively imagined alternative modernity. Second, by highlighting the unique position of Johor, the Malaysian state bordering Singapore, in the Sinophone media circuit, the article demonstrates how geographic proximities can sometimes be more significant than national boundaries or policies in regulating cultural traffic. For decades, Chinese Johoreans have watched television channels in Singapore, since they can "illicitly" receive satellite signals from across. In light of Singapore's Speak Mandarin Campaign, which banned "dialect" programming, they have historically been more exposed to Mandarin programming than other Malaysians, who more likely consumed transnational Chinese cultural products in their original (non-Mandarin) languages. The unrelenting presence of Singaporean media has enabled a distinctive Johorean identity and a spatial reconfiguration of home.

To place all of this in a broader theoretical context, this article engages the Sinophone concept alongside scholarship on "global China" (e.g., Lee 2017, 2022; Rofel and Rojas 2023; Pavlićević and Talmacs 2022). Committed to decentering China studies, while the Sinophone challenges the field's Han-centric analytic applications for understanding transnational Chinese cultures, global China studies calls for expanding the boundary of China studies beyond China's geographic territory. Although seemingly contradictory in their critical agendas, both frameworks consider China's imperial influences as multiple and co-optive rather than as operating through direct force. In the field-changing monograph *The Specter of Global China*, Ching Kwan Lee (2017) articulates global China as a multifaceted phenomenon through an ethnographic comparison of China's state versus private capital in Zambia's copper mining and construction industries. In a recent *China Quarterly* special issue, Lee (2022: 316) further called for approaching "global China as a power, rather than a policy or geographical, phenomenon," as a way to capture "the decoupling of state and civilian objectives." Indeed, the special issue in which this article appears illustrates that China's global reach takes many forms other than state-led foreign capital investment, including through migration, higher education, and media circulations. The study of global China is a study of dynamic, uneasy processes that often lead to unintended consequences. As Lee argues, "Power is relational, so we should attend to resistance, bargaining, accommodation, appropriation and adaptations by players in this power project not as an afterthought or secondary supplementary study but as *constitutive* of global China" (317). By presenting a bottom-up, human-centered view of the historical workings and contemporary contestations of Sinophone media in Malaysia, this article attempts to show that a Sinophone framework helps illuminate how global China is resisted and challenged by everyday cultural and affective practices.

The findings presented in this article are the result of ethnographic research and interviews conducted in person in Malaysia and Taiwan, as well as via virtual conferencing platforms in 2019–21. The interviewees, in their twenties to fifties and of diverse ethnolinguistic family backgrounds (including Cantonese, Foochow, Hakka, Hokkien, and Teochew), grew up and had spent extended time living in states across Peninsular Malaysia, including Perak, Johor, Penang, and Selangor. Moreover, most of them were in diaspora, living temporarily or permanently in Hong Kong or Taiwan. As this article will demonstrate, this diverse sample of interviewees across age and geography highlights the temporal and spatial continuities and disjunctures of Chinese-language media consumption in Malaysia and other parts of the Sinophone world. Further, I propose that the interviewees' present-day consumption of non-PRC Chinese-language media exemplifies a Sinophone logic of cultural and affective mobilities that resists the dominance and homogenization of PRC media in Southeast Asia. The following sections outline the theoretical contexts that inform the study.

The Translocal in/as the Transnational

In the last two decades, a wave of media and cultural studies scholarship has examined the consumption of East Asian and Chinese-language media as a transnational experience, arguing for the significance of their impact on cultural lives across and beyond the region (e.g., Chua 2012; Chua and Iwabuchi 2008; Hong and Jin 2021; Iwabuchi, Muecke, and Thomas 2004; Martin et al. 2020; Kawashima and Lee 2018). According to Seok-Kyeong Hong and Dal Yong Jin (2021: 1), "Since the beginning of the 21st century, there has been an active development of the exchange and convergence of East Asian pop culture—referring to the new collective condition represented by the reciprocal merging and penetrating within the once-separated practical, industrial, and business aspects of popular culture under the influence of digital culture." Chua Beng Huat's (2012) now-classic book *Structure, Audience, and Soft Power in East Asian Pop Culture* provides an extensive examination of popular media produced in and circulated across Japan, Korea, and what Chua calls "Pop Culture China": a site of articulation linking Chinese-speaking audiences across Hong Kong, Taiwan, the People's Republic of China, and Singapore. Recent studies have also directed our attention to Australia as a site of trans-Asian media flows (e.g., Khoo, Martin, and Yue 2020; Martin et al. 2020). For example, Fran Martin et al. (2020: 4) have argued for "East Asian media's potentials for enabling forms of imaginative and affective attachment across distance and difference." Their findings suggest that the consumption of East Asian media has not only enabled Australians' transcultural learning but also cultivated their cosmopolitan ethos—in other words, their openness toward cultural difference (see Hannerz 1990). Such studies demonstrate how the political economy of entertainment industries, national policies, and audiences facilitate and regulate *trans*national cultural flows. However, little attention has been paid to *intra*national differences in relation to East Asian and Chinese-language popular media consumption. My findings suggest that the nation-state framework, which is the assumed framework for analysis in these studies, sometimes fails to capture the nuanced effects of transcultural processes. Instead, this article demonstrates that a translocal perspective is crucial to reveal the experiential unevenness of transnational cultural flows and that Malaysia is an exemplary site for such an analysis.

Critical geographers Katherine Brickell and Avona Datta (2016: 3) have pointed out that "the history of translocality itself . . . has emerged from a concern over the disembedded understanding of transnational networks." To overcome the limitations of taking the nation-state as the basis of analysis in transnational studies, scholarship since the mid-1990s has formulated different approaches through the alternative framework of translocality, examining various forms of local-to-local mobilities and interactions as a "space in which new forms of (post)national identity are constituted" (Mandaville 2002: 204). Arjun Appadurai (1996), for example, has pointed out how locality is heterogeneously and disjunctively shaped by multidirectional flows of people, media, ideologies, and capital. Using neighborhoods as an example, Appadurai sees localities as social formations that are produced relationally and contextually rather than scalarly or spatially. Given that locality is itself a social construct, "the locality of local knowledge is not only, or even mainly, its embeddedness in a nonnegotiable here and now or its stubborn disinterest in things at large" (181). In Appadurai's formulation, the translocal, in distinction from the transnational, encompasses multiple social fields connected by mobility and global processes within and beyond the nation-state that, in turn, enable new social formations (see also Mandaville 2002; Oakes and Schein 2006). Geographers in particular have moreover drawn our attention to recognizing "groundedness" amid globalizing processes (Brickell and Datta 2016; Greiner and Sakdapolrak 2013; Hedberg and do Carmo 2012), or as Brickell and Datta (2016: 3) put it, "situatedness during mobility." Indeed, as David Conradson and Deirdre Mckay (2007: 169) point out, "The formation of migrant selfhood is usually more closely related to localities within nations than to nation-states" (see also Conradson and Latham 2007; Huang and Yeoh 2007).

In a geographical contribution to Asian media studies, Wanning Sun and Jenny Chio (2012: 3) argue that "there are now many 'Chinas' within the nation-state entity that is the People's Republic of China." In the introduction to their edited volume *Mapping Media in China: Region, Province, Locality*, they make three points about the contested relationship between local and national media: first, regionalization leads to the formation of local power structures; second, local media often need to respond to local pressures; and third, local media have increasingly become a site of negotiation with the central state. They argue that in the early 2000s, the translocal interactions enabled by local satellite television consumption across different Chinese provinces destabilized not only the hegemony of national media but also viewers' senses of Chinese identity (see also Wanning Sun 2012; Wusan Sun 2012; Zhao and Xing 2012). This article demonstrates that Malaysia illustrates an even more decentered relationship between Chinese-language media consumption and ethnic Chinese identity formation. Specifically, it highlights the distinctiveness of Malaysian states such as Johor as sites of translocal interactions that enable transnational engagements with other parts of the Sinophone world, especially Hong Kong and Singapore. Thus, it is this article's objective to translocalize Pop Culture "China" (where, following Chua [2012], Chineseness is culturally rather than nationally defined). This is why we need the Sinophone.

The Sinophone as Uneven Ethnolinguistic Experiences

If area studies paradigms like China studies shore up national boundaries in knowledge production, Sinophone studies disrupts them. In the now-classic *Visuality and Identity: Sinophone Articulations across the Pacific*, Shu-mei Shih (2007) conceives the Sinophone as a cultural sphere that links Sinitic communities through their diverse localizations of Chinese languages outside China. In Shih's formulation, language rather than race or ethnicity is strategically utilized to decenter the Han-centric understanding of Chineseness and set limits on the time span of diaspora: the moment one no longer speaks Chinese is when one becomes a local. For a study of Malaysians' consumption of Chinese-language media, I argue that this attention to language is vital. This is because, as I will demonstrate, my interviewees' present-day language use—specifically, their fluency in Cantonese or lack of it—is the most apparent marker, and a historically specific legacy, of uneven transnational cultural flows across the country. Yet despite the Sinophone's potentials as an ethnolinguistic concept, many studies of Sinophone cultures, with a few exceptions (e.g., Hee 2019; Lu 2007; Lau 2021), have been more inclined to foreground nonlinguistic elements (for example, visual or production elements) in their analysis of Chinese-language media.

In the recent book *Reorienting Chinese Stars in Global Polyphonic Networks*, Dorothy Wai Sim Lau (2021: 9) argues that "Chinese stars inhabit an indeterminate, erratic space where the linguistic boundaries are increasingly porous to negotiate the power dynamics and ethnic politics." Examining the polyphonic construction of Chinese stardom in Asian and Hollywood cinemas as well as digital multimedia spaces, the book highlights how diverse languages and accents in the Sinophone media sphere have enabled multiple articulations of ethnicity. However, while this attention to language is productive of new understandings of Chineseness, what is overshadowed in Lau's analysis and others' is the role of audiences in facilitating these transnational cultural flows vis-à-vis their own linguistic identities and practices. This is perhaps connected with the methodological orientation of both Sinophone studies and the field of transnational Chinese media studies, which persistently privileges the textual over the ethnographic. Indeed, a linguistic turn in the study of Chinese-language media raises the unavoidable (yet frequently avoided) question: What better way to study present-day, living language use in overseas Chinese communities than ethnography?

Temporal (Mis)alignments: Hong Kong and the Presence of Its Past

In Malaysia's Chinese-speaking communities, as in many other overseas Chinese societies, "dialects" often do not exist in relation or addition to a "language" (i.e., Mandarin).[1] This is especially true for middle-aged and senior Chinese Malaysians who did not go to Mandarin-medium schools; to them, "dialects" are often not an option but the only kind of Chinese they speak. This was the case for my interviewee Ken, a business professor from Ipoh in his fifties, who could only speak Cantonese and English. But sometimes, such "dialects" are not transmitted intergenerationally at home but instead are used in contexts beyond the family. As a Hong Konger living in Malaysia, new acquaintances would often speak Cantonese to me before they came out as non-Cantonese through variations of the following conversation:

> "I am not Cantonese."
> I would usually say, "What?"
> "I am Hakka."
> I would feel (or later, politely act) confused and say, "How come you speak Cantonese so fluently, just like a native speaker?"
> "I learned Cantonese by watching your television dramas."

The dramas these research participants watched were mostly produced by the same television broadcasting company: "Thanks to TVB,"[2] as Yanny, a native of Penang in her late twenties, responded to the same question. Unlike today when Korean and P. R. Chinese cultural products dominate the Malaysian mediascape, Hong Kong television dramas and popular music were once widely consumed by Chinese Malaysians, ethnically Cantonese and non-Cantonese alike. Rooted in a city with a population of only seven million (five million in the 1980s), TVB has long targeted overseas markets with sizable Cantonese-speaking populations, such as North America and Southeast Asia, especially since the 1980s when the local market began to shrink as "wealthy and younger citizens began to seek out alternative modes of entertainment, such as movie videos, karaoke, and video games" (Curtin 2007: 111). Thanks to the global reach of Hong Kong's entertainment industry, Chinese Malaysians know a great deal about the city, its people, and their ways of life and struggles. More often than not, new acquaintances would assertively ask me where I lived in the small city, a question I have almost never been asked anywhere else in the world other than Hong Kong. What usually followed was a demonstration of cultural knowledge, as respondents threw at me names of streets I didn't know and celebrities who were no longer locally active but had left to earn Renminbi in China's mainland. This cultural knowledge was pervasive to the extent that it was sometimes an effortless embodiment. For example, having moved to Hong Kong a year before our interview, Kelly, an art curator from Kuala Lumpur in her early thirties, now spoke Hong Kong–accented Cantonese (which would be deemed pretentious if spoken in Malaysia) and used culturally specific slang so fluently that locals could not tell her apart from themselves.

Michael Curtin (2003: 203) writes that the media capitals of Bombay, Cairo, and Hong Kong "represent centers of media activity that have specific logics of their own; ones that do not necessarily correspond to the geography, interests or policies of particular nation-states." This global positioning has, in Hong Kong's case, enabled "logics that motivate the development of the medium" that "are not primarily governed by the interests of the Chinese state, or even the Special Administrative Region (SAR)" (204). This pre-1990s market orientation away from China has cultural as well as political implications, since "traditionally these Chinese-language media outlets have maintained a guarded—if not hostile—distance from Communist China" (Wanning Sun and Sinclair 2016: 5–6). As Wanning Sun and John Sinclair (2016: 6) write, "Although small in number and local in impact, . . . older generations of local Chinese media [in Hong Kong] were also an integral part of the 'diasporic Chinese public sphere' and were characterized by their independence from China." Indeed, to many members of overseas Chinese communities, the Hong Kong relevant to them is pre-handover Hong Kong.

A few days after the 2020 Lunar New Year, when COVID-19 was still a major media story, my friend Alvin, a native of Ipoh in his early thirties, invited me to his house for a party. An enthusiast of all things Hong Kong, Alvin's emotional attachment to the city extended beyond the realm of popular culture: his Facebook posts showed that he had been actively following the then ongoing Anti-extradition Law Amendment Bill movement. During the party, Cantopop—dominated by 1990s hits including the songs of Jacky Cheung, Leslie Cheung, and Anita Mui—was playing in the background while we drank beer and chatted in Cantonese with Alvin's childhood friends from Ipoh. Their presence reminded me of countless afternoons spent at the Nam Heong branch near my residence, an iconic café with sixty years of history that promises to preserve the nostalgic flavors of Ipoh heritage.[3] It was not the egg tart or famous white coffee that made me a regular customer but the 1990s Cantopop, always in the background, which gave me the taste of home. In defining Pop Culture China, Chua (2012: 40) calls it a "a soft-bedrock of shared 'Chineseness,' of a sense of 'community' without a permanent cultural center and not necessarily amounting to a dominant identity for anyone in particular, remains discursively imaginable and materially realizable." This imagined community, I argue, also reconfigures senses of time and space, as in this instance, where we see Cantopop used to represent histories and cultures outside its place of production. *The nostalgic flavors of Ipoh were, in one way or another, the nostalgic flavors of Hong Kong.* This displaced configuration of time and place is perhaps most succinctly captured by Liew Kai Khiun (2016: 1–2) in their work on transnational cultural memories. They write, "If the contemporary trails of 'now-ness' in the transnational popular cultures of East and Southeast Asia are characterized by traits of novelty and trendiness, familiarity and continuity are the affective traces of 'pastness.'" In encounters with the Cantonese language like these, I learned that distanced attachment could be and was indeed a privilege: while many in Hong Kong found it out of place to celebrate anything, even Lunar New Year, in the time of political crisis, those outside the territory could still pick and choose (likely dated) versions of the city that best suit their moods and narratives of home.

Other than resulting from the business-driven transnational media activities of previous decades, my findings also suggest that Malaysians' present-day consumption of Hong Kong's past manifests a temporal displacement of their aspirations for an alternative modernity. For example, when asked to give examples of television dramas he liked watching, Ken immediately named *The Greed of Man* (*Dashidai* 大時代) (1992) as his favorite:

> At that time the "middle-income"[4] [Malaysian] people didn't have a lot of money. They saw them [Hong Kong people] living in public housing and how they faced modernization. They could feel it; my parents could feel the struggles [of Hong Kong people]. So, seeing their struggles made [Malaysian] people identify with the sadness and joy [of modernization]. . . . There were scenes [in *The Greed of Man*] showing how people look for employment and fail to secure a job, how some people do not

earn enough and have to borrow money. That kind of situation made them [Malaysian people] binge-watch those dramas.

Ordinary people's social aspirations and struggles as represented on Hong Kong television dramas coincided with Malaysia's recent wave of modernization in the 1990s. It was a time of rapid economic development resulting in both joy and sadness. As Wong pointed out, inpouring foreign investments contributed to a widening gap between the rich and the poor, increasing urban-rural differences, as well as widespread corruption. Another TVB drama Ken liked was *Instinct* (*Xiaokanfengyun* 笑看風雲) (1994), and he highlighted its significance to him as a young man in Ipoh witnessing the country's transformation:

> Many [Malaysian] people longed for such social justice. They wanted such a ["heroic"] figure to rescue them from the corrupted business world. So, many [Malaysian] people liked Adam Cheng's role as a righteous person who provides opportunities for younger people to climb the career ladder and not be subject to corruption. That feeling was a very hopeful one, especially in the 1990s. . . . Those dramas have [a] moral teaching: people suffer miserably but there is always somebody who will come to rescue them. So, it [*Instinct*] really highlighted the collective hope [of Hong Kong and Malaysian people alike] for a better future. So, they [Malaysians] really enjoyed watching those dramas.

Shortly after arriving in Taiwan to take up his faculty position at a national university four years prior, Ken had bought a DVD box set of *The Greed of Man* and rewatched the show, as he longed for a taste of home. As Koichi Iwabuchi (2004: 153) has pointed out, "The transnational evocation of nostalgia is highlighted when it is employed to confirm a frozen temporal lag between two cultures." But, for Ken, the function of Hong Kong television in enabling his emotional attachment to Malaysia had an expiration date. He stopped watching TVB dramas in the mid-1990s when they no longer represented the struggles of "middle-income" people. The mid- to late 1990s was marked by the popularity of *The File of Justice* (*Yihaohuangting* 壹號皇庭) (1992) and *Healing Hands* (*Miaoshourenxin* 妙手仁心) (1998) as well as the many subsequent legal and medical dramas released in the decade that followed (Liew 2012). As Ken said, those dramas were no longer "political" or "connect[ed] to society," as they only depicted the working lives of young wealthy professionals.

In examining Japanese fans' consumption of Hong Kong popular culture in the 1990s, Iwabuchi (2004: 153) argues that transnational cultural circulation has produced "a condition that finds people constituting memory on the basis of mass-mediated cultural forms originating from elsewhere." Through Hong Kong stars and the films of Wong Kar-wai, Japanese fans associated the city "with Japan's past and losses" (164), referring to vanished "social vigor" and cultural styles. In other words, Hong Kong provided "a different mode of Asian modernity, one which antithetically demonstrates what has gone wrong with Japan's modernization process" (166). But for Southeast Asian Chinese audiences, this nostalgic longing, as a phenomenon of frozen temporal lag, is constituted by a wider geographical shift in Sinophone media consumption. When asked about their impressions of Hong Kong based on their media consumption, my interviewees tended to associate their knowledge of the city with popular texts produced before the early 2000s. While they were aware of Cantopop idols who rose to fame in the local popular music scene since the early 2000s such as Eason Chan, Joey Yung, and Twins, the examples they named were more likely to be legendary singers whose careers were launched before many of their own births, such as those whose songs were played at Alvin's party. Moreover, they were barely familiar at all with most post-2000 Hong Kong television dramas; their often-referenced "most recent" dramas included *Armed Reaction* (*Tuoqiangshijie* 陀槍師姐) (1998), *Happy Ever After* (*Jinyumantang* 金玉滿堂) (1999), *Return of the Cuckoo* (*Aomenjie* 澳門街) (2000), and *War and Beauty* (*Jinzhiyunie* 金枝慾孽) (2004).

In the 2010s, Hong Kong popular culture became considerably less relevant to the lives of Chinese-speaking Malaysians. This was not simply because of its decline in and beyond the city as Taiwanese popular culture began to gain prominence in the Sinophone world. The clear-cut shift from Hong Kong to Taiwan was, moreover, motivated by technological and infrastructural developments, as highlighted by Kelly, who called herself a passive consumer of Chinese-language media, since she would watch and listen to anything most accessible to her rather than deliberately seeking out specific cultural products. Born and raised in a Cantonese-speaking family in Cheras, Kelly grew up watching TVB dramas on national television while having dinner on weekday evenings until, in the late 1990s, her family subscribed to Astro, a Malaysian satellite television operator that offered many Chinese-language television channels broadcasting programs from Taiwan in particular. She stopped watching TVB dramas after the Taiwanese teenage drama *Meteor Garden* (*Liuxinghuayuan* 流星花園) came out in 2001, and she had bought every Jay Chou album since his debut in 2000.

If the favorable global reception of Cantonese dramas led to the success of Hong Kong television in Malaysia, idol dramas (and variety shows) were what defined the Taiwan era in the 2000s. Adapted from the Japanese manga *Boys over Flowers*, *Meteor Garden* was brought up by three of my interviewees who described it as a turning point in their media consumption from Hong Kong to Taiwan. Hsiu-Chuang Deppman (2009: 93) argues that *Meteor Garden* and subsequent Taiwanese idol dramas provided "an alternative vision of East Asian modernity, one that seems to reconcile traditional values (i.e., filial piety, respect for authority, and civic duty) with ideals of progress (sexual freedom, gender and racial equality, democracy, romance, and civil liberty)." Compared to that of Hong Kong, this version of modernity is perhaps more closely aligned with the aspirations of the generation of Malaysian audiences who grew up in a more economically developed society. For example, Min, a native of Kuala Lumpur in her midtwenties who had a literature degree from Taiwan's National Chengchi University, told me that the reason she went to Taiwan was because her idol Ariel Lin, who rose to fame for her role in the 2005 idol drama *It Started with a Kiss* (*Ezuojuzhiwen* 惡作劇之吻), had studied the same subject at the same university.

Yet, from the 2010s, this alternative desire for a "post-materialist" modernity was soon driven out by PRC media and the global capitalist success it signifies. In their volume *China's Media Go Global*, editors Daya Kishan Thussu, Hugo de Burgh, and Anbin Shi (2018: 3) write that "the unprecedented global expansion of Chinese media and communication networks over the past decade raises important questions about the changing global media landscape and the role of China within it." Recent years have seen an increasing convergence of PRC media and the Malaysian Chinese mediascape. For example,

Astro, which now reaches 77 percent of Malaysian households (Shackleton 2019), began delivering content from China's online video platform iQiyi in 2019. Lauren Gorfinkel (2018: 155), moreover, points out that "media reaching out to overseas Chinese is backed by organizations with competing interests" and "the CCP has been active in its attempts to promote its official state version of Chinese identity to overseas Chinese, with television programming playing an important role." Indeed, the current widespread consumption of PRC media has significant political implications for overseas Chinese communities. According to a recent report on the spread of disinformation during the 2019 Hong Kong protest (*Malaysiakini* 2021), "Mainstream Chinese language media in Malaysia were found to be among the main 'importers' of disinformation originating from China state media and other pro-CCP media in Hong Kong," resulting in overwhelmingly anti-protester sentiments on Malaysia's Chinese-language internet. But even while PRC media dominates the overseas Chinese-language mediascape and shapes Chinese Malaysians' political attitudes and memory, as well as archiving affective traces of pastness and a frozen temporal lag, is productive of a Sinophone logic of relationality. This is seen in Ken and Alvin's media consumption, which connects them emotionally with past ways of life as Chinese Malaysians and the present struggles in Hong Kong.

Spatial Convergence: Constructing Home via Singapore

On the day of the 2020 Chinese New Year, I spent the early afternoon at Zoe's family home in Johor Bahru. Zoe was now based in Taiwan, where she had been living since graduating with a master's degree two years earlier, and went back to Malaysia to visit her family at this time every year. Like many families in Johor Bahru, her parents had, until their recent retirement, made daily commutes to Singapore via the Johor-Singapore Causeway in order to earn a higher income than they could in Malaysia. As we gathered in the family sitting room organized around a television, a Chinese-language historical drama played while we ate homemade taro cakes and exchanged notes on how Lunar New Year was celebrated differently in Hong Kong and Johor. Our conversation was interrupted when a kitchen knife flew through the air toward a male character on the TV screen. I was shocked to see supernatural elements in a seemingly historical drama. On the spur of the moment, I shouted, "Wow, is it about ghosts?"

Zoe's sister answered, "It is *The Ghost Bride*."

I responded, "Oh, so that's the new Netflix original series everybody's talking about?"

"Yes."

Now realizing the drama was set in the nineteenth century, I impulsively asked, "Why are they speaking Mandarin? People didn't speak Mandarin at that time, at least not this kind of [rather standard] Mandarin, right?"

"That's not the point." Zoe, obviously not a fan of the show, instead called my attention to its visual representation: "Look at their costumes and the sets. They are way too glamorous to be real."

A Taiwanese-Malaysian coproduction based on a novel by the Malaysian writer Yangsze Choo, *The Ghost Bride* (*Bianzhijia* 彼岸之嫁) (2020) tells the story of a Chinese Malaysian woman's marriage to the deceased son of a wealthy family in colonial Malacca in the 1890s. While I am unsure why we were bothered by the lack of historical accuracy in a ghostly drama, Zoe's dismissal of its language (spoken Mandarin) as *less* of a marker of cultural inauthenticity than visual elements exemplifies a Johor-specific pattern of media consumption, marked by the normalization of the Mandarin language—that is, distinct from those in other parts of Malaysia. Later that afternoon, Zoe drove me to visit her old friend Johnson, a Johorean in his mid-twenties. Playing on television in his sitting room, packed with many relatives, was the replay of a variety show aired on a Singaporean channel. Despite living on Malaysian soil, it was the norm rather than an exception for people in Johor Bahru and the state of Johor in general to easily and "illicitly" receive satellite signals from across the border, enabled by the geographic proximity between the two countries.

While many research participants made a connection between Hong Kong TV dramas and their learning of Cantonese, this was not the case with the Johoreans. Just like people from the rest of Malaysia, Chinese Johoreans used to regularly consume Hong Kong dramas. But unlike their counterparts who watched them in Cantonese with Malay subtitles on national television, the TVB dramas Johoreans watched on Singapore television were dubbed into Mandarin: this was the result of Singapore's still ongoing Speak Mandarin Campaign, launched by the then prime minister Lee Kuan Yew in 1979. As an initiative to "strategically realign the dominant ethnic community for 'Chineseness' in the twenty-first century" (Leong 1999: 25), the Speak Mandarin Campaign emerged as a social policy at a time when Mandarin was neither the native language of nor popularly used for communication among most Chinese Singaporeans. Other than promoting the use of Mandarin by making it compulsory in education, "the use of other Chinese languages, already officially marginalized as dialects, was banned from all public broadcast media" (Chua 2012: 62). While the Speak Mandarin Campaign proved to be a successful national policy, for better or for worse, in homogenizing the Chinese-speaking community in Singapore (see Tan 2016), its effects on people's language use have reached beyond the nation.

Back to Alvin's party, where I met Emily, a Johorean in her mid-twenties, who had moved to Kuala Lumpur for work a few years earlier. Later in the evening, we joined Alvin and his schoolmates from Ipoh to play Ring of Fire, a party game that requires players to take turns drawing a card and following the corresponding rule. A few minutes into the game, Alvin drew a Jack, the "Make a Rule" card, and decided that "Everybody must speak Cantonese."

Emily helplessly complained, "But I can't speak Cantonese . . ."

Someone shouted, "Just say no problem [*mou man tai* 無問題]!"

Like Emily, my other interviewees from Johor Bahru, including Katy, a journalist in her mid-twenties with a Cantonese father, also could not understand Cantonese, let alone speak it. For many Johoreans, Mandarin is the only Chinese language they speak. This border-crossing cultural experience perhaps explains why Zoe, who grew up watching programs in or dubbed into Mandarin on Singaporean television stations, could easily tolerate the linguistically decontextualized Mandarin-speaking colonial Malacca in *The Ghost Bride*. Indeed, watching Singapore television was prevalent to the extent that Johoreans rarely felt the need to reflect on their own situatedness. When asked about why she and her family had always watched Singapore television channels, Katy said:

Katy: You wouldn't ask why we watched Singapore channels. Because we watched them every day. When you talked to other kids in school, everybody watched the same thing. So, we have never really asked ourselves why. . . .

Author: But you had a choice to watch Malaysian television, right?

Katy: Our television has always had an antenna attached to it. When I was young I actually didn't know whether we would be able to watch Malaysian channels without the antenna. It was not until the time preceding the 2008 Malaysian general election when a series of protests such as Bersih took place that my father started watching the news on 8TV [a Malaysian Chinese-language channel]. Because you wouldn't see these on Singapore television. . . . Before that everything seemed very normal, we never deliberately chose [to watch Malaysian television]. I think I lived within the result of that choice [i.e., that was beyond my choosing].

Singaporean television's central place in Johoreans' leisure lives is much more than a matter of convenience. In fact, their media consumption is driven to a great extent by personal investments and transnational desires. This is evident in the visually distinctive cityscape of Muar, a Johorean town bordering Malacca on the Western coast of Peninsular Malaysia, where extremely tall antennas are attached to residential houses to receive Singaporean satellite television 165 kilometers away from Singapore. The ownership of such equipment is so common that a random search of streets in Muar on Google Street View results in images of multiple antennas reaching up into the sky.[5] Such a deterritorialized translocal television infrastructure resonates with Wanning Sun's (2012: 14) observation about Chinese provinces after 1998, "when almost all provincial television stations were given permission to switch from cable to satellite transmission." She points out that satellite technology enabled Chinese viewers to watch television programs in and, in turn, identify with provinces other than their own. As "provincial television is deliberately and consciously challenging central television's monopoly of representing 'China'" (15), this mediated translocality had the potential to transform viewers' Chinese subject formations since "the state media no longer [held] a monopoly over the definition of what is Chinese culture" (23).

Media consumption also reconfigured my interviewees' sense of geographical belonging and constructions of home, and this was most marked in the practices of those in the diaspora. Noel, a student in his mid-twenties now living in Taipei, said it had always been easier for him to identify with

Singapore than with the rest of Malaysia. This was evident in his choice to watch Singaporean over Malaysian news on national television when he was at home in Johor Bahru. At the time of our interview in September 2021, he had not returned home to visit his family for nineteen months due to COVID-19 travel restrictions. To emotionally connect to home in Malaysia, Noel began to pay attention to the happenings in the Southeast Asian Sinophone mediascape and would watch "every Malaysian or Singaporean film" screened in Taipei. During our interview, he showed me a photo of the recent films he had watched, including DVDs of the Singaporean director Anthony Chen's *Ilo Ilo* (2013) and *Wet Season* (2019), and film tickets to a screening of three Malaysian and Singaporean short films at the Golden Harvest Festival, including Malaysian director Chong Keat-aun's *Cemetery of Courtesy* (2017), and Singaporean directors Boo Jun-feng's *The Casuarina Cove* (2009) and Anthony Chen's *Ah Ma* (2007).

If being in Johor made Katy (above) lose her sense of situatedness due to a normalized cross-border media environment, Noel's diasporic experience reveals how the situatedness of Malaysia is spatially relational and becomes obvious when one is confronted with alternative media choices. By specifying the locality of Johor as a site of Chinese-language media consumption, we see an ongoing development of transnational cultural flows that is distinct from the rest of Malaysia and has enabled different imaginations of the nation that continue to decenter Chinese identities, past and present. Johor-Singapore translocal connections have enabled a Sinophone logic of identification that challenges the nation-state framework of global media analysis as well as the view of PRC media homogenization and domination that such a framework enables.

Conclusion

By investigating the differences in Chinese Malaysians' cultural practices, including language use and sense of belonging across different localities within Malaysia, this article has historically contextualized audiences' distinctive and divergent patterns of Chinese-language media consumption and highlighted the implications of these for conceptualizing Malaysia's present-day Sinophone mediascape in the context of the rising regional dominance of PRC media. By tracing media traffics arriving multidirectionally from Hong

Kong and Singapore, and examining their lived impacts on audiences in different localities in Malaysia, I have moreover argued for the importance of understanding transnational cultural flows as necessarily translocal phenomena, as evidenced in interviewees' experiences of consuming Chinese-language media that are differ distinctively between Johor and other parts of Malaysia.

By "reimagining China beyond China, connecting, contextualizing, and comparing 'Chinese' development with that in other parts of the world" (Lee 2017: xiv), this article advances our understanding of how "global China" is resisted in media audiences' everyday cultural and affective mobilities. As Lee (2022) argues, "The intellectual payoff of seeing global China as a power project is that we will ask questions about agency (who), interest (why), method (how) and consequences (so what)" (316–17). Through qualitative inquiry, I hope to have offered an alternative view of Chinese Malaysians' Chinese-language media consumption that counters mainstream narratives pointing to the homogenization of PRC media in Chinese-speaking communities globally. By considering Malaysia's ethnolinguistic realities and the role of everyday language use in these processes of resistance, this article highlights the potential of the Sinophone framework in revealing the complexities of translocal cultural flows both within Malaysia and across the Chinese-speaking world today.

Notes

1   This observation is less applicable to the state of Johor. See the next section for an elaborated discussion.

2   Television Broadcasts Limited—a major broadcaster of Cantonese television shows for audiences in both Hong Kong and Chinese-speaking communities worldwide.

3   "About Us," Nam Heong Ipoh (website), http://www.namheongipoh.com/about-us/ (accessed September 8, 2021).

4   By "middle-income" people, Ken referred to the working-class Hong Kong people who were upwardly mobile due to emerging middle-class occupations in the time of rapid economic development in the 1970s–90s. For an extensive discussion of the East Asian middle class, see Hsiao 1993, 1999.

5   Google Street View image capture, October 2019, https://www.google.com/maps/@2.062615,102.5901263,3a,47.5y,192.58h,111.52t/data=!3m6!1e1!3m4!1sehcWR_NfeHEEem-O3V82pA!2e0!7i16384!8i8192.

References

Appadurai, Arjun. 1996. *Modernity at Large: Cultural Dimensions of Globalization*. Minneapolis: University of Minnesota Press.

Brickell, Katherine, and Ayona Datta. 2016. "Introduction: Translocal Geographies." In *Translocal Geographies: Spaces, Places, Connections*, edited by Katherine Brickell and Ayona Datta, 3–20. New York: Routledge.

Chua, Beng Huat. 2012. *Structure, Audience, and Soft Power in East Asian Pop Culture*. Hong Kong: Hong Kong University Press.

Chua, Beng Huat, and Koichi Iwabuchi, eds. 2008. *East Asian Pop Culture: Analysing the Korean Wave*. Hong Kong: Hong Kong University Press.

Conradson, David, and Alan Latham. 2007. "The Affective Possibilities of London: Antipodean Transnationals and the Overseas Experience." *Mobilities* 2, no. 2: 231–54.

Conradson, David, and Deirdre Mckay. 2007. "Translocal Subjectivities: Mobility, Connection, Emotion." *Mobilities* 2, no. 2: 167–74.

Curtin, Michael. 2003. "Media Capital: Towards the Study of Spatial Flows." *International Journal of Cultural Studies* 6, no. 2: 202–28.

Curtin, Michael. 2007. *Playing to the World's Biggest Audience: The Globalization of Chinese Film and TV*. Berkeley: University of California Press.

Deppman, Hsiu-Chuang. 2009. "Made in Taiwan: An Analysis of *Meteor Garden* as an East Asian Idol Drama." In *TV China*, edited by Ying Zhu and Chris Berry, 90–110. Bloomington: Indiana University Press.

Gorfinkel, Lauren. 2018. *Chinese Television and National Identity Construction: The Cultural Politics of Music-Entertainment Programmes*. New York: Routledge.

Greiner, Clemens, and Patrick Sakdapolrak. 2013. "Translocality: Concepts, Applications, and Emerging Research Perspectives." *Geography Compass* 7, no. 5: 373–84.

Hannerz, Ulf. 1990. "Cosmopolitans and Locals in World Culture." *Theory, Culture, and Society* 7, no. 2–3: 237–51.

Hedberg, Charlotta, and Renato Miguel do Carmo, eds. 2012. *Translocal Ruralism: Mobility and Connectivity in European Rural Spaces*. Dordrecht, Netherlands: Springer.

Hee, Wai-Siam. 2019. "Accented Style: On Namewee's Sinophone Malaysian Film and Rap Songs." *Interventions: International Journal of Postcolonial Studies* 21, no. 2: 273–90.

Hong, Seok-Kyeong, and Dal Yong Jin, eds. 2021. *Transnational Convergence of East Asian Pop Culture*. New York: Routledge.

Hsiao, Hsin-Huang Michael, ed. 1993. *Discovery of the Middle Classes in East Asia*. Taipei: Institute of Ethnology, Academia Sinica.

Hsiao, Hsin-Huang Michael, ed. 1999. *East Asian Middle Classes in Comparative Perspective*. Taipei: Institute of Ethnology, Academia Sinica.

Huang, Shirlena, and Brenda S. A. Yeoh. 2007. "Emotional Labour and Transnational Domestic Work: The Moving Geographies of 'Maid Abuse' in Singapore." *Mobilities* 2, no. 2: 195–217.

Iwabuchi, Koichi. 2004. "Time and the Neighbor: Japanese Media Consumption of Asia in the 1990s." In *Rogue Flows: Trans-Asian Cultural Traffic*, edited by Koichi Iwabuchi, Stephen Muecke, and Mandy Thomas, 151–74. Hong Kong: Hong Kong University Press.

Iwabuchi, Koichi, Stephen Muecke, and Mandy Thomas, eds. 2004. *Rogue Flows: Trans-Asian Cultural Traffic*. Hong Kong: Hong Kong University Press.

Kawashima, Nobuko, and Hye-Kyung Lee, eds. 2018. *Asian Cultural Flows: Cultural Policies, Creative Industries, and Media Consumers*. Singapore: Springer.

Khoo, Olivia, Fran Martin, and Audrey Yue. 2020. "Introduction: Australia in the Field of Trans-Asian Media Flows." *Media International Australia* 175, no. 1: 3–5.

Lau, Dorothy Wai Sim. 2021. *Reorienting Chinese Stars in Global Polyphonic Networks: Voice, Ethnicity, Power*. Singapore: Palgrave Macmillan.

Lee, Ching Kwan. 2017. *The Specter of Global China: Politics, Labor, and Foreign Investment in Africa*. Chicago: University of Chicago Press.

Lee, Ching Kwan. 2022. "Introduction: Global China at Twenty; Why, How, and So What?" *China Quarterly*, no. 250: 313–31.

Leong, K. Chan. 1999. "Communication, National Identity, and Cultural Identity in Singapore: Graphic Responses to the 'Speak Mandarin' Campaigns." *Design Journal* 2, no. 1: 24–38.

Liew, Kai Khiun. 2012. "Informatization-Dramatization: Communicating Health in East Asian Television Dramas." *International Journal of Communication*, no. 6: 2040–56.

Liew, Kai Khiun. 2016. *Transnational Memory and Popular Culture in East and Southeast Asia: Amnesia, Nostalgia, and Heritage*. London: Rowman and Littlefield.

Lu, Sheldon. 2007. "Dialect and Modernity in Twenty-First Century Sinophone Cinema." *Jump Cut: A Review of Contemporary Media*, no. 49. https://www.ejumpcut.org/archive/jc49.2007/Lu/index.html.

Malaysiakini. 2021. "The Hong Kong Infowar in Malaysia: How 'Fake News' on the Hong Kong Protest Reached Our Shores." August 11. https://pages.malaysiakini.com/hk-misinfo/en/.

Mandaville, Peter. 2002. "Reading the State from Elsewhere: Towards an Anthropology of the Postnational." *Review of International Studies* 28, no. 1: 199–207.

Martin, Fran, Koichi Iwabuchi, Grace Gassin, and WaiLing Seto. 2020. "Transcultural Media Practices Fostering Cosmopolitan Ethos in a Digital Age: Engagements with East Asian Media in Australia." *Inter-Asia Cultural Studies* 21, no. 1: 2–19.

Oakes, Tim, and Louisa Schein, eds. 2006. *Translocal China: Linkages, Identities, and the Reimagining of Space.* London: Routledge.

Pavlićević, Dragan, and Nicole Talmacs, eds. 2022. *The China Question: Contestations and Adaptations.* Singapore: Palgrave Macmillan.

Rofel, Lisa, and Carlos Rojas, eds. 2023. *New World Orderings: China and the Global South.* Durham, NC: Duke University Press.

Shackleton, Liz. 2019. "Malaysia's Astro Pacts with Chinese Streaming Giant iQiyi." *ScreenDaily*, June 17. https://www.screendaily.com/news/malaysias-astro-pacts-with-chinese-streaming-giant-iqiyi/5140449.article.

Shih, Shu-mei. 2007. *Visuality and Identity: Sinophone Articulations across the Pacific.* Berkeley: University of California Press.

Sun, Wanning. 2012. "Localizing Chinese Media: A Geographic Turn in Media and Communication Research." In Sun and Chio 2012b: 13–27.

Sun, Wanning, and Jenny Chio. 2012a. Introduction to Sun and Chio 2012b: 3–12.

Sun, Wanning, and Jenny Chio, eds. 2012b. *Mapping Media in China: Region, Province, Locality.* New York: Routledge.

Sun, Wanning, and John Sinclair. 2016. "Introduction: Rethinking Chinese Diasporic Media." In *Media and Communication in the Chinese Diaspora: Rethinking Transnationalism*, edited by Wanning Sun and John Sinclair, 1–14. New York: Routledge.

Sun, Wusan. 2012. "Top-Down Policies versus Grassroots Resistance." In Sun and Chio 2012b: 62–75.

Tan, E. K. 2016. "In Search of New Forms: The Impact of Bilingual Policy and the 'Speak Mandarin' Campaign on Sinophone Singapore Poetry." *Interventions: International Journal of Postcolonial Studies* 18, no. 4: 526–42.

Thussu, Daya Kishan, Hugo de Burgh, and Anbin Shi. 2018. Introduction to *China's Media Go Global*, edited by Daya Kishan Thussu, Hugo de Burgh, and Anbin Shi, 1–13. New York: Routledge.

Zhao, Yuezhi, and Suoxin Xing. 2012. "Provincial Papers, National Power: The Scaling Up of the *Nafang Daily* Media Group." In Sun and Chio 2012b: 31–46.

Contributors

Fanni Beck recently received her PhD from the Department of Sociology and Social Anthropology at Central European University.

Haijing Dai is associate professor in the Department of Social Work at the Chinese University of Hong Kong.

Qian Gong is senior lecturer in the School of Education at Curtin University, Perth.

Christina Ho is associate professor of social and political sciences at the University of Technology Sydney.

Shuheng Jin is assistant professor in the Department of Social Work, Guangdong University of Technology.

Anita Koo is professor of sociology at Hong Kong Baptist University.

Shih-Diing Liu is professor of communication at the University of Macau.

positions 32:4   DOI 10.1215/10679847-11306880
Copyright 2024 by Duke University Press

Fran Martin is professor of cultural studies at the University of Melbourne.

Jacqueline Nelson is a research fellow at Anti-Slavery Australia at the University of Technology Sydney.

Pál Nyíri is a professor at the Institute of Global Studies, Budapest University of Economics (Corvinus).

Ngai Pun is chair professor and head of the Department of Cultural Studies, Lingnan University, Hong Kong.

Dallas Rogers is associate professor in architecture and environments at the University of Sydney.

Lin Song is assistant professor in the School of Journalism and Communication, Jinan University, China.

Huan Wu is a senior research services coordinator in the College of Asia and the Pacific at The Australian National University.

Ting-Fai Yu is a fellow at the Netherlands Institute for Advanced Study in the Humanities and Social Sciences.